Prologue

REME – The Magnificent Bastards. Stories and anecdotes told in a soldier's way, in a soldier's language, the real way, no punches pulled. Recruitment to demob and all the exciting and sometimes sordid stuff in-between. UK, Germany, Canada, and Northern Ireland. Infantry, tanks, and helicopters. Beer, Brandy, Fags and Rugby. This book has it all.

'Cheeseboard' and I turned and walked back to the RUC Landrover. I approached the back door, gave the handle a twist and yanked it open. I was instantly staring down the barrel of a very big revolver that had been thrust into my face. The hand holding the revolver was shaking and the eyes behind the outstretched arm were very wide under the peak of the dark green police forage cap. I was in deep, deep, shit, and I knew it.

REME – The Magnificent Bastards

DEDICATION

I dedicate this book to my wife Nicola, for all her patience and tolerance. She has heard much of the content of this book many times over; she complains not.

Also, to NJR, and to Jimbo for their advice on aspects of the book. To David and Anne for their proof reading.

Often, in this book where I state 'I' it could just as well be 'We' or 'Us', this is after all a 'British Army' story, and we are never alone.

And finally, and most importantly, to all those 'Magnificent Bastards', REME and 'Other Arms', for their friendship and their sacrifice.

Thank you all.

AetM

Ron

Best Wishes

Tyrone Rees

South Wales 2023

TAFFY REES

AetM.

2

Front Cover

Jethro Tull and I staring at somebody with a camera
while having a fag on a 14th/20th Kings Hussars
Chieftain ARV after 'track-bashing' on Soltau
Lunenberg Training Area c1979

REME – The Magnificent Bastards

Table of Contents

REME – The Magnificent Bastards

The Weetabix Year

I had always, as a child, wanted to be a soldier or a police officer. Raised on a diet of 'Commando' magazines, and Hotspur and Victor comics. The heroes, always British soldiers, won their battles against the odds, inevitably they were the good guys. Dixon of Dock Green and 'Z' cars were ever present. It was always stirring stuff.

I had part time jobs as a 'Corona' pop-lorry loader, a shelf stacker in the Co-op, a Plasterers Labourer, and a farm tractor driver. At aged sixteen I left Grammar School as an unsuccessful under-achieving know nothing, know everything teenager. I had so much to learn.

My first full time job was a printer's assistant in a cardboard box making factory at 'Jacob Beatus Printers and Carton Manufacturers", in the Rhondda. My job was to put hundreds of thousands of flat, printed, large cardboard sheets into a big hydraulic machine, that drew them through onto a steel bed and stamped them in a press creating cuts and creases so they could be folded into boxes. In my case it was Weetabix boxes - by the million. If you ate Weetabix between 1974 and 1975, I probably had a hand in making your Weetabix box. The job was numb skullingly boring. No skill, no adventure, no future.

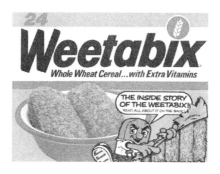

MILLIONS AND MILLIONS AND MILLION!

The machine operator, and my boss, was a gentleman called John Jones from Caerphilly, same place as the cheese. John was old school factory floor. Always well-presented he wore his patterned tie outside his patterned pullover, over his check patterned shirt and took great pride in his work. His shoes were always spotlessly clean, and he never swore. Everybody else in the factory did, but not John. He was always chasing the bonus payment for cutting and creasing extra sheets of card. I recall it wasn't much extra money, shillings for me. My first wage was £11 a week which didn't go far. I was always skint by the Tuesday following the Friday pay-day. I would borrow back the 'lodge' I had paid my mother. I was quickly into a routine; pay Friday, Rugby Club Friday night, play rugby Saturday, at home Sunday, rugby training Monday, to the cinema with the rugby boys in Cardiff on Tuesday after permanently borrowing off mam. Wednesday Rugby training, Thursday night in and so on and so on. It was quickly becoming a rut.

I decided to join the police. Off went my application to South Wales police and I didn't hear anything for weeks.

A friend of mine had come into the possession of a cut-off leather frilled leather jacket, too big for him, he gave it to me. It was covered in 'Hells-Angel'

badges, threats to kill and other demonic things. It certainly wasn't me; I was no hells-angel or anything like one, but it was well made.

Some of my household chores were keeping the garden tidy, chopping wood for the coal fire, keeping the coal supplied and being the eldest of four I fell into the role of babysitter, chief cook, and bottle washer. So, one day I'm at the back of the house chopping wood. The hells-angel jacket served usefully as a protective garment, and I kept it hanging in the wood and coal shed for that purpose alone.

One day the coal was delivered straight from the colliery by tipper lorry. A couple of tons as was the way. I'd donned the leather jacket and spent an hour or so bucketing-in the coal to the coal shed. I was black faced and covered in coal-dust. Straight after the coal I began to chop wood for kindling using a huge menacing looking hook cleaver that we'd had for years and served perfectly for the job.

My mother called me, 'There's somebody here to see you', she shouted from the house.

I walked in, black faced, sweating, wearing a hells angel doom and threat-laden leather carrying a menacing cleaver in my hand.

The gentleman who had come to visit turned out to be a Police Inspector from South Wales Police on an unannounced home visit to assess me for suitability to join the force. It didn't go well.

I wasn't prepared. I stammered and stuttered through his questions. And I think, worse of all, was my appearance. Fifteen stones, unclean, sweating, wearing a jacket of doom, and wielding a mass murderers' weapon. No, it didn't go well at all.

I received a letter from South Wales Police sometime later stating that I was deemed unsuitable for police employment due to my wearing contact lenses and that Police Cadets, for which I had applied, did not accept people without perfect unaided vision. They

16

added that I would not be excluded from applying to South Wales Police as an adult police officer when I reached nineteen years of age. I think they were being as kind as they could be in their rejection of me.

They could have written 'South Wales Police do not require a fifteen stone, unclean, sweating, doom jacket wearing hells angel wielding a murder's machete with poor eyesight'. Bless them; so, it's back to Weetabix boxes. Bugger!

The factory was a grind. Decent working people but it wasn't for me. Three years there till I was nineteen would be unbearable. How many Weetabix boxes is that. Oh God!

The Penygraig rugby club was good. I loved the game; it formed a big part of my life. At the club I met Dai who frequented the club after leaving the army. He had served twenty-two years as a member of the 17th/21st Lancers. A tank regiment with a Skull and Crossbones for a regimental badge. We spoke regularly about his time there. To me everything he talked about was exciting and different; travel, tanks, army life and all the different things he had done and all the places he had done them in. All the while I was in the Rugby Club routine and feeding flat Weetabix boxes into a press. Chats with Fred kindled my military ambition, I was thinking more and more about it.

Two things happened in the factory that were to set me on a path out of there. Firstly, one Saturday morning I was asked to work overtime for a few hours at a second factory premises the firm owned. On arrival there I was tasked to move one pallet of cardboard on a hand trolley about twenty yards across a warehouse floor. This took about two minutes; I then asked the supervisor, whom I was quickly to discover was a man of perpetual boredom, what next? He told me there was nothing more to do and that I should just sit around for three or four hours then clock out. While I sat, bored to death, the old-timer regaled me with tales of his long years working in factories. It was slow torturous death by factory floor stories.

The second motivating factor for me to leave was when I was instructed to bail the waste cardboard using a large hydraulic bailing machine. I spent the day stuffing cardboard cut offs into a steel cage, compressing it with a ram and then binding it with wires. Death by bailing.

I got home that evening and told my dad it was going to be the army for me!

My dad wasn't too keen. He had done two years national service in about 1955 in the Royal Welsh Regiment. Though he wasn't keen I had often heard him tell with fondness stories of his time in the army. Stories of sport, good friends, and a fab time at Lunenberg in Germany. My mind was made up. I did a bit of research at the local library and spoke with some older gents at the rugby club. I had an uncle, Trevor, known as 'Bowler' because of his rugby talent, who had been a Royal Signaller, and he recommended the Royal Signals; but they weren't for me I later learned they were more commonly known as 'Scaly-backs'.

It was going to be the Welsh Guards for me. A Welsh regiment with a good rugby history. Fabulous and exciting

Army Careers Office

On a cold January morning in 1975, my dad and I walked into the army careers office at Gelliwasted Road in Pontypridd. My father spoke to the Sergeant there and he told him I wanted to join the army. The Sergeant looked me up and down and asked me to sit in a nearby office alone. After about ten minutes the Sergeant walked in and asked me which regiment, was I thinking about joining. I told him the Welsh Guards. He asked why and I stumbled some dross about proud of Wales, rugby and being a smart soldier. As it happened the senior Warrant Officer in the building was an RSM from the Welsh Guards. The Sergeant left the room and returned with the

RSM. He was wearing full, what I later learnt was No.2 dress uniform. Resplendent in smartness, badges, medals, and belts. He looked imposing and in my mind's eye a future me. I was flattering myself!

ME ONE DAY!

He chatted with me politely, noticed that I was quite a big lad, asked me if I could run and if I played sport. I proudly told him the name rugby club I played for, Penygraig RFC, and at what position. He broadened

21

into a big smile and assured me my choice of Welsh Guards was excellent and I would be very welcome, and I would enjoy the regiment immensely. I was delighted I'd only been in the career's office for about fifteen minutes, and I was assured of a place in the Welsh Guards, and I had a brand-new best friend. How little I knew! How much I would learn!

So, some paperwork was filled out, questions answered, and appointments made for entrance exams, medical examinations, and a wait was arranged while other checks were made with the police. I left the careers office feeling as if I had embarked on my career already. I could see myself in a red tunic outside Buckingham Palace impressing the Queen and tourists from all over the world. Onward and upward, 'Cymru Am Byth' – 'Wales For Ever'.

I attended for an entrance examination back at Pontypridd a week or two later. I recall sitting for what seemed like hours ticking boxes and writing

short answers. There were hundreds of them, but I managed to finish the papers well before the allotted time was up.

Some short weeks later I was asked to attend a medical.

So off to the big city, Cardiff, for a medical. I was stripped to my pants, poked, prodded, weighed, listened to, and peered at through instruments. There wasn't much conversation. I was told the examination was over, to get dressed, and to be on my way. I left to go back to the valleys without so much as a nod and a wink.

The next step was a return to the Pontypridd careers office for what I was told was to be a final interview. I considered this to be a formality and they would give me a joining date to go to the Guards Depot at Pirbright. (I learned a depot is where they train soldiers). It was going to be an exciting day.

The interview was very formal. I was placed in a chair before a person who I believe was a Major, but certainly an officer. He asked my intended ambitions with the army, and I reiterated to be a good and smart Welsh Guardsman, to do my duty and to play rugby for the regiment. At which point he ruined my career and told me the Welsh Guards were not for me. He pointed out that I had done very well in my tests and that I was more suited to the Royal Electrical and Mechanical Engineers (what a gob full) or known more widely as the REME pronounced 'Reemee'.

I wasn't expecting that. It took me a moment or two for it all to sink in. The first job he suggested was Instrument Technician, about which I had no clue. He went on to talk about vehicle mechanics and other trade jobs. Whatever, but the Welsh Guards were out of the question.

The upshot of the interview was that there was an offer of the REME on the table and which trade could be decided at the army selection centre at Sutton Coldfield where I would spend three days.

I was asked what I had to clear before I was able to go. Well, I would have walked away from Weetabix boxes there and then, but I had a driving test booked for March and an end of season rugby tour to France with my club. So, it was agreed I would go to the selection centre in the first week of April.

I left the careers office a little troubled the Welsh Guards door had closed, it wasn't explained to me why, but the REME door was open. However, my immediate choice was the REME or Weetabix. I had a month or two to think about and besides there were French rugby clubs that needed beating.

Army Selection Centre at Sutton Coldfield

My surname is Rees, I am Welsh, I have an undeniable Welsh accent, so I was called 'Taff Rees'; obvious. I was 'Taff' Rees for the next 12 yeas 309 days. There were lots of others called Taff and Jock and Geordie and Yorkie and Brummie and Scouse. How is it people from the south of England and the West country don't have proper names?

It's a wet April morning and I'm off to Sutton Coldfield. The army had sent me joining instructions and a rail warrant. I was to catch a train from my local train station to Cardiff where I would change for Bristol Parkway, change for Birmingham, change for Sutton Coldfield; quite an adventure for a seventeen-year-old relatively untravelled valley boy. I'd packed the evening before, nothing but clothes. I didn't have anything else. My mother told my father to give me some advice. He wasn't expecting the command and said to be sure to wash under my arms and my

crotch. That was it. As it turned out that was very good advice.

My mother took me to the station for the early morning train. It was pouring with rain. An un-ceremonial awkward brief goodbye and I was on the station, in the rain, suitcase by my side wondering if I was doing the right thing.

The train journey was lonely and incident free. The connections were made, and I arrived at Sutton Coldfield in good order.

As I walked out of the station wondering where to go, I could see a, what I now know to be a Bedford RL three tonner. A green army lorry with a cab and a canvas covered back. There were other young men or boys milling around, each looking as lost as me and each carrying or standing by a suitcase or Lage bag. We just milled around near the lorry, all unsure and nobody speaking.

There was a soldier in uniform sitting in the cab of the lorry, he was smoking and totally disinterested in us. Another train pulled in the station and another group of bemused young men joined us. The soldier, a one-stripe Lance Corporal got out of the cab and firmly told us to get in the back of the lorry. We did so, but it was probably the first time for all of us to do this, it certainly was for me. How tough can it be to climb into the back of a lorry with a suitcase for the first time? The answer is – it's bloody awkward and tough.

We jerkily bounced along in the lorry in the way that only an army lorry can jerkily bounce. Arriving at the camp we were told to get of the lorry and wait outside a building where we would be called in one by one. We chatted small-talk amongst ourselves, where are you from? My name is! Got any fags mate? What regiment do you want? and so on.

Eventually it was my turn. I was given a room number, a wad of documents to read and fill in and for the first time told my regimental number along with instruction to memorise it by the following day. I did, the full eight digits, it's been on the tip of my tongue ever since. We were told to wait outside until we were directed to our accommodation.

After we had all been through the office a Corporal gathered us together and started barking at us. He told us to get in formation of threes, to turn when he told us to and to put our left and right feet forward when he said so. What a complete and utter shambles. It's difficult to walk to somebody else's instruction, carrying a case didn't help, and not knowing where you're going just topped it off. Eventually after a lot of shouting and swearing we arrived a barrack block and told to fall out! What did that mean? Fall out of what?

We were instructed to find our allocated room, dump our suitcases, and return outside to collect a mattress and bedding.

Outside once again, we gaggled off under instruction to a store where we collected a mattress, blankets, sheets and two pillows. Then we returned to the accommodation carrying our bedding in the same shapeless mess we had earlier displayed. This army thing was a lark!

We were given directions to the cookhouse and told to make our beds.

First Army Bollocking

In the evening, we were all in the NAAFI, having a beer and making acquaintances. We talked of where we were from, our ambition for our different regiments and corps and other 'new to each other' stuff. At the end of the evening, a very tall, large Corporal appeared. He loudly told us all to 'Fuck Off' to bed. On my way out of the NAAFI I stopped to get a drink from a vending machine. Suddenly the Corporal turned on me and started yelling. Apparently, I was a useless scumbag. No good for anything, and if I wanted to stay in his army, I'd better

get a 'Fucking Grip". I daren't ask grip of what? I just went. My drink paid for but uncollected. I had received my first bollocking by a professional bollocker. There would be many more.

My first night in barracks wasn't very pleasant. I learned that young men away from home with two beers inside them can be absolute twats. Childish, gobby, pissed, yelling, and generally messing about.

I remember two of my room companions were aspiring to be aircraft technicians in the REME. One of them was named Parrott and answered to 'Polly' the others surname was Lancaster, and obviously, answered to 'Lanky', his regimental number was of course another eight digits, one from mine. I've not seen or heard of them since.

The next day started with breakfast. Army food was good and would remain so for the entire length of my service. On that first day we all queued for haircuts. I had a short back and sides only a few days before in preparation. Never mind, they gave me another one. We were packed off to a gymnasium where we had to run back and fore, do press-ups, sit ups, climb a rope, get weighed, get skin measured and other novice things.

The next day was a series of presentations and lectures about different regiments and corps and what jobs were available and what we could expect with each job. Everybody thought Royal Engineers train driver looked good. We were ushered about, only marginally more successfully without luggage or mattresses.

The following day was interview and allocation time. I found myself sitting in front of a Major, what regiment he was from I know not. He asked me if I could kill someone. I replied that I could if the person had done something wrong. That answer wasn't good enough I realised, and he asked me again. He wanted an outright 'of course I could no problem'. That's what he got. We settled into a bit of a one-way chat and when I left, I was I was heading for the

Training Battalion and Depot REME located at Arborfield in Royal Berkshire. Royal mind you! I was going to be an Instrument Technician which, as far as I knew, meant I would be looking after binoculars, gun-sight, theodolites, and the like. It was a brave new world.

Onto a jerky green lorry armed with a warrant to the train station and onto a train to Reading where I would change for Wokingham station.

On the journey I was accompanied by another young hopeful who was off to the Guards Depot at Pirbright. He was tall and skinny, wore spectacle and was very, very spotty. He kept telling me he was going to be the smartest guardsman ever. I wonder if he ever made it.

1ˢᵀ BOLLOCKNG – THAT'LL TEACH ME TO BE THIRSTY

Training Battalion and Depot REME

The Training Battalion and Depot REME is where adult REME recruits were sent to be transformed from civilians into trained soldiers. Same welcome as Sutton Coldfield only this time by a green army bus. Army buses are designed to be the most uncomfortable in the world. Tinny, rickety, noisy, cold, or hot, hard thin seats prone to break-down.

Poperinghe Barracks, Arborfield. This was a whole new world for me. First thing I learnt was that I was going to live in a 'Spider'. A Spider! Who lives in spiders? Was this a reason for termination by arachnophobia I thought. Turns out that a spider is a wooden barrack block constructed in the shape of a spider. There are six legs in our case, not eight, and the centre body of the spider is an ablution block of toilets, sinks, showers and maybe a bath. In my instance seventeen young soldiers in each spider leg.

Our spider leg was old and in a poor state of repair, rumour had it that it had been condemned many years before. It was functional and certainly gave us a special military 'feel'.

Each bed space in the spider had a steel frame bed with a metal wire base, a large six-foot metal locker and a small two shelf bedside cabinet. The luxury element was a thin mat measuring about two feet by three. That was it.

My first platoon was called 'build-up' platoon. In this platoon you sit around and do nothing all day. No uniform, no instructions other than to keep out of the way and not to talk to anybody. So, we did just that. We were waiting for enough new recruits to 'build-up' until there were enough to form a full platoon of about fifty recruits. The way the army named things lacked originality in my very new view.

The only incident I can recall about 'build-up' platoon was that one languishing day, about six of us were lounging on our beds in the spider chatting when a chap in a tracksuit walked in through the front door of the spider leg and out the back door. He was older than us and clearly experienced soldier material, I could tell by his porn star moustache. I didn't know who he was, but he looked serious, he made eye-contact with us all. I was the only person in the group who stood up, awkwardly I might add. As he left the room, I had a bad feeling which was proven to be justified about twenty minutes later.

It turns out the track-suited serious looking chap was S/Sgt Chippie Wood. He would be our platoon Senior Non-Commissioned Officer (SNCO) and our 'God' for our time at the Training Battalion and Depot REME.

At about the twenty-minute point two Corporals came in and went to town on us for about ten minutes. Apparently when a senior Non-Commissioned Officer (NCO), particularly your own, enters the room you stand to attention and don't move. Corporals (Cpl's) Davies and Macron, I was to learn their names later, enjoyed shouting and bawling insults and apparently, we were worthless and unlikely to make soldiers unless we got a serious grip of ourselves, shaped up and sorted our miserable lives out. I mentioned to the Corporals that I had stood up, but that was a mistake; mentioning it that is. They rounded on me a little louder and of the group of recruits present I was the most worthless, needed to get the biggest grip, had the most miserable life and I was the least likely to make a soldier.

2ND BOLLOCKING – THAT'LL TEACH ME TO DO THE RIGHT THING!

It was my second army bollocking. I considered that as I had stood up showing some respect, I didn't know who the bloke in the tracksuit was anyway, my bollocking was for doing the right thing, and for not knowing something I couldn't have possibly known anyway. I was learning this army thing fast!

Eventually enough recruits arrived to form a recruit platoon. We were No 2 Platoon of 1975. An original name, I wonder wondered who thought that up?

We numbered about fifty or sixty and we were from all over the UK. The occupants of each spider leg formed a section. My spider leg had three Jocks, two Taff's (the other being Selwyn Harris from Newport) and about ten others. We quickly got to know each other's names and where we were from. Friendships were formed quickly. Our ages range from seventeen (that was me, the youngest) to thirty (Roger Dawkins), many had previous work experience and I had stories of Weetabix Boxes to tell.

So, on the first morning of being a platoon we were formed into three ranks and marched off (gaggled more like) to the Quarter Master's store to collect kit. I learned the Quarter Masters Store is forever after called the QM's. I also learned that everything, absolutely everything, in the army is called 'Kit'.

Inside the very large tin hut that was the QMs there was a long counter along which we passed and people behind the counter gave us uniform, equipment, webbing, cutlery, mugs, hats, badges, gym kit, coats. It was given to us all in one go and with a little help we were loaded up with it all and told to make our way individually back to our spider.

It was a challenging journey, kit was dropped, rolled away, retrieved, dropped, and rolled away again. Eventually we were in our spider with a great huge pile of stuff on each bed. It would be impossible for all this stuff to be put into our one solitary locker each.

So, we put on uniforms for the first time, and I discover several things. The shirts are very hairy and very itchy, they are also very long generally knee-length. We are also issued with another type of shirt which is not hairy, doesn't itch, and it fits well, but we are not allowed to wear it.

The berets are unruly and stick out and too tight or too loose. There is no hole in the beret in which to fit a REME badge.

Army boots, called DMS (I still don't know what the letters mean), are thick rubber soled, leather uppers and stiff and unwieldy. We get two pairs each and I have yet to learn why. Also, there is a special way to lace them, which I have at this point yet to learn. I am told that how you 'lace' your boots will determine if a Gurkha beheads you with his Kukri or not. Bit of a worry at this early stage in my military career. Check your laces and keep an eye out for Gurkhas!

We get a pair of black daps, or trainers or plimsoles' what they are called depends on where you come from. In the Welsh valleys its daps. Cheap as chips and useless.

A green pullover, cotton pants and vests, all too large or too small. A very intriguing army tie which looks and feels like a short flat rope. Eating utensils come in the way of a knife, fork, and spoon ever after known as KFS and a green plastic mug for tea. Tea is ever after known as 'Char' and made by the gallon. An unabsorbing green army towel is issued but toiletries such as soap, toothpaste, shampoo, boot polish, razors etc., are your own responsibility and can be bought from the NAAFI.

The NAAFI standing for Navy, Army Air Force Institute is the onsite shop, café, bar for us to use. Everything any young soldier needs can be bought there including 'Blanco' which was new to me, nobody 'Blancoed' anything in the Rhondda.

'Puttees' are worth a special mention. They are probably a yard long length of a sage material sewn onto which is a further yard of thin khaki coloured rough ribbon. They are wound around the top of your DMS boot and make a seal between your boot top and your trouser bottoms. I think they are to stop dangerous snakes and lizards going up your trouser leg, but I'm not sure because nobody ever told me. How many dangerous snakes and lizards are there in Royal Berkshire? It's a challenge to learn to put them on, tie them off correctly and make them look decently smart. It happens eventually and the addition of a pair of elastics atop the puttees in which to tuck your trouser bottoms makes all the difference.

Puttee Definition –

A puttee is a covering for the lower part of the leg from the ankle to the knee, alternatively known as: leg wraps, leg bindings, winingas, or Wickelbänder. They consist of a long narrow piece of cloth wound tightly, and spirally round the leg, and serving to provide both support and protection. They were worn by both mounted and dismounted soldiers, generally taking the place of the leather gaiter.

We were also given two REME cap badges. The REME cap badge has a distinctive shape. It's a composition of a horse, a globe, a streak of lightning and a royal crown. I was told it meant –

> *The horse stands on a globe and above it is a scroll inscribed 'REME' surmounted by a crown. Behind the horse there is a lightning flash. This symbolises electrical engineering while the globe stands for the world-wide role of the unit. The chained horse symbolises power under control.*

There you go. Later in my service I would be given other explanations but none quite so formal or correct. Such as –

> *REME work as hard as horses, as fast as lightning, and if you break the chain and drop a bollock, you'll get crowned.*

> *REME also had numerous connotations as often expressed by bored soldiers.*

- *Rough Engineering Made Easy*
- *Royal Engineers Minus Education*
- *Ruin Every Maiden Eventually*
- *Ruin Everything Mechanical and Electrical*

and more

The 'Beret' with which we had been issued was an unwieldy woollen cow-pat. It had to be shrunk-to-fit. We were shown how to do this by an instructor.

SHRINK TO FIT, HOT, COLD, HOT, COLD, HOT, COLD .....

It goes like this - You get two sinks of water, one very hot the other cold. You soak the beret alternatively into the hot and cold and then after a while you wring the water out and you place the wet beret on your head. Then firmly pulling the slack in the beret to the right and rear you press it onto your head. Then you walk around with a wet beret on your head until it is almost dry and has taken on its new shape. A slit is cut into the cap badge holder of the beret and the regimental badge affixed and pressed in. The badge is worn over the left eye. Berets are brushed clean with boot brushes but no polish. Berets gather dust and debris easily and have been the cause of many serious bollockings over the years. We were no exception.

Learning to be Shouted and Sworn At

Military training in the REME is taught by REME soldiers who have opted to train as Regimental Duty soldiers 'RD'. To qualify they must pass a Regimental Duty Qualification course known as RDQ (original name I know). This qualifies them to shout and swear more than anybody else and they can be very good at it. So eventually recruit military training begins, being taught by people who are qualified to shout and swear.

There is a lot of shouting and swearing in the army and the place where it excels is on the drill square. The REME are as good at shouting and swearing as any other regiment or Corps in the British or any other army. So, in a move to take the recruits away from the shambling chaotic drill of untrained soldiers they teach drill. I can't understate how much shouting and swearing this involves at this stage.

I was familiar with a range of profanities and insults from the rugby fields of South Wales, but the British Army takes it to a whole new professional level. Consider the disparity between the Vauxhall Conference and the Premiership, massive.

Young soldiers very quickly learn that the parade square is a sacred place, very sacred. Nonchalantly strolling across the parade square is not on. Doing so normally has two subsequent effects. Firstly, if your seen doing so by any person with the words

'Sergeant Major' in his title you will cause him to go into an apoplectic fit and he will instantly display his prowess at shouting and swearing; being a 'Sergeant Major' he will have qualified highly in shouting and swearing. Secondly it will cause the unsuspecting trespasser to either spend some time in the guardroom jail or cop for a few extra duties.

I was not told at the time, but I learned years later that the parade square was sacred because –

> *After the battle when retreat was sounded, and the unit had reassembled to call the roll and count the dead a hollow square was formed. The dead were placed within the square, and no one used this space as a thoroughfare. Today the parade ground represents this square, and hence a unit's dead. It is hallowed ground soaked with the blood of the fallen and the area is respected as such.*

No wonder the Sergeant Majors went apoplectic, and rightly so. Respect for fallen comrades is everything; I would personally learn this as my career progressed.

Drill

We all gather shambling and chaotically near the parade square which is a giant car park without cars, or parking metres or anything else for that matter.

Here the RD staff begin shouting. They put us all in a straight line, fifty of us, and place the tallest of us on the right. In our case it was Michael Cavell from Newport, tall and skinny. Then in descending height-wise from Cavell we form a straight shoulder to shoulder line on his left right down to the shortest soldier on the end. In our case Taff Harris from Newport (what is it with height disparity in Newport) who the Jocks had christened 'Wee Taff' as opposed to 'Big Taff' which was me. More originality I thought.

Shoulder to shoulder facing front one of the Corporals' shouts at us to 'number from the right'. So, Cavell on the right is One, then two and so on down to Harris who is fifty something. Then odd numbers take one pace forward and even numbers take one pace back. 'Cavell the tall' stands still and the remainder of the front-rank turn towards him, the rear rank turn to their left and are told to follow around on the front rank. As they march (loosely used term at this stage) forward the instructor pushes them into either the front, centre or rear rank all based on Cavell's position. Its magic. When we all stop the platoon has somehow morphed into a symmetrically shaped clever thing. One end are tall people, the height of the soldiers then decreases symmetrically to the platoon middle before increasing in height to the other end. 'Wee-Taff' is in the middle. It was probably the first thing that surprised and impressed me in the army. We are now told this is our formation and this is our shape to learn drill.

Drill is where the army teaches you to walk in a particular way at a particular speed. It also teaches you to start, stop, turn, change direction, walk around a bend (wheel), walk in one place, and stamp your feet a lot. We're all supposed to do the same thing at the same time decided by somebody shouting and swearing at us.

There is also 'Rifle Drill'. This is where we learn to carry a rifle in different ways, move it from hand to hand, lay it on the floor and sometimes 'slap' it. Again, all decided by somebody shouting and swearing at us.

With 'Drill' are many new phrases to learn and act upon. Quick march, slow march, left turn, right turn, mark time, step short the inside man, step out the outside man, collars in the back of the neck, press down on the thumb, left wheel, right wheel, about turn, break into double time, break into quick time, saluting's to the right and left, and so on. 'Fill your

chest with pride'! was one of my favourites. 'Suck your gut in', not so much.

There are more difficult things to pick up and decipher eff ri eff ri eff ri eff. At least its repetitive and easy to remember. Agghh. Stand aaaaa eeeez. Staaand Eazzzy. And so on.

All this drill stuff is no good unless you can tell the time correctly. Not o'clock time but proper army time. Namely - One Two Three, One. Or 1-23-1. To get the drill movements together we start of by shouting, as loud as we can, 1-23-1 making an action on each digit to practically every movement we make. This ensures we begin to synchronise as a team. As we became more proficient, we shouted 1-23-1 under our breaths to ourselves and further along we just thought it as a matter of course.

What's the time? 1-23-1, same as it's always been! Still is today.

Every day we spend hours drilling. Many mistakes are made but they number less and less as time passes. You can tell how long the platoons have been in training by the way the march. At the start we are jerky and unsure, but it quickly becomes effortless, and we can look on more junior platoons as having a lot to learn. Veterans already are we.

Grow or Shrink – It'll Fit

No 2 dress. Is to be our best dress; we are not worthy of No 1's. Its Khaki in colour and comprises a button up tunic with a belt, trousers, the non-itchy-shirt, and the flat rope tie. For issue we are marched along to the QM's where we are each given tunic and trousers and told to put it on. Not one of them fits. Not one! So, we are all stood in a line, fifty or more of us, and along walks the tailor. If the uniform is too big, he says 'You will grow into it', if it's too small he says, 'You will shrink into it'. That was it, no measurements, no tapes, no scissors, no chalk, nothing. Oral tailoring. Funny thing was he was

absolutely bang on and at the end of basic training all of us looked splendidly well turned out in proper fitting uniforms. Clever bloke that tailor!

<u>Shooting and ranges</u>

We are all marched to the armoury to be issued rifles. The gool old Self-Loading Rifle (SLR), army designated L1A1, a thumping favourite of a 7.62mm high velocity long rifle based on the Belgian FN. Twenty round magazine, open iron sights. We're given a sling, bayonet and scabbard, cleaning kit. We're also given hours and hours of rifle drill until it becomes an extra limb.

Before we get to fire the rifle, we are taught how to dry fire, to strip and assemble. We learn how to 'pull-through' to clean the barrel and oil. Using dummy rounds we load, unload and deal with imaginary misfires, time and time again. We practice speed magazine loading and learn the 'marksmanship principles' of how to position our bodies, align the rifle and breathe. We do this kneeling, standing,

sitting, and lying down; and any other body contortion we can think of. We repeat it all blind-folded also. There is a lot to it.

Eventually we get to the range. It's an exciting day. Live ammunition and targets at 100, 200 and 300 yds. Blimey 300 yds are a long way off.

So, you've learnt your drills, passed your dry run tests, listened to your Corporals and now you must fire the actual rifle for real.

You do everything right, but it still doesn't prepare you for that very first almighty crack and thump into your shoulder. What the Fuck was that! But you've done it, and you do it again and again. Your shots get scored, some good, some not so, then you collect the brass, clean your rifle.

Then there's a leaving the range declaration to the officer in charge. "I have no live rounds or empty cartridge cases in my possession Sir". What a difficult gob-full that is to remember at first. Very

quickly it all becomes second nature, we become more proficient, better shots, quicker rifle cleaners and prompt and correct declarers.

The SLR a real thumper

Lessons

We had lessons in first aid, map reading, ironing clothes, beret shrinking to fit, boot polishing, bed making, regimental and Corps history, fieldcraft, target acquisition and other essential military specific things. Every lesson was started by the instructor telling you it might save your life one day. The motivation was always the same, it was the army way. Tying your laces the correct way saves your life – remember Johnny Gurkha and his Kukri.

NBC training was my least favourite. Nuclear, Chemical and Biological (NBC) warfare training was no fun. The NBC hooded suit was rough and charcoal, with a hood and rubber gloves. The S6 (I still don't know what that denotes) Respirator was hard rubber, a tight fit and sucked at your face when you breathed, Running or any activity demanding more breath-intake was massively more challenging. Running around in a closed tin shed full of CS gas was no fun. While in there, off with your mask and forced to speak till you must draw breath. Oh joy. Then outside, facing the wind, running nose, teary eyes, burning sweaty bits. Yep, joy of joys. The stuff stayed with you for hours.

The RD staff were, for the most part, decent people. Time served REME soldiers doing a decent job. They had absolute power over us and vastly superior military knowledge. Our future careers hung on their opinion of us, so we tried our best to please. Of course, it was in their interests for us to do well also. There was keen competition between the different sections. Rivalry is and always has been an excellent stimulant.

They were tough on inspection of kit and spider. Sometimes everything went out the window and that was a bind, particularly if hard and long worked on bulled-boots landed on their toes. I wonder who opened the windows beforehand?

Cleaning of barracks is cleaning, the only thing militarily different was 'bumpering' the floors. Polish was spread on the wooden floors and a heavy metal block attached to a long wooden handle was used to polish the floor. It was called a 'bumper', I suppose because it bumped into things; I don't really know. It was efficiently augmented with the laying of an old army blanket on the floor and wrapped around the bumper. Sometimes a soldier sitting on a blanket was used as a substitute bumper, to polish as he was pulled around and across the floor by others. Innovation and teamwork.

Drill, shooting and smartness, stimulated and refined by shouting and swearing, gets better as time passes and we develop a growing sense of pride and importance in what we can do and how we perform.

The food in the cookhouse was prepared by the Army Catering Corps (ACC) more colloquially knows as Andy Caps Commandos or less flatteringly the 'Slop Jockeys'. In truth they were the only Corps in the army that relentlessly put themselves up for criticism three times a day. In my view they did a fabulous job for all my service, often in the 'field' under the most trying of conditions. I had to learn what 'In the field' meant. Its anywhere outdoors on exercise, scheme, or active service. 'In the field' morphed into the "Ulu" sometime later. It's the same place. My garden today is the "Ulu". My vocabulary was growing.

I learnt my rifle was a 'Bundook", washing was 'Dhobi; washing powder was 'Dhobi Dust', a sandwich was a 'Sarnie'. I was becoming more and more worldly wise every day.

How to Piss

Many of the lessons were supplemented with Army Training Films made by the Kinematograph Service which was formed during the war in 1941 to meet the demand of the explosion in training needs. By the time I was watching them they were well dated. Normally projected from an 8mm projector they were flitty and faded and often broke and had been spliced many times over. They were always accompanied

by that old pucker English voice portraying a sense of urgency and how trusted the content was.

Most of the films I've long forgotten but what I do remember was the one that taught us it was ok to shag prostitutes and how to piss.

The script went like this; the scene is in some distant oriental country and a couple of British soldiers are out on the lash, as all British soldiers do. Its traditional. During the evening the soldiers pull two birds. Both birds are stunners, one of them is a whore and charges for her services the other is a schoolteacher and it's a freebee (Oh yes!), they all have a great time with a 'happy ending'.

Next scene the soldiers that went with the whore, she was a looker mind, is shown playing sport, enjoying a good time in the NAAFI and is the picture of health and happiness.

GEOGRAPHY TEACHER

Next scene shows the soldier that got across the schoolteacher and he's there looking ultra-embarrassed and squirming in front of a very stern-faced Medical Officer (MO) seeking treatment for his dose of 'clap'.

Moral of the story – shag whores and not schoolteachers.

The film moved on to explain an array of precautions that could be taken to reduce the risk of VD. Condoms, no entry and so on. The part of the film that has stuck with me is where the speaker says it's good to, after having had your way with a schoolteacher or whore, go for a piss.

When pissing pinch, the end of your foreskin (if you have one, I think we all did, but I didn't check), so that a balloon of piss gathers around you bell-end, then slowly release your pinch so that a slow flow escapes. Thus, circulating your piss around your bell-end, so it gathers any unwelcome bacteria and foreign bodies.

Those bloody unclean schoolteachers. I still practice this to this day, I'm expert at it. The pinched pissing that is, not the shagging of whores and schoolteachers.

Spider life.

Reveille was six am, but people often got up earlier to iron shirts or polish boots because they hadn't had the foresight or sense to do it the night before. There is nothing more annoying than being woken by the harsh early morning rubbing of polish onto boots.

Out of bed and into the 'ablutions' which was another new word to me. Shower shit and a shave was the essential morning routine. Fifty young men, generally naked or in underpants only, feuding over ten or twenty sinks, six showers and maybe ten crappers. A close shave was vitally important any less could mean a bollocking by one of the many professional bollocker's in town. And we daren't go on a first or muster parade with the slightest hint of shaving scream or soap on our faces. To do so was akin to a capital offence. A torrent of personally directed scumbag, dirtball, heathen, unclean, contaminated abuse would come our way.

Once abluted and dressed we made our beds, turned down hospital fashion and dead flat, then it was a run along to the cookhouse for a 'full English' or 'full Welsh' or 'full Scottish' depending on where you were from. They were all the same with an excellent choice of everything breakfast.

Now fed we'd walk back to the spider with a green plastic mug full of char being drunk along the way. Arriving at the spider a final wash of KFS and mug, an after-breakfast teeth brush for some followed by 'block-jobs'. A list of who had to do what had been pinned on the spider notice board.

There were different areas allocated for cleaning. Each person allocated was responsible for the cleanliness and tidiness. There were corridors, windows, main floor, ablutions, outside areas, bins and so on. It's very unpleasant cleaning away another person's skid marks. But, that type of thing was soon sorted. We were assuming a collective responsibility and looking out for each other.

Next was the essential smartness check before muster parade. Boots clean, no fluff on uniform, beret on straight and pulled back to the right and rear, cap badge over left eye, buttons done-up, no bulges in pocket.

We'd form up outside, Cavell always as right-hand marker, Wee Harris in the middle, always the same place. The instructors would then begin shouting and swearing and off we would go to the muster parade on the parade square.

The senior platoon would be on the right and the less senior platoons diminishing to the left. On parade there was always an excess of shouting but no swearing. We'd march onto the square and form-up. There would normally be an inspection by someone in authority. Most of the time it was the SNCO, in our case S/Sgt Chippie Wood. Sometimes there would be an officer, maybe a platoon commander or a company officer. I don't remember any of them as we didn't see them a great deal and when we did, they always spoke quietly to the instructors which was consequently translated into shouting and swearing for our benefit lest we were unable to converse normally. After a while we got used to the shouting and swearing and it became normal communication. Some of us began to mimic it and for all of us our swearing was improving magnificently.

Muster was generally followed by an hour or so of drill. Guess what? yep, shouting and swearing!

About 10am would be NAAFI break. That's where we all go to the NAAFFI for char and smokes. Normally half an hour before we move onto another military lesson in some shed, or utilitarian spider or grassy bank if the weather was non-inclement. See how my new vocabulary is creeping in!

Then lunch, then more lessons. The end of the day normally terminated with something physical such as a platoon run. This is where all of us in PT vest, combat trousers and those bloody heavy stiff DMS

boots went for a two- or three-mile run. Soldiers at the front and back wearing fluorescent tabards and instructors shouting and swearing alongside. Squad running isn't so bad, you quickly get into a breathing and jogging rhythm. All in step, the slap of the boots on the ground takes you along, but it's always good to reach the end. Quick shower for some and off for the evening, and main, meal of the day.

Following the meal its kit ready for tomorrow, boots, ironing and so on, unless you were an early morning annoying polisher.

Guard Duty

After about six weeks we were deemed responsible enough to carry out guard duty. There was no fun in guard duty. The first couple of times guard duty is novel but it soon wears off.

Twelve men and an NCO are ordered for guard duty. The dress code is always full combat uniform, beret, clean shaven, belt and boots. All must be clean and well presented. The orderly officer normally, or SNCO on duty inspects the guard and the inspecting person has the prerogative to award 'stick man'. This award was given to the smartest turned-out soldier on the parade. That soldier was then excused duty and was free to do as they wished. I suppose it was an incentive to encourage smartness. I don't know the origin of the term 'stick-man', I can only think that as the inspecting officer normally carries a stick, the stick-man would be the person chosen by pointing the stick at them. In that case he should rightly be called the 'end of stick man'. But I don't really know, still don't.

After the parade the guard move into the guardroom where, normally the second in charge a JNCO, divides the guard into shifts, normally of four soldiers each. The shifts were called 'stags', I don't know why this is either; I always thought a stag to be a male deer. The stag pattern was normally two hours on and four-off. The four-off being spent in the guardroom making tea, reading, smoking, or sleeping. Guard duty was normally an unexciting onerous pastime.

British army guardrooms I found to be universally uncomfortable places. Furnished in a utilitarian manner without not an ounce of comfort. The chairs were always of metal or wood, square and hard. The beds or bunks were steel framed, and steel sprung. No blankets each soldier brought along their issue sleeping bag; known affectionately as a 'green maggots'. I always 'itched' all over when I was on guard.

The guardroom char tasted the same the world over, the guardroom itch was the same annoying itch the world over and the tiredness the following day was the same tiredness the world over. We didn't get the day off because we had been awake all night, we just carried on as normal but more tired.

Those soldiers not on 'stag' had to get rations from the cookhouse for the duration of the duty. It was always the same stuff. Tea, tins of condensed milk, sugar. Sandwiches of dry-bread, dry ham with the corners upturned, and thin dried cheese. There may be an apple or a kit-kat if our luck was in, sometimes the kit-kat would be in-date.

At the depot the guard commander NCO had the opportunity to either impress us new recruits with exaggerated war stories or outright lies; we didn't know the difference. Or on the other hand we could be totally ignored by the vastly experienced old sweats.

Two men would be posted on the main gate, two more would form a perambulating foot patrol. The guard were armed with pick-elves, that's pickaxe handles without the pick on the end. Jut the metal collar to which it would be attached. They were heavy unwieldy things which were good for battering stuff. That was it.

Those guard duties at the REME depot were particularly onerous. The IRA stole some guns from the guardroom in the sixties so at some following

point in history some wit had decided that a good security measure at the depot was to build a glass cage on the front of the guardroom. It had probably been there for eons. The guardroom overlooked the front gate to the camp at which two members of the guard were always on duty. The glass cage was literally that – a glass cage. Placed in the centre of the cage was a solitary hard chair. It was the world's most uncomfortable chair. We spent a whole two-hour stag in the glass cage. It was purgatory.

I assume the reason we were imprisoned in the glass cage, maybe to keep an eye on the guard on the gate with a view to raising the alarm if necessary. I don't think there was any way to raise the alarm other than shout and bang the glass.

The locked door was at the back of the cage, three sides of glass, spartan in the extreme. The most boring, soul destroying, mind numbingly dreadful place imaginable. Two hours were an eternity. At night or quiet weekends even more so. Those two

hours of fridge cold, or tropical hot, discomfort would stretch into days which stretched into weeks and on into months through years to eternity.

I learned of one young recruit soldier who was locked in that oven on his first ever guard duty, he fell asleep standing up, it took forever to wake him up, and he got fourteen days jail. After that the stag length in the glass cooker was changed to forty minutes duration. Some young men spent their eighteenth and twenty-first birthdays in there, others impersonated goldfish for two hours. What was the point?

Character building? I think, in this instance, not.

Soul destroying? Probably!

On character building experiences some things are, and other things are not. The old or senior soldier often takes pleasure in espousing the 'back in my day when men were men' philosophy, and I understand a lot of it, and it can be valuable experience. But some stuff was just senseless.

Often these REME recruits were highly intelligent and embarking on careers of exceedingly technical requirements and the REME locked them in glass cage!

I don't think I experienced an exciting stint of guard duty in twelve years, with the significant exception of Northern Ireland of course.

Field Exercise

Towards the end of training, we go on a four- or five-day field exercise where we put into practice all the things we have learnt (supposedly) in and around the barracks. Platoon and section tactics, skirmishing, cover, camouflaging, basher (one man tent) erection, trench digging, defensive deployment, field signals, cross country movement, platoon attack, movement at night, hand signals and so on.

It's a trying time. First exercise and putting it altogether is difficult. No sleep, unwashed, hungry, even less sleep accompanied by a bit of shouting and swearing.

I was tasked along with a cockney lad called Michael King to dig a trench. He had a clear cockney accent and had never been outside London. He wore a permanent five o'clock shadow and got no end of grief for being unshaven. As we were digging the trench, we got down a few feet and suddenly he shouted and leapt from the shallow trench. 'A snake', 'A snake' he shouted. He was in quite a panic. I investigated the trench but could not see anything. One of the instructors came across to us to see what was going on. I can't recall his name, he was a Lance Corporal (L/Cpl) form the Queens Lancashire Fusiliers, wiry and experienced and harsh looking. He enquired what was going on and King told him and pointed to the snake. The L/Cpl jumped into the trench and came out with what I now know to be a 'slow worm' in his hand. King looked on agog as the L/Cpl cleanly bit the head off his snake and threw it into the bushes as he spat the head out of his mouth.

'There you go' he said, 'Get on with it and stop fucking about' and walked off!

I'd never seen anybody bite the head off anything in the Rhondda Valley. King just stared at me with his mouth open. I had nothing to say and carried on digging. It was the very first 'real' thing I encountered in my adult life. I was a young seventeen-year-old and people in my presence were biting the heads of snakes. It disturbed me a little and I pondered what I had seen for hours. I grew up a tad there and then. How young and naïve was I?

Character building? Hell yes!

Return to camp in jerky green army lorries. Kit to be cleaned and stowed, weapons cleaned and locked away then into the spider for ablutions, food, and sleep.

Passing Out Parade

Passing-out parade was fast approaching. We practiced over and over. We also practiced indoors in another 'biggest shed in the world' in case of inclement weather (see what vocabulary athleticism I did there). Drill perfect, uniform perfect – bring it on.

The passing out parade was witnessed by our families. It's quite a spectacle for those who haven't seen one. Proud as punch.

The officer taking the parade was a Colonel from the parachute Regiment (Brutal trained killers that they are!). He was resplendent in No 1 blues and his maroon beret and as he walked along the ranks he stopped and chatted selectively with us. He stood in front of me and asked where I was from 'Rhondda Valley Sir' I replied. 'Do you play rugby he asked, 'Yes Sir', 'What position'? He asked. 'Prop forward Sir' I replied. 'Good' he said. He turned to the REME Colonel accompanying him and said, 'All the best prop forwards come from the Rhondda Valley'. I

thought, what a fabulous Para Colonel this man is, and, in a way, he was correct because in my subsequent twelve years of service I would play rugby against, I think, all the airborne units and never be on a losing side.

It's the end of basic training. The shouting and swearing have stopped and is replaced by reasonable conversation and instruction. Its handshakes and good wishes all around and we're off on home leave prior to reporting to our next training unit.

For me as a potential Instrument Technician it's going to be the School of Electrical and Mechanical Engineering at Havannah Barracks at Bordon in Hampshire.

'SeeMee'

The School of Electrical and Mechanical Engineering (SEME)

This was where soldiers who had passed basic military training were sent to embark on courses of mechanical training. Additionally, upgrader courses were taken in furtherance of trade training.

On completion of leave we returned to the depot where we gathered before those of us going to the School of Electrical and Mechanical Engineering (SEME), pronounce 'SeeMee', were loaded onto green jerky buses for the journey to Bordon. On arrival I was posted to 'A' Company at Havannah Barracks, its where the potential Instrument Technicians went. I shared a room with four new friends, a more eclectic group you couldn't wish to meet. Nic White who became a lifelong friend, inspector in the Hong Kong police and a (legitimate) International Arms Dealer. Richard 'Dick' Pickering who had been a dispensing optician and would be

commissioned to the rank of Captain, and Gerry Blears who would be Captured in Kuwait from which he would emerge safe and sound. It was a ground floor corner room near the ablutions (how quick am I picking this up?) and the cookhouse and facing onto the front of barracks parade square.

A million times more relaxed than the depot. The junior NCOs were mostly students on courses who had been locally promoted and the platoon Sgt's were experienced soldiers who were on the Artificer Course which is sort of advanced training for SNCO's in trades. I believe it guarantees them promotion of sorts. They are generally very 'keen' people which I learnt could be a little annoying.

The format at SEME is you wait for enough 'like' potentials to arrive and then a course is formed. Trade training takes place Monday through till Friday, Wednesday is always a sports afternoon, for me it was always rugby. Military training takes place on the occasional weekend. There were rare guard and fire picquet duties. That's it.

Regimental Police

I had a while to wait for sufficient potential instrument technicians to arrive so some wag in the duty's office sent me to be a 'Regimental Policeman' at Martinique Barracks. I had no clue what it meant but, in the army, when you're a young soldier, you do what you are told.

Wearing a forage cap as opposed to a beret I reported to the guardroom in Martinique. I was given a white belt and a wide black armband with two letters 'RP' embraided on in red. That was it, I was a Regimental Policeman. How important was I?

The provost Sergeant was a man called John Butcher; likeable and a little extrovert in every way. He wore his hair over his collar which was particularly 'risqué' for the provost Sergeant whose main duty was to enforce discipline. He drove a huge black Rolls-Royce; his army retirement after twenty-two years was impending, and he had an ambition to become a waiter. His rationale was that a good waiter could make a person's evening out very enjoyable, and he would get great satisfaction from doing that. He was, of course, very correct.

The provost Corporal, and my direct boss, was on the other hand a very undeterminable kettle of fish. Corporal Edward 'Scouse' Aubrey did have, I think, either haemorrhoids or chronic toothache or more likely both afflictions. It must have been something of that nature. For him nothing was right, everything was worth shouting and swearing about. He was a direct rumbustious character and a man of constant agitation, but when we got to know him, he wasn't at all bad. Just loud.

Within weeks the powers that be promoted me to acting, unpaid, unwanted Lance Corporal. That meant I had one stripe by virtue of being a regimental policeman. How more important was I?

The Regimental police duties consisted of manning the camp front gate during daytime hours, guarding sentenced prisoners in the guardroom, and marching them around a bit to get showers, food, and exercise and to oversee them doing gardening and litter picking fatigues. It was an easy job, and the prisoners were no different to us other than by virtue of their incarceration. A guard room military criminal is a generally very petty offender sentenced by the Commanding Officer (CO) for less that twenty-eight days detention. Normally for short terms of being Absent Without Leave (AWOL) or scrapping or anything miscellaneous and considered contrary to good order and military discipline which was a coverall offence.

During this policing period, I learned to give orders, speak to people as a grown up to get them to respond and to shoulder responsibility. It was to be good training for the future. Glenn Ewen was a fellow Regimental Policeman and he and I were to become firm friends for many years of our service.

Eventually, sufficient potential Instrument Technicians arrived, and I was released from RP duties to join my course.

Instrument Technician?

Instrument Technicians require skills in fine mechanical matters and electronics. Dexterity of hand is required due to the sensitive and concise nature of the work. I didn't have the required skills involving patience and I found the course difficult and demanding. It just wasn't interesting me. However, what was interesting me was the tanks and armoured recovery vehicles I could hear and see on the tank training area close to our classroom.

One day on the course we had to, using a very small and delicate instrument lathe, manufacture a speedometer needle. The length of metal was about two inches long and we had to lathe it into four or five different diameters along its length. It also required two tapers of exacting dimensions to be manufactured to. I was crap at it. I remember fiddling

with the lathe, breaking more than one needle (probably many more). The instructor wasn't impressed with me and despite his best efforts it just wasn't going to be my bag. The tank engines were calling. I was going to apply to be a Recovery Mechanic.

Recovery Mechanic?

The role Key Responsibilities are described as -

- Help to recover damaged vehicles and rescue stranded soldiers.
- Work at the heart of the action
- Be adept at numerous recovery methods.
- Use cranes, lifting gear and mechanical theory to work out how to retrieve immobile vehicles.
- To keep the fighting forces moving forwards

Yep. That was more me and at just about eighteen years of age I was going to get to drive tanks to boot.

It was agreed I change my status from potential Instrument Technician to Potential Recovery Mechanic. I knew it was going to be a drop in pay and less promotion prospects, but, in my view, better a good Recy Mech than a crap Inst Tech.

The first things Recy Mechs must do is to learn to drive lorries. So off to the driving school at SEME Bordon. I already have a car licence so first things first I learn to drive Bedford Four Tonner, a standard general service wagon.

It was Bordon to Southampton and back every day with the last hour spent manoeuvring on the driver training square at SEME.

Enroute to Southampton one of our regular stops was a roadside café which was overrun with chickens. The standard fayre was a cup of char and an egg banjo (egg sandwich (sarnie)). It seemed every egg was double yoker, all well and good, but every day!

I successfully passed my HGV3 test first time. So on to HGV 2 and a ten-ton AEC. Same format, same routes, even the double yokers stayed the same. HGV 2 passed successfully.

I was one of the lucky few who managed to squeeze in a HGV1 course. Same format, same routes and same non-articulated double yokers.

I was eighteen years old, undergone and passed basic military training, taken, and passed three HGV driving toasts and I was an expert in double-yoker egg sandwiches. Not a Weetabix box in sight. Oh joy!

Tracked Vehicles

Next up prior to starting my Recy Mech course was the necessary requirement to hold a group H licence, tracked vehicle that is. I start learning to drive tracks in a 432 Armoured Personnel Carrier, (APC) known originally as a 432. A metal box on tracks, a foot throttle, two long metal sticks for turning and braking and that's about it. It's a hard vibrating ride along the road. Easy to drive with your head out in the wind and the rain. Test passed no problem.

However, on a Recy Mech course there's not a lot of call for 432 driving. What there is a call for is to drive heavy tracked vehicles of about 50 tons in weight.

At Last! Bring on the big boys, time to drive a Centurion Main Battle Tank! The Dogs Bollocks! Now we're talking. Fifty tons of steel, a 27,000cc Rolls Royce Meteor Engine (of Spitfire fame), a crash unmeshed gear box and a giant thirst of four gallons of petrol to the mile. Fabulous and very exciting!

Delighted that I wasn't paying for the petrol I started my Centurion familiarisation course. I was taught to drive a centurion gun-tank at Bordon by a polish guy called Ray Stopinski. He could drive the Cent second to none. 27000cc, crash box, stick changes, double de-clutching, no brakes of any use. Real proper driving.

Even with 27000cc to move it about the Cent takes some skill to get moving. Particularly so in mud, on sand, and across uneven ground.

Tank driver training grounds tend to be uneven, muddy places and all the mud and unevenness wants to do is stop your Cent from moving. Stick in the mud.

So off we go. In a cent there are three conventional pedals, except their huge. The gearstick rises between your legs and the steering is through two tillers at either side of your seat. Pull the right one to turn right and vice versa on the left. Start the engine, clutch in, into 2nd gear and off we go. On the hard standing its straightforward. Into third gear, double-declutch, same as a lorry. Match the engine revs to the transmission and road speed. Up and down the box. Five up and down, two reverse. Gently pull on the tillers and the Cent changes direction on its central axis. Fabulous and easy, how good is this. Next day onto rough ground, 'The 'Ulu" all rough

ground is 'The 'Ulu''. Off the hardstanding, it's been raining and onto 'The 'Ulu''. Onto mud.

The Cent becomes a strange abrasively argumentative new animal. Whereas on the road its easy and obedient on the mud it doesn't want to go. Add a little angle of hill and it just stops. Try again, pull off, stop. Try again, pull off, change gear, just stop. Try again, pull off, build up revs, go a little faster, change up, die a death, and stop. For fucks sake!

Ray Stopinski waves his red circle traffic lollipop. Try again, same thing starts, try. Stop. For fucks sake. Have a fag sitting on the gun barrel. Ray explains that the mud and the wet and the angle all serve to stop the vehicle moving. I can't get it from 2nd to 3rd. Ray explains I need to 'stick-change'. What is a stick-change?

He explains that stick change is a simultaneous three-way action involving the clutch, the gearstick and a steering tiller that must be done super quickly.

So that the next gear is selected before the speed attained in the 2nd gear isn't lost before the clutch is re-engaged and the engine power re-applied. Oh! Why didn't you say so. It's as clear as the three feet deep mud we are attempting driving in.

It's a complicated thing to explain to a relatively inexperienced driver. It's even more complicated if it's explained in a thick polish accent, with a wet fag in your gob, while gesticulating wildly with a red traffic lollipop and sitting on a centurion tank barrel in the rain parked in three feet of sticking mud. But it worked and I got it.

Once you've got it you've got it. It's just suddenly there. A fabulous feeling of achievement and strangely enough the more you practice the slicker you get. A real skill. I'd go so far to say If you could drive a Centurion properly you were the 'creme de la creme' of drivers in the entire British Forces. Much better than 'any' other drivers, there was more to it. No automatics, no synchromesh. If you can get one of these fifty-ton steel beast moving quickly, especially when towing on 'The 'Ulu'', then you are a master and can drive anything. You were the 'best of the best'.

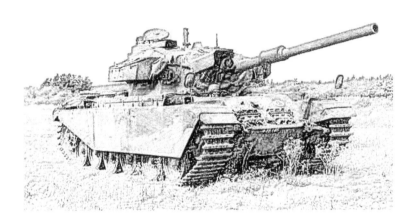

THE DOGS BOLLOCKS!

<u>Recy Mech School</u>

So, armed with HGV1 and the ability to drive a Cent cross country it's onto the Recy Mech course proper. We were an eclectic mix of trainee Recy Mechs. Most of us had passed through Bordon. Paul Haines had seen the light and rebadged from the 17/21st Lancers; Dave Ali had joined us from the Light Infantry (fed up with walking I guess). Leroy Breselford Wellington was from the Jamaican Defence Force. Graham (Hoppy or Cider) Hopkins from Gloucester. John Hodson and Lester Newman. I think there were about a dozen of us. We formed three crews of four. It was going to be graft; such is the nature of Army Recovery.

Off into the classroom we go. There's much to be learned. I quickly discover Army recovery is a 'dark art' and there is so much unthought of stuff to cover.

There are tests all along the way, more akin to a college than a workshop. I suppose after all we are in a school!

We learn recovery systems, planning and procedures followed by safety issues of men and materials. We had to learn to plan recovery tasks consider affecting factors, our state of readiness, the route and topography to the task. The tactical situation: I mean, who wants to do recovery behind enemy lines?

Arriving at the scene of the stricken vehicle we had to consider a huge range of factors such as soil recognition. Soil, I hear you say, well soil affects how easy or otherwise it is to move a vehicle along. Think of driving along a meadow field of firm soil compared to driving through three-foot-deep sucking mud, or on gravel. It's all different.

If a vehicle was well and truly 'stuck' we'd learn to consider important things to enable us to calculate how to get it out and what equipment, we could use. The key issues were type and weight of the vehicle, type of soil, any degree of slope the casualty vehicle had to be pulled up, and if there was any damage to the vehicle. Then calculating with 'Recy Mech Maths' we would assemble enough tackle in a suitable combination to move the casualty vehicle where we wanted it to go. Though sounding complicated once we got the hang of it along with a bit of practice it was quite straight forward.

The best part of practising vehicle recovery was that we had to purposefully bog in vehicles before we could recover them. The 'Dump Crew' as they were called had great fun in making recovery as difficult as possible ramming fifty-ton tanks into bogs, down steep hills, into deep water, over ravines, into forests. Official vandalism, but no matter how hard the dump crew tried or how ingenious were their efforts everything was recovered. Such was the level of training and use of equipment we were taught. Credit to our instructors, all experienced and long served Recy Mechs.

We also learned special techniques relevant to recovery. Towing and pushing vehicles, emergency

track shortening. Cutting taut thrown tracks with oxyacetylene burning equipment and blowing tracks off with explosives. It was also the Recy Mechs' job that in the event of a withdrawal we were tasked with destroying equipment to make it of no use to any advancing enemy. Authorised legitimate vandalism on a grand scale. In any other forum it would be criminal damage; it was fabulous fun.

We had to know about dangerous loads such as fuel and explosives and how to recover and deal with such laden vehicles.

We learnt many types of hand signals so we could have dismounted control of vehicles, winches, and cranes. All this in different types of weather from the very hot to the painfully cold.

We towed tanks and trucks and land rovers and anything else the army had to offer with rigid towbars and with ropes and chains.

Radio training.

"Enemy aircraft
over Dover
And over
Andover
Over"

Some of the course involved us rope splicing steel and fibre ropes. It was taught by a skilled elderly man called Price who had a clear and precise Welsh accent but was from India, or so he told me. I thought it was more like Tonypandy.

After leaving training we found most of the stuff we had learnt useful, but the rope splicing, not a bit of it.

Soldiering at SEME

SEME wasn't all trade training, there was ancillary military duty stuff which we all had our share of. One day I was on guard duty at SEME main gate during an exercise. This brigadier pulls up and I ask him for his ID card. I examine the card and it shows him as being a Lt Colonel. I say right person wrong rank; he compliments me on my observation, and he goes on his way. I thought he was a good bloke.

3RD BOLLOCKING - KNOB! LESSON LEARNT

A short while late a Major arrives, and I ask for his ID card; he is shown as a Captain. I say right person wrong rank. He goes off on one and gives me a bollocking for what I had said. I thought he was a knob. For a young soldier lesson learnt there.

Bordon Anecdotes

Lester's Reward

One day we were on the ranges carrying out shooting practice. One of our crew was a chap called Lester Newman he was a man exuding constant knowledge, a tall Englishman of buoyant character. Apparently, he'd fucked up on the range and the Corporal in charge sent him off into the woods to reconsider his life and so on. As Lester was walking through the woods, he saw some men digging a hole. These men saw an armed soldier approaching them and they ran to their car and sped off. Lester, whilst in the process of reviewing his life investigated the hole the men had been digging and he found £1,100,000 the proceeds of a robbery.

The find was handed over to the authorities and there was a ten per cent reward to be had £110,000. The army said they should have it, but Lester stood his ground, went to court and was, after a length of time, awarded the money. Good for Lester. I saw him a few short years later at 94 Locating Regt RA in Celle, Germany. He told me he'd got the money and had gone home for a weekend and all he could spend was £26,000. He'd bought a house and a car. I've not seen or heard of him since.

LESTER – GO RECONSIDER YOUR LIFE!

<u>Merry Christmas You Tiffy Bastard</u>

As an eighteen-year-old acting, unpaid unwanted Lance/Jack at Havannah Barracks Bordon in I copped for Xmas duties so on Christmas Eve I was NCO/ic Fire picquet with 12 other guys under my command.

We paraded with the guard, stick men (stick men were the smartest turned out and if selected were excused the duty), were selected and we retired to the fire picquet hut, a spider leg, for what was going to be a 'whizz' Christmas.

As the NCO/ic I arranged for a few of the lads to visit the shop in the town for some goodies. One or two asked if they could get beer. Being Christmas, me being a social and moderate sort of guy I agreed. We chatted about it and decided on getting a 24 pack, less than two cans each. The visit to the shop was made.

An hour or two into the duty the lads and I are sitting in the hut watching telly, eating goodies and one or two are drinking one of their possible two beers. In walks the orderly officer a 'new' Tiffy S/Sgt he was clearly a man of constant self-importance, I cannot remember is name, I don't want to.

He takes one look at the two lads drinking beer and assumes we are all pissed. He is of course wrong, but because he is a very important new 'Tiffy' he decides to put us through the mill. We spent the next four or five hours exercising 'firefighting'. We were knackered at the end of it. He had us crashing out to non-existent fires, dragging an ancient red wooden, probably Victorian, fire cart festooned with buckets and spades and picks and hoses and hand pumps. We were hosing gallons of water all over the place. The cart was useless and knackered. If the Tiffy had let us drink the beer I'm sure we could have collectively pissed more forcefully.

What had happened and what did it achieve?

1. The 'Tiffy' had totally misread the situation, less than two cans per man doesn't equal pissed by any standard.
2. His management style and manner did absolutely nothing to earn respect from the lads; in fact, all he did was earn a loathing and disrespect.

So, wherever he is today 'Happy Fucking Christmas' I hope somewhere over the years you had the same dished out to you. I hope you choke on your two Christmas beers. Throughout my working life I have remembered this experience as a way not to treat people and I never have.

Merry Christmas it's a Food Fight

The army cookhouse is notorious as a favoured venue for Christmas food fights. The biggest I ever witnessed was at SEME at Havannah Barracks; Don Barnes a 'Man of Kent' and a vehicle mechanic changing trade to Recy Mech and a good friend of mine picked up a can of beer, shook it violently, and sprayed all on the opposite table. That was the starting gun. Within seconds the place was in uproar, turkey, spuds, and gravy everywhere. Officers and SNCO's serving the food bolted for cover and the cookhouse was trashed. It took about two minutes and that was the end of Christmas dinner. Mass exodus of unfed soldiers transfer to the NAAFI for beer. Merry Christmas everybody.

Comfy Bum

Army issue toilet roll was universally crap (pun intended), it was common garden government issue, slightly abrasive on one side. Very smooth on the other. It was adorned with a 'war-office' crows foot it was that old and was ineffective for wiping one's arse. It seldom worked efficiently tending to spread and smear rather than gather and clean. The consequence was that soldiers often bought their own 'comfy-bum' from the NAAFI. An essential sanitary commodity to be sought and cherished. We used to keep our own 'comfy-bum' in our lockers for pre-planned crapper visits.

However, sometimes when about the camp a visit was essential but access to our lockers would be denied because of distance or time or location. So, the visit would necessitate the using of the 'crows-foot' useless commodity. Occasionally if we were very lucky, we would find that some forgetful or careless soul would have left their personal comfy-bum 'behind' (see what I did there), and it would be available for our use.

There is nothing more pleasurable or satisfying than be able to cleanly wipe your arse at somebody else's' expense!

Character building? Hell yes!

SOMEBODY ELSES EXPENSE – FABULOUS!

<u>Eamon's Caubeen</u>

Whilst at Bordon during the famous never to be forgotten 1976 very hot summer there were a lot of wildfires about the south of England. Around the town of Guildford was particularly bad and the army were summoned to assist the fire brigade to fight the fires. Hundreds if not thousands of us were loaded onto green Bedford lorries of all types and driven to the area of the fires at Guildford. We were dressed in green army combat suits and each man was issued with a stout fire-beater. The fire beater was a thick wooden handle about six foot in length with an eighteen-inch square of thick rubber fastened on the end. The plan was that we would form lines approach the fire and beat out the flames. It was a serious conflagration; strong winds and the flames were tall and leaping everywhere. It was a very dangerous situation.

Our section leader was Eamon Teague (Name changed) a transferee NCO from the Royal Irish

Rangers. A man of complex and melodious Irish dialogue, I enjoyed his company immensely. Every time he spoke, he closed his eyes, and you could see his eyeballs agitating behind his lids as if searching for words. He still wore his Royal Irish hat which is called a 'Caubeen it's a green pudding like thing with a green feather about six or eight inches long sticking straight up behind the 'Harp' cap badge. I liked the look of it. The rest of us were in normal black army berets.

EAMONS CAUBEEN

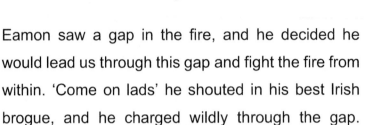

Eamon saw a gap in the fire, and he decided he would lead us through this gap and fight the fire from within. 'Come on lads' he shouted in his best Irish brogue, and he charged wildly through the gap. Collectively we said, 'Fuck that!'.

It was a ridiculously lousy and dangerous proposition. We looked on as Eamon thrashed about within the flames for a few seconds before charging out about ten times faster than he went in. He was minus his beater and his caubeen was ash covered and smoking and only the charcoal stump of his green feather was left. His face was bright red, and he was spluttering and gasping for breath. His eyebrows had disappeared; singed away. We pulled him away from the fire brushed him down and doused him with water and sat him in the safety of a truck. He was a good lad and a good friend of mine but his decision making, and leadership were shit. Bless him and his caubeen.

A Proper REME Soldier

Another memorable occasion was when we were on a regimental weekend where 'we', that's the military 'we', were sent out to do military things.

I was young and inexperienced, but I had an HGV licence, I was the designated Bedford RL (a four-ton petrol engine general service truck) driver for the exercise.

We were 'crashed-out' from our bivouac in the middle of the night. It was freezing. White, very white frost everywhere. Very, very cold.

In the darkness we had to move. The Sergeant in charge of my section was on his 'Tiffy' course. I can't remember his name, but he was a Jock with ginger hair and slightly balding. He must have put up with a lot of military banter previously because of this.

He was fabulous. He was the first military man to talk and treat me like an adult, rather than just barking orders RD style. He had a leadership job to do, and I had a soldier's job to do, and we both knew it.

It was cold, we were tired, we were getting 'fucked about' from above, and he, superb as he was, hovered just above it all. He spoke calmly, assuredly and with confidence and ordered me one to one, explaining the rationale for his order and the wherewithal of his decision. He displayed rare commodities. He respected what I was doing and guided me, where required, the correct way. He was a 'proper' Senior NCO.

Even though I can't remember his name (and I have struggled to do so) I have never forgotten him. I can picture him in that same circumstance, in that same RL, in that same white-cold night to this day. He left a positive indelible, life long, impression on me that I have tried to emulate throughout my military and later civilian working career, and that I try to achieve to this day.

He had no great aspiration, no hidden agenda, he was just doing the right thing at the right time for the right reason. There was no more correct or proper thing to do.

I know that since then many younger people who I have trained or tutored over the years, and there have been many, who will have undoubtably benefited from the quality and ethos and manner that I learnt that one freezing cold night in the company of an exceptional leader, and I have since passed on. How remarkable that the one short encounter with a 'quality' man can have such an important lifelong legacy. So, Ginger haired Jock 'Tiffy' Sergeant on your Tiffy course, whoever you are, wherever you are I tell you this; you were and still probably are a 'proper' man, a good SNCO and a good example of a soldier and I 'Thank You'.

Character building? Hell yes! He was the best of the REME.

SEME Rugby

Rugby at SEME was strong. There were three sides put out under the leadership of Tim Pratt, a man of constant rugby enthusiasm. He was the Corps rugby Captain, SEME club Captain and first team Skipper. We trained twice a week and played every Wednesday playing other army sides and the likes of the police and fire service. The rugby was different to the rugby I had learnt in the Welsh valleys. The army rugby was physically tough however the skill levels were varying. It was great fun. At this young age, and despite having played in a WRU level club at home, I initially played in the second and third XV's. The clubhouse was a spider leg; a lot went on in spider legs. There was always beer, only ever beer, it was generally flat and warm. We drank, and we sang filthy songs, and we played foolish drunken games. It was fab.

Character building? Hell yes!

It was at SEME when I first ever Skippered a rugby team (Skippered is such an English term). It was the 'A' Company 7 a side team in the inter-company sevens played on a hot Saturday on a hard dry pitch. I can't remember how we got off in the competition, but I do know that every single one of our team reported sick on the Monday morning with something cracked, pulled, or strained. A re-union in the Medical Reception Station (MRS). Nobody was badly hurt, and we were dressed, stretched, bandaged, and creamed and all sent back to work.

There were famous and infamous REME rugby players at Bordon. I didn't know them very well there, but I got to do so as I progressed up the force's rugby ladder. Tim Pratt, my hero, was one such obvious player. Others were the hard Fijian Wam Bam Tawaki, Dave Spawforth, Taff Wishart and many more. At SEME I played alongside Taff Moogan, George Raw and Steve Ogarra for the first of many times. Top men and tough rugby players.

My last point about rugby at SEME is that it was the only place where I kicked off at 7am in the morning, twice. We did this because we had time pressures to play games in some inter-company competition or other. One wakes up very quickly at the bottom of a 7am ruck!

Character building? Hell yes!

1st Unit – The 13/18th Royal Hussars

The 13/18th Royal Hussars were a famous Yorkshire recruited cavalry Regiment. At this time, they were composed of a Headquarter Squadron and three sabre squadrons each of sixteen chieftain main battle tanks.

13TH/18TH ROYAL HUSSARS

Arrival

It's the middle of a cold winter and I'm posted off to Germany as a Class 3 Recovery Mechanic, I also have a new title its 'Craftsman Rees'. My local L/Cpl stripe had gone and as a qualified tradesman I'd earned the title Craftsman as opposed to Private.

It's my first non-training unit. I'm joining the Light Aid Detachment (LAD) of the 13/18th Royal Hussars. A very famous Yorkshire recruited cavalry regiment equipped with chieftain main battle tanks based at Hohne in Northwest Germany.

I fly into and am collected from Hannover Airport in one of those green tinny army buses and deposited at block MB 37 in Hohne station. A second world war Wehrmacht and SS barracks now occupied by NATO forces. This was the real thing. I walk into the barracks, get told to drop my bag and case and follow this man who takes me about twenty yards around the corner into the side of the building and into the LAD bar.

It's a small bar with a dozen guys drinking beers and shorts; Asbach Brandy and lemonade. Its handshakes all around and I am made very welcome. I'm immediately continuing as 'Taff'. I'm introduced to everybody and told their names, but I instantly forget. I know we're in the bar till about 3am at which point I'm a bit pissed. I go to bed and sleep on springs, no mattress, no blankets, but it's no matter the beer and brandy are working.

We're in 'rattle' accommodation which is temporary as the proper accommodation is being refurbished. I awake about six with a hangover. Its ablutions and I dig out my uniform. The dress code for the regiment is green coveralls and a green plastic webbing belt, DMS boots, puttees, and beret. I'm to work in the main LAD and I get a lift to the workshop. When we get there its muster parade. There's about thirty of us on parade. There's a roll call and my names not called out. We fall out and I'm approached by my Sergeant. His name is Roy Allan. He's a decent bloke and he takes me to his office which is the Recy

Section at the rear of the workshop. We have a cup of char and I'm introduced to the two other LAD Recy Mechs. Alan 'Spud' Murphy and Tony 'Clutch' Patterson. We chat away with introductions and small talk. The Sgt has a very noticeable stammer, but he gets there eventually. Spud has two or three years in, and Clutch is about a year ahead of me. The welcome is good they are all decent blokes. Spud and Clutch show me around. We walk around the workshop where I get introduced to lots of people. The OC, the ASM, and Walter an elderly German who makes the coffee for everybody mid-morning; 'Kein Geld, Kein Kaffee ', (No money, No Coffee), no negotiation. He was a decent chap.

We get a land rover and I'm taxied around the tank park. Dirty great big Chieftain tanks everywhere, dozens of them. Soldiers all over them, Yorkshire soldiers, Royal Hussars. This was the real McCoy.

We draw a mattress and bedding and extra coveralls from the 13/18th QM's. I'm given the afternoon to get

sorted. Make my bed, unpack, get settled. There's four of us in a small rattle room in two sets of bunk beds. One of the four is Glenn Ewen my oppo from Regimental Police days. Another chap in the room was Peter Rudd an unusual character with a breathing through his nose issue. He was also a world class snorer, and I bunked above him. It was sometimes very challenging. I quickly learned that from my top-bunk, while he was lying on his back and snoring for England with his mouth open in the bottom bunk, if I dropped something into his mouth, anything small enough to fit, he would splutter momentarily and stop snoring for a while. Doused fag ends and peanuts were good ammo.

Regular visits to the LAD bar were expected.

Muster parade every morning and my Sgt Roy Allan is calling the roll. His stammer gives him difficulty in pronouncing his R's. My surname is of course Rees. It goes something like this-

"Elson", 'Sir', "Jones", 'Sir', ''Patterson' 'Sir', 'Phillips', 'Sir", R..,R…R….R….R… 'Fuck it - Taff' 'Sir'. So, it went on when Roy called the roll. All were amused and he got it off to perfection and when he eventually got to 'Taff' everybody would shout it out to help him along.

Pulley Block Lift

In my first week Roy told me that all decent Recy Mechs could pick up an ARV pulley block and hold it over their head for a minute. Blimey I thought that's a challenge. A pulley black was part of the recovery kit and was big and sturdy enough to take ninety tons of pressure. Heavy, very heavy indeed. I knew I could lift one but above my head for one minute was another thing. So, it's a new unit, the man throwing out the challenge is my Sgt, and it looks like it's a career test. Not very confidentially I grab the pulley block, feet shoulder width apart I lift the block to my thighs and leaning back slightly I curl it up to my chest. Then it's a bit of a snatch affair and I get it up over my head, straighten my arms and lock them out. Through gritted teeth, while sucking in huge amounts of air I say to Roy to let me know when the minute is up. It seems like forever, and he eventually calls it and I lower the steel block to the floor where it clangs onto the stone. Roy is staring. I realise it was a wind-up and I wasn't expected to do it. None of the others had or could. Nevertheless, I had set a small mark in my new unit, and it stood me in good stead as my new Sergeant was impressed.

My allocated vehicle was a Leyland Heavy Recovery Vehicle which was ok, and I could operate it efficiently, but it wasn't an ARV. I couldn't expect more as a class 3 Recy Mech at the main LAD. I spent my first few months using the crane on the Leyland for pack (tank engines are called packs) and gearbox lifts with the squadron fitter section. This was good because I was getting to know people and I was close to the tanks.

The Yorkshire Hussars were fab. Difficult for me to understand Yorkshire accents were everywhere. "Thee, Though, thannus (though knows)" were the order of the day. Regrettably the regiment were strong on football and cricket but had no rugby team. WTF! So, it was no rugby for a season which I supposed left me to get on with learning to be a Recy Mech and LAD member. There was always something going on. Recovery work, squadron runs, gym work, pack changes, vehicles to be towed to larger workshops, equipment's to be moved around. It was a busy time.

The NAAFI was a fair walk from the LAD workshop but nearby was a German army canteen that we were allowed to use. It was limited in the food and drink it served but it worked well for us. The choice was traditional German sausage, bread rolls and coffee or soft drink. Bock wurst – boiled sausage, my favourite. Brat wurst – grilled sausage. Curry wurst – grilled sausage covered in ketchup and curry powder. The mustard option to accompany the

sausages was known as Senf or 'baby-shit', the same consistency and colour. I preferred ketchup over baby-shit.

I got to drive the occasional Centurion ARV when the Corporal Recy Mechs were on leave I would cover for them at Squadron, but the tank park work was mostly towing dead tanks about.

First Recovery Job

On my very first real recovery job I accompanied my Sgt, Roy Allan. Taking the Leyland and a heavy trailer we drove to the Lunenberg Heath to recover a British soldiers wrecked ford escort. It was early morning, cold and frosty. The two soldiers in it had got well pissed and driven straight ahead at a bend and into the biggest, widest oak tree in Germany. Both were killed outright. They had hit the tree head on, and the car was concertinaed to about half its length. It was an eery and very real scene and the hairs on the back of my neck were standing. The very young and inexperienced me was taking it all in.

Roy was walking around the car, and I was stood at the rear he was mooching in the wrecked vehicle I was about ten yards away from him. Here Catch! He shouted and threw a trainer arching through the air towards me. As it was mid-flight and I prepared to catch it he shouted, 'There's a foot in it". Fucking Hell! I shit myself and jump back avoiding the trainer. Roy thought it funny, he even stammered when he laughed. I was on a learning curve. The army of course is for grown-ups. There was no foot.

We dragged the wreck away from the tree, gathered up the car debris and threw it inside the car then winched the car onto the trailer, strapped it down and drove back to camp.

I drove and I learnt that the trailer characteristics change with a load. The Leyland and trailer had a propensity to snake from side to side and it could be moderated with a speed and steering change. Every day is a school day, in more ways than one. We parked on the LAD square and the trailer on which

the wreck was strapped was immediately surrounded by the LAD Vehicle Mechanics (VM's) imparting their professional opinions on the likelihood of the vehicle ever being made roadworthy again. In my humble Class three, brand new, Recy Mech opinion it was 'well fucked'.

Character building? Hell yes!

First Duty Recovery

As a Recy Mech I didn't do guard duty or fire picquet, instead I would be allocated Duty Recy Mech duties which we took turns with all other units in the division having recovery elements attached. We could be called out at any time of the day or night to anywhere in driving distance.

One night after midnight we are roused from our beds by the Royal Military Police (RMP ('Monkeys')) they tell us that a ford escort has broken down on the autobahn about forty miles away. We are crewing a Leyland Heavy Recovery Vehicle, a 'wrecker', Spud

Murphy is the experienced Recy Mech and driver, and I'm observing and learning. Spud knows the location and off we go. It's my first duty callout and I am excited like a little boy.

We get to the area in which we have been informed the vehicle is located and there is nothing to be found. Not a sausage. We have a searching drive around for about an hour without success. We drive back to Hohne where we are told by the RMP that the driver has phoned in and said he had been told to change his location by the German Police, to the opposite side of the Autobahn. So, we drive back out to the new location and succeed in finding the broken-down escort. There is the driver and a passenger. The passenger is the wife of a soldier who has been admitted to hospital and she has been visiting him in the escort with the allocated driver.

We suspend tow the half ton escort, onto the back of the twenty-ton wrecker, its massive overkill. We begin our journey back to Hohne camp. There isn't much room at all. Spud, very wisely for him, is driving. The escort driver is seated between Spud and I and the lady is sitting on my lap. It's a very uncomfortable, cramped journey. The escort driver and the lady both fell asleep on me, I daren't move. Eventually we arrive at Hohne, drop the vehicle off at the workshop and the passengers at the RMP post.

It was an unexciting first duty call-out. There was confusion over location, frustration over the search, and the job took twice as long as it needed to have. It was, unknown to me at the time, very typical of recovery call-outs.

The only good thing was on our return to camp in the early hours, recovery completed, we were entitled to rouse the duty 'Slop Jockey' who served up a first-class breakfast as they always did. Thanks.

A Proper Bollocking

Shortly after arriving at the 13/18th 'Part One Orders', which are the daily published orders for the regiment for the day listed me among others as having to attend for a dental appointment. I didn't see the order and I missed the appointment. Consequently, I was summoned before the Regimental Sergeant Major where I was anticipating a bit of shouting and swearing. His name was Henderson, and he was a Scotsman. He was known as 'Piggy' but obviously not to his face. He was a round fat bloke and facially he had piggy features. He looked to be an unpleasant person. Wasn't that all RSM's?

He informed me very loudly that I had missed a dental appointment that had been posted on part one orders. I was new, unfamiliar with lots of things, and he went to town on me.

He was calling me 'Reeze', with a heavy pronunciation on the Z. It must be a Scottish thing.

He was telling me I had no future, no career, and that I was doomed to a terrible time while I was with the regiment. He went on for quite a while getting louder and louder and using the 'Reeze' pronunciation more and more.

After an age he had finished and told me to get out of his office and sort my life out.

As I left, I turned to him and said, 'I'm Welsh Sir, my name is Rees pronounced Rees not 'Reeze' Sir', impersonating his accent.

4ᵀᴴ -BOLLOCKING – A PROPER ONE

To be perfectly honest what I had said was a big, big mistake. Very big. I shouldn't have said anything. I should have just left. After that anybody could call me Reeze if they wanted.

By the time he'd finished with me I had experienced one of the two finest bollockings I was to be on the receiving end of in twelve years. He was a professional bollocker. One of the best. incidentally my top of the charts best all time No 1 bollocking was to come from another Scots RSM a few years later. RSM Berry of the Black Watch a Scots infantry regiment. He was a class bollocker. Premiership. Must be a Scottish RSM thing!

Exercise Wild Winch

I was sent on my Recovery Mechanic three to two upgrader course. If I passed this course, I would be able to work alone and unsupervised. The army were taking a chance on me!

Recovery upgrader courses are given appropriately manly names reflecting the acknowledged requirement of muscles and manliness to be a good Recy Mech. The most popular of the upgrader course names is 'Samsons Pride'. The course I was to upgrade on was staged by 7 Armoured Workshop the largest divisional REME unit. The upgrader course was to be called 'Wild Winch'. Quite a snazzy and appropriate name I thought.

Essentially the course takes place on the huge Soltau training area. There is night and day recovery. It's all conducted on the 'Ulu', and we live under canvas for a fortnight.

The course manager is Warrant Officer Pete De Jong, he is on detachment for the Australian REME, I don't think the UK REME Recy Mechs had warrant officer ranks at that time.

The course is split into crews of four or five and each student (I'm making it sound posh) takes turns at being crew commander. There's an element of instruction, some classroom work in tents but mostly its showing what you've retained from your basic course and displaying what you've learned in your units. I had been fortunate in this respect with my posting at an armoured unit, a fab Sergeant in Roy Allan, and helpful colleagues by the way of Spud and Clutch. There had been no bullshit, just hard work, and a good variety of it. Some of the guys told sad tales of being posted to units, large REME workshops where all they had done was paint vehicles and sweep the floors. I felt for them. At the end of the course there were to be two prestigious prizes: Best Recovery Mechanic and Best Crew.

Everybody was marked throughout the course. Enthusiastic participation and taking control were important. As crews we quickly gelled, and the best crews and individuals were identified quite quickly. I was lucky enough to be in a hard-working crew that enjoyed the work. There was wheeled vehicle recovery which was OK, and armoured recovery at which I thrived.

The 'dump crew' was provided by qualified Recy Mechs from 7 Armoured. They loved their job and performed with gusto at making our jobs as difficult as possible. The deeper, the wetter, the more challenging the better. They thrived on it and took pride in their vandalism and chaos. They were a fab group of people and, of course, we were aspiring to be where they were.

We worked long hours, tactically, under mock attack, in darkness and so on. It was a challenging, hard-working environment. There were chefs doing the field cooking, and they, as they always did, dished up a great food. Everybody was well fed. There was an improvised bar in a tent, and we were able to have a can or two of beer when not engaged on course work. Truth be told, sleep was the best commodity, the beers would have to wait.

I was lucky enough to finish with the 'Best Recovery Mechanic' award. I had pipped Hoppy on the theory. A small, inscribed pewter mug was given to me and I have it to this day. Every time I look at it it's the 'trout raid' (see below) I think of before anything else.

Character building. Hell yes!

Trout Anybody 1

There's a river on the Soltau training area called the Schwindebeck, which has caused the demise of many an aspiring troop or tank commander for failing to appreciate the wet sucking nature of the ground and how quickly tanks can become stuck – for days. However, the good thing for us on this course was that along the Schwindebeck there was located a sizeable trout farm. Coupled with this knowledge was the fact that one of the Sergeant instructors, let's call him 'Toddy' he had a great sense of adventure (massive understatement), and he was in possession of plastic explosives which we used for track-cutting and demolition purposes.

So, a plan was hatched. Toddy and a trusted few, I might have been included, were going fishing. It was very exciting, and involved camouflage, map reading, tactical night driving, tactical approach, mission execution, casualty (trout) gathering and extraction and withdrawal.

Toddy decided that four ounces of plastic would be enough to stun the trout and as they floated to the surface, we would gather them quickly and make good out withdrawal.

The four ounces of plastic was primed with a detonator, and a short length of safety fuse crimped in. Toddy and maybe I crept to the pond and laying low Toddy lit the fuse and as it spluttered into life, he slipped the explosive into the walled trout pool, and we retreated a few yards expecting a muffled detonation and the trout to coming floating to the surface.

Our muffled detonation expectation was an exercise in misplaced optimism. There was an almighty BANG! A wave of water rushed off the small pond wall and soaked us, then water and trout began to fall all around us. Fucking Hell! The pressure was on. We quickly scurried around grabbing trout and stuffing them inside our jackets and anywhere else they would fit. I'm sure we left a fishy trail as we rushed back to our Landrover. We piled in and made a light-less escape from the area.

The very fresh trout were fabulous eating, much better than the usual composite ration. The ACC cooked trout well. I learned a lot that night, another trout opportunity would present years later.

Character building? Hell yes!

Junior Military Certificate (JMC)

I wasn't too long at the unit before they decided to send me on a Junior Military Certificate (JMC) course. At the depot we had passed the Basic Military Certificate (BMC) course. Before any promotion to L/Cpl came along we had to have passed JMC.

The course was at, an Armoured Workshop in Germany, a large REME workshop with greater repair facilities than our LAD. The Directing Staff (DS) Were REME RD Soldiers. We were anticipating the traditional shouting and swearing for a few weeks, and we weren't let down.

Collection of bedding, allocation of a bed in a barrack block (no spider), and a quick guide around the camp by a course JNCO.

I knew a few on the course. Graham Hopkins from my basic recovery course was there so to was Peter Rudd from the same unit as me.

Muster parade first morning and we were assured we were an absolute shower the like of which had never been seen before. I was beginning to understand such welcomes are traditional. Drill, skirmishing, tactics, NCB lessons, map reading, first aid, section attacks and so on.

About a week into the course, we went on an unannounced forced march. The pace was set by the S/Sgt, I think his name was Shepard. It wasn't a running pace, but it fell just short. He was wearing the uniform the same as us, however, we were in addition, all wearing battle kit and carrying rifles with tin helmets atop. We weren't expecting to be on the march, we didn't know how far it was going to be nor how long it would last. All annoying things. I decided to tuck in behind the S/Sgt, keep my head down and get on with it. I wasn't the fastest of runners over distance, but I could handle this pace carrying equipment.

It was bloody hard work, and we covered, I suspect, about eight miles. The pace didn't stop and a few of the course fell out. Either hurt from blisters or just plain knackered. I just kept going tucked in behind the S/Sgt not thinking about it. I recall carrying the rifle of another chap on the course and trying to drag him along. Eventually we finished and came to a stop. Talk about bolloxed. Sweating, knackered, thirsty, all the usual things. Those that had finished sat drinking water from our bottles and waiting for the stragglers and walking wounded to come in, then back to barracks, ablutions, kit cleaned and readied for the morrow then off to the NAAFI for a beer or town for a 'Bratwurst and Baby Shit'.

I learned that next day from one of the course L/Cpls that irrespective of what happened on the remainder of the course I had passed because of sticking with it and helping another. The S/Sgt was impressed.

The noteworthy thing I remember about the course was that on one occasion we found ourselves skirmishing up and down the length of sports pitches. Skirmishing is moving forward under fire and taking an evasive zig-zagging route. its demanding work. Add to it full battle kit and weapons it gets tougher. Up and down, up, and down, side to side, never ending. Then, when your all-in 'Gas. Gas, Gas' quickly get your respirators on which makes it ten times harder, difficulty breathing, not enough oxygen. Now it's tough!

Working as sections, looking out for each other I noticed one of ours stumble and begin to fall behind. It was Pete Rudd from my unit. Hoppy and I grabbed him and screaming and yelling at him dragged him along to the end of the course. A fair distance and length of time. We stopped dragging him and he fell to the floor. We flopped down beside him respirators off, sucking in air and loosening clothing. Pete Rudd lay still. I turned him over and I couldn't see his face, his respirator was full of blood. I pulled his respirator off and loads of blood splashed about. I quickly wiped it off and suddenly he started spluttering and gasping for air and shouting incoherently. It took him a few minutes to regain his composure. It transpired that he had a breathing issue caused by some sort of physical obstruction in his nose, hence his world class snoring.

Hoppy and I had almost caused his demise by doing the 'army thing' and not letting him fall behind. Then saved his life by removing his respirator and clearing the blood from his airways. Thus JMC was passed.

At the end of the course there was an end-of-course piss up in a German pub. The beer flowed and it was rowdy night. When it came to paying the substantial bill there wasn't a single member of the training staff

to be seen; practising their camouflage skills I suppose.

ARV Life

I was the driver on my first ARV, a Centurion, fifty tons and a big engine with a crash gearbox. They are hard unforgiving vehicles but if looked after with regular servicing and upkeep they are the most reliable of machines. The engine is superb, though governed to twenty-one and a half miles per hour they would run all day. Cpl Jim Corrie, a long time served Recy Mech, was my first ARV commander, and I learned much from him. For some reason he was always saying 'Oh, dearie me, its number three', in his Scots accent. I don't know why he repeated it time after time, certainly more than three times.

I learned how to build penthouses over the rear engine decks. An old steel tubular frame off a Bedford lorry, slotted onto steel track-pins welded onto the four corners of the rear of the ARV. Over the frame we would fit a selection of canvases and tarpaulins; fitting them so we had a rain and wind proof penthouse. The more complicated 'penthouses' had metal stowage bins welded to the inside of the frame. These bins would contain essential recovery equipment such as Cherry Brandy for cold nights, Baileys Cream Liquor to be added to early morning Char. Always a selection of tea and coffee and anything else that was wanted quickly to hand.

The front and backs of the penthouse would be 'flapped' so we could open them when moving, and quickly close them when parked. In the winter they were great for heat retention from the engine. Sometimes we would go to sleep on the back decks, and if it had been a particularly hard drive we would be lulled to sleep by the brewing and bubbling of the petrol in two sixty-gallon rear fuel tanks situated underneath the decks. The ARV was always popular because of its home comforts and independence and there was never a shortage of volunteer crews.

CENTURION ARMOURED RECOVERY VEHICLE & LUXURY PENTHOUSE

We had sufficient room on the back decks to carry metal bed frames on which we would lay our sleeping bags. Enough room to carry armchairs and on one occasion a discarded household fridge that had been repaired. TVs were sometimes carried, but the signal strength was generally unreliable as was the choice of TV channels.

We also had lots of stowage room for beer, Herforder Pills which came in cardboard 'Yellow Handbags" and was often used as currency for favours and reward for achievement. The yellow handbag referring to the yellow coloured, handled carrying box they came in.

We also had plenty of room for rations which were normally four-man packs. There were ten different menus. Word was that A-H contained a binding agent and J a mild laxative. There was certainly some bowel interference going on and regularity was a stranger in the 'Ulu'. Some crews made all-in stew for every meal. I always thought a bit of presentation went a long way to improving the meals. Additions of eggs and bread were always welcome.

Once, after having been advised by an old artisan Sergeant, I fried eggs in hydraulic oil. The oil was a rich red in colour as were the eggs when cooked. My advice - only pass on the recipe to somebody who needs character building.

The ARV also had the customary British Army Boiling Vessel (BV), used to boil water for brews, shaving, bollock washing and to heat cans of food.

Sometimes one boil would be for multi purposes, it could also be boiled on the move.

Any decent ARV crew would also be in possession of a 'Benghazi Burner'. This was a water heater fashioned by a friendly metalsmith (of which there were many, and popular they were too), from a five-gallon oil drum. A circular hole was cut in the bottom and a crude chimney placed in the hole and welded watertight. Three or four legs were welded to the bottom of the oil can. Underneath was placed a metal box-tin full of sand or earth and soaked in petrol. The can was filled with water, the petrol placed centrally underneath and lit. Whoosh, almost instant hot water. Enough for, washing, dishes, shaving, showers etc. a fabulously useful bit of kit.

If we were on dry ground washing pans and mess tins would be done in earth or sand. Same as washing in water but with abrasive dry earth. Saved on washing up liquid and drying cloths.

<u>Centurion ARV Driving</u>

If you could drive a Centurion well, you were the best. If you could drive a Centurion ARV towing another; you were the 'best of the best'; that's one hundred tons of weight. If you had the opportunity and the occasion to drive a Centurion ARV, towing another Centurion ARV, whilst towing a third Centurion ARV then, then very clearly, you are the best of the best of the best! That's one hundred and fifty tons of weight. I did so once. Driving the centurions, particularly so as a Recy Mech, it was a special skill. Consider the following experiences.

<u>'Ulu' Driving</u>

It's the last day of a three-week exercise. You are a Recy Mech, and you have a Centurion ARV with a well experienced crew of three. After the three weeks of scheme, you are dirty, knackered, very knackered even, desperate for a sleep and a hot bath. In the middle of the 'Ulu' there is battle tank that is a non-runner, it needs a pack (engine) change and there are none available, so the Tiffy tells you it must be towed back to camp, a journey of about fifty miles. The first three of which are on the 'Ulu'.

You need to make sure your ARV is fit for the task. Full of fuel, two hundred and forty gallons of petrol brimming all three tanks. You find a stretch of hard standing to make sure your steel battle tracks are tight. You don't need track-slap or to throw a loose track on the way home. Tight tracks give you optimum steering and driving centurions you need all the form in your favour, particularly when towing another fifty tons. You will be somewhere between one hundred and one hundred and ten tons moving down the road. Make sure the ARV kit is well stowed, no clutter, and there is plenty of brew kit to hand. So off to the 'Ulu' to get your broken tank, you have either a grid reference number or an oily finger-mark on a well-worn and tatty map.

Driving across the wet and muddy 'Ulu' is great fun on a solo ARV. Driving a tank or ARV across well used training areas is akin to sailing a choppy sea in a small boat. Stick changes are the order of the day. The worn 'Ulu' undulates and is all bumps and dips. Bump after bump, dip after dip. The dips full of sloshing dirty mud silted water, the bumps rounded and smooth. Tracks in forested areas are two deep water filled ruts the width apart of a tank's tracks. The centre ridge smooth and square where the belly of the tank has ironed flat the soft mud.

As you drive along you pick out your ground, trying to make the journey as smooth and as quick as possible. A driver who crashes and smashes his way along does no good for the comfort of his crew, the orderliness of his stowed equipment nor the health and function of his vehicle.

Undulating bump after bump. Accelerate firmly up the bump, ease off the throttle as you crest the fulcrum, accelerate down. Don't change gear going uphill, use the ground to help you. Change up going downhill, use gravity to help you along. Change on the flat if its mud or hard going, then stick changes are a must. Try not to use any brakes whatsoever. The brakes on a Centurion are rubbish and don't last long. Save then for a real emergency if possible. The water and mud slosh up under the front track guards occasionally splashing over the glacis plate and into your face. Nobody gets out clean. Driving through water is always interesting. You don't always know how deep it is or if there are large potholes hidden, or if there's something just under the surface that might foul your tracks. As you go through deep water keep an eye on the depth, you don't want the water filling the tank, or the air intakes. All tanks have bilge pumps, but prevention is better than a struggling bilge pump. Push the inevitable bow wave in front of you, If you catch and overtake it, you'll fill you lap with shitty water, which will be guaranteed to be freezing. Who needs freezing muddy knackers?

So, you arrive at your tank to be towed. A switched-on tank crew will have already removed the quill shafts from the drive, readying the tank for towing.

You'll need to connect the casualty tank to the back of your ARV. You do this with steel A bars. Heavy steel bars connected to the front of the broken tank with towing adaptors secured to the towbars by pins. Only these pins weigh about six or seven pounds each and are about six inches thick and about eight inches long. The two bars are collected to the back of the ARV causing a triangle with the pinnacle at the ARV. When moving along the towed tank will naturally follow. So, once you are connected it's all crews on the ARV and 'away we go'.

Driving across the 'Ulu' with a tank on the back is a new ball game. No frivolous joy-riding or mud surfing, no more pirouetting bump crests, it's now a serious job of work. Concentration and timing are paramount, every action must be pre-determined, every manoeuvre has a consequence, every consequence a further development; its never-ending. If you go over a bump, you must consider that another fifty tons has yet to come over, also, as you go down the bump the following fifty tons will push you along, as you go up the following fifty tons will drag you back. If you turn the fifty tons behind you will try to, firstly hold you back from the turn, and then secondly push you to oversteer. Such fun and games. The parameters and positional considerations constantly change. Stick changing has elevated from a mechanical process to an art. That's it Recy Mechs are Artists.

Character building? Hell yes!

Road Driving an ARV

Eventually you move off the 'Ulu' onto the road. It's a different type of driving skill once more. Before getting on the road, you stop and clean your lights, erect your 'winky-wanky' (Amber flashing light), and clean the worst of the mud off your tracks. The same applies to the tank you are towing.

Driving an ARV on the German road network is a challenge. You can only see directly to the front, so you are a team with your ARV commander who is atop and has a three-hundred-and-sixty-degree view. You are connected by radio. As a driver you are dependent on the commander giving 'clear' or not at junctions, for informing you of overtaking vehicles and for pointing out any other considered hazards. Never say 'No' its easily confused with 'Go'. I once knew of a 'no' that was translated as a 'go', resulting in a Scimitar Armoured Reconnaissance Vehicle being squarely embedded into the side of a school bus; nasty.

Driving on hard standing, tarmac, is easier than the 'Ulu'. Traditional double-the-clutch is the preferred option. Timings on gear changes synchronised by ear with the orchestra of the engine is the way forward. Smooth and comfortable. The centurion is governed to twenty-one and a half miles per hour. Even so, I do know that going down the road, on tracks, weighing one hundred plus tons at that speed 'out-phallics' any Porsche that ever there was!

The German Road network is pretty good and it's easy to get up to top speed. The look-ahead is essential, remember shit brakes. The civvy drivers do well to stay away from us, it's no competition in the event of a collision. Steering on the ARV is by two sticks, one either side of the driver's seat. No ARV I ever drove went in a perfect straight line, they always veered slowly off in one direction or the other. Gentle finger pulling on the sticks would right the course, but you must be alert to it. While you are driving along your well-trained crew would have been boiling a brew using the ever-popular BV. One of the crew would clamber over the front of the ARV and deliver a hot green plastic mug of Char. The best crews, and mine always were, would ensure there was a warmer in the Char. Asbach Brandy was popular.

After about twenty miles, which would have taken hours or more, it's wise to pull over and check the load. Tracks tight, road wheels secure, any heat in

the hubs, lights working and so on. Back on the road, that bath and sleep are waiting.

Driving through towns and villages is a challenge. Many old German town houses have balconies that stick out into the streets. Particularly irksome when towing something with height such as a Royal Engineer Bridge layer. More than one balcony found itself on an armoured journey. The civilian population would stand and stare. Many of the older Germans would give us the old Churchill 'V' for victory sign. We would always return it. We were after all there for good reason, the Iron Curtain and the huge Red Army were only a few miles away.

You crack on, hopefully without breakdown or without any other tanks breaking down. As the ARV it would be your job to go and get it if it couldn't be repaired on the roadside. Remember that bath and sleep are waiting.

Eventually you pull into the tank park, its journeys end. If you're not last in, you unhitch the towed tank and park it appropriately. You do this because you may have to go out again. If you are last in and don't have to go out again it can wait till the next working day. The weapons are put in the armoury, and its bath and sleep time. Fall asleep in the bath.

Steel Tracks and Snow

Steel tracks on the Centurions, they were called 'battle tracks', were fabulous for cross country driving. They gave great grip and helped to power the Centurions along. However, bring on the ice and snow on a tarmac or concrete road and it was another matter. The Centurions, all fifty tons of them would just skim long the surface of snow or ice. You could be driving along. Ease back the tiller to turn right, the tank would turn and face the direction intended but the ARV would carry on in a straight line, sideways along the load. No brakes to speak of no way of stopping. It was often roulette, and if you were towing it was even worse. Many a centurion smashed sideways into objects and caused a great deal of damage to vehicles, roadside furniture, the occasional building and sometimes people. It was a dangerous business!

Down steep hills could be an unsmiling challenge. In second or third gear, twenty-seven thousand cubic centimetres of Rolls Royce power smashing on the governors, backfiring like a badly timed machine gun. No power to turn, no brakes to stop. If the downhill run was straight, you were in with a chance. Select the correct gear and gently nurse the beast along. Anticipate the road and its features, be patient, Centurion patient!

Add some impact factors. A fifty-ton tank on tow, down a steep narrow hill; road or track it made little difference. Configure-in some tight bends and an acute 'camber', dropping into a ditch. Add rain or snow, ice is the most challenging, snow atop ice even more so. The fifty ton you are towing finds a mind of its own and it wants to push you along. You must anticipate every angle, every undulate, everything. Concentration is the byword, you can't relax for even a second, the one-hundred-ton plus you are cuddling along will bite your arse in an instant.

Looking ahead you survey the route, anticipate problems, and evaluate a safety plan. If it looks as if it's going to run-away or overturn, do you try to get out? If so which way, left or right or climb over the back! You have another option, to drop your seat and get down inside the driver's compartment. Down inside a runaway fifty-ton steel box loaded with up to two hundred and forty gallons of instantly flammable petrol, two tanks of which are alongside the red-hot engine that has been smashing the governors. The runaway one-hundred-ton combination will easily smash through buildings, mow down trees, crush anything in its path. Jac-knifing would create a real problem, one hundred tons of pressure fixing you fast and always in a bad place like on a hill or narrow trail. I encountered this issue in Canada, thankfully not my ARV. (I refer to it elsewhere in this book).

Towing uphill in ice or snow requires the Centurion ARV driver to be super-efficient at stick changing. You'll get nowhere without it. Armoured Recy Mech driving is a serious sobering business requiring skill and courage. And we did it time after time. It's a testimony to the professionalism and superior driving skills of the Recy Mechs that there were so few tragedies. Well done boys!

Hohne Anecdotes 1

Loudest Place in the world.

Herself thinks I am hard of hearing and she's probably right. I can say with some authority that the loudest and noisiest place in the world is when your tasked to manage the range flag on the tank firing line during live firing on Hohne ranges.

So, you park your ARV tight up to the flag which is located on the extreme side of the firing line but directly adjacent to battle tanks. You sit on your ARV with coffee and book waiting for the control tower to tell you which colour flag to fly. Red is the important one, the tanks are going into action. The message comes across 'flag to red' and you scurry to the front of your ARV to change the flag.

As its your first time on the ranges you sit on the front of the ARV looking along the front line of the tanks. You have an excellent view from here. A first-class seat, you can't buy this.

The .50 ranging guns fire first, bursts of three, seeking 'on' for the main armament. Bang-Bang-Bang! Very loud and I can see the fall of shot about two kilometres forward hitting the ground in front of a 'hard target' which is an old rusty hulk of somebody's tank. Your very impressed, great view, great seat, best in the house. Your very impressed with the accuracy and efficiency of the Hussars. Your extra lucky because it's the nearest tank to you that is firing first; it's about 3-5 yards distance, not far at all really. The next three shots from the .50 Bang Bang-Bang again. This time I can see the fall of shot on the hard target. It's like white lightning flashes and small puffs of smoke.

Having found the range, the neighbouring tank fires the first 120mm shell down the range 'BANG', it's the biggest BANG, it's the crack of all thunders and the opening of all the heavens. 'HOLY FUCKING HELL! WHAT THE FUCK'?

No amount of instruction or anticipation can quite prepare you for the unexpected sound and shock of a 120mm letting loose from very nearby. Coffee spilt; book dropped. Shocked and just a little confused. Lesson learnt.

Character building? Hell yes!

I heard many troopers say, whilst on the ranges -

> *There's a Yank*
> *In a Tank*
> *On the Bank*
> *Having a Wank*
> *Knock him out!*

Poor yank I used to think.

120mm of FUCK OFF

We were on the ranges with the 13th/18th tanks. Not much for a Recy Mech to do while the tanks are stationary on the concrete firing apron. The ARV crew put the range flag up and down, red for firing and green for not. If the weather fine, it's a cushy time; brews and reading. I'd occasionally help with the ammo-bashing, those shells, hundreds of them, are heavy. The regiment decided we, the REME, could have a shoot of the main guns. Fabulous.

The S/Sgt gunnery instructor, I think his name was Ernie, put me in the gunner's seat inside the tank turret; he sat above and behind me in the commander's seat. There wasn't a great deal of room, very cramped and the position would suit smaller soldiers.

I looked through the reticuled gun-sight, Ernie pointed out the necessary controls I would use for elevation and traverse and of course the trigger for firing the gun. The tanks then normally used .50 Browning's for ranging but nothing so complicated for me. With my eyes tight against the gunner's sight Ernie moved the gun around pointing out targets and explaining, in layman's terms, the reticule sight. I was to fire two shells. I would aim at a hard target down the range, which was a rusty old tank that had been shot at a thousand or more times before. I would fire the one hundred and twenty millimetre rifled main armament and if I hit the target then all well and good, just do the same again. If I missed the target, I was to note the point on the sight reticule where the shot fell and then for my second shot 'lay it on', meaning put the point on the reticule where the shot fell over the intended target. Optimistic I was not.

I'd been very close to the main guns firing when outside the tanks and it was the noisiest place in the world; I was anticipating the same within. I laid the sight on the intended target, pulled the trigger, and off went the shell. There was no almighty bang, there was no sharp explosive crack. Just a dull whoosh as the shell flew down the range and the recoil is absorbed by the gun mechanism. I'm sure there is a gunnery term for this, but I don't have it. A bit of an anti-climax really.

I had missed the target, my shot falling yards of to the right but at the same level as the target. Ernie guided me in, and I placed the reticule point where the shot had fallen directly on my target. The loader loaded, he was as fast as lightning, there was shouting going on, but its understanding was beyond me. Ernie gave the OK and I let the second shot go. The same dull woosh but this time I watched the shell hit the target directly. Brilliant. Tank gunner extraordinaire; I. am the Sgt York of Recy Mechs. how cool was I! Ernie congratulated me with a decent back-slap, and I climbed from the gunners' seat and out of the turret. My bragging rights intact.

I never fired anything of a bigger calibre for the rest of my service. When the troopers were talking about their shooting on the ranges while over a beer, they didn't say 'I pulled the trigger' or 'I fired the gun'; they would say something like 'FUCK OFF'.

Character building? Hell yes!

Egg Banjos a Culinary Delight and Tradition

While at the 13th/18th Royal Hussars I was first introduced to egg banjos. Egg Banjo's were a regular meal on exercise and eggs were also readily available in the cookhouse.

Exercise Egg Banjos I remember as being made from stale or almost stale army white bread and a liberal dosing of margarine that came out of a tin. The egg would have been fried to within an inch of its life in the same margarine. The fried egg itself would be a crispy brown/black on one side and slimy yellow and white on the other or they could have been brown and black on both sides. A thick covering of red or brown sauce was personal choice. Some soldiers substituted the sauce with jam or condensed milk. Heroes in my mind. The 'club' version would possibly have included slices of fried tinned meat or an addition of a greasy tinned sausage or two.

If you had not cooked it yourself when the Egg Banjo was passed to you the hand that did so was invariably covered in engine oil and other scum material which would colour the outside of the banjo with a grey and black lubricant. Some of them, not all, were very tasty. Banjos were generally accompanied by a huge mug of army char complete with the obligatory scum floating on top.

<u>'Egg Banjo' How To.</u>

Egg Banjo – is an oft used common military term for an 'egg sandwich'.

Staple to the diet of the British Army for many years as an easy and quick snack or meal often provided and easily made. There are number of permutations for preparing the 'egg banjo'; there are individual preferences and traditions but no hard and fast rules. Here's a guide -

Ingredients
The following list of ingredients

1. One egg (two or more may be used)

2. Two slices of bread (fresh or stale, mouldy or otherwise; any colour).

3. Oil or margarine (engine or hydraulic oil can be used in emergencies).

Utensils

1. Frying pan (hot exhaust cowling, any reasonably level hot surface).

2. Spatula (any flat broad metal object, wooden object, or non-melt plastic object).

3. Means of heat i.e., gas cooker (Benghazi burner, campfire, oxy-acetylene torch).

Situation

1. A couple of days into exercise.

2. 02:00 return to camp after patrol.

3. Any time after leaving the army for nostalgic purposes.

Method (This is not rigid methodology, but it is tried and proven).

> *1. Be sure to be knackered due to lack of sleep, physical exertion, prolonged exposure to shit weather.*
>
> *2. Ensure you have the necessary ingredients and utensils. If not improvise and steal some. You can barter with a proposed egg banjo in acquiring ingredients and utensils.*
>
> *3. Ignite your heat source (being extra secretive if tactical) and lay your flat metal on top of the heat source.*
>
> *4. Add your cooking oil (be mindful of flash points if using engineering oils (particularly if tactical)).*
>
> *5. Prepare your bread. Black, dirty, oily hand marks are expected. Cut off green mould (optional).*
>
> *6. Spread bread with thick lumps of tinned margarine, lard, or anything else slippery and possible edible.*

Place bread nearby on flat surface (it doesn't have to be a clean surface, just nearby).

7. Crack eggs and place in the oil. Cook till brown or black (optional) and crispy on the bottom whilst maintaining a soft runny yolk (vital – your military future depends on this).

8. Place expertly cooked egg onto marge covered bread; make a big theatrical deal about this, you will have an audience.

9. Sprinkle egg with salt and apply ketchup or brown sauce or both.

10. Place second piece of bread on top of egg, marge side down. Press down firmly with dirty hand leaving oily handprint so the recipient knows which side is up.

11. Pass to friend telling him it's probably going to be the best banjo he's ever likely to have.

Consumption

Upon receiving banjo.

1. Always say 'thanks it looks fabulous'

2. Hold firmly in two hands with greasy black handprint on top.

3. Slowly and knowingly, revolve the banjo looking for best attack angle.

4. Identify best attack angle and using both hand push as much of the banjo as you can into your mouth, taking a big a bite as possible. This is a display of experience and gratitude.

5. After taking your first giant bite, hold banjo high in your left hand and sweep away the runny yolk that has dripped onto your chest area with a strumming action of your right hand (hence the name banjo) thereby spreading the yolk further rather than cleaning it off.

6. Greedily and quickly finish off your banjo in the hope of being ready for a second.

7. Swill mouth with hot sweet tea from a green or black plastic mug.

Formalities

1. Always express profound thanks, keeping the possibility open for future banjos.

2. Always state it was the very best banjo you ever had, and there will never be the like again.

3. Never ever ask for the yolk to be broken.

4. Be sure to take your turn at banjo making.

Oddities.

Tankies and REME banjos tend to have the blackest oily handprints. It's art.

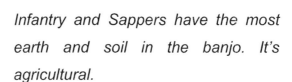
Infantry and Sappers have the most earth and soil in the banjo. It's agricultural.

Gunners and Signallers must always use stale mouldy bread. It's laziness.

Footnote.

Air, Intelligence, Dental and Education Corps are not allowed to cook their own banjos in case they are clean, fresh, and edible. However, they can be invited by any of the above to have one, but this is only for entertainment purposes while watching them trying to eat it without gagging.

<u>Convoy Lob or Convoy Cock?</u>

Nobody ever told me about convoy lob until it came to me (pun intended). Not in basic, or trade training. It's a sensitive issue and something every army driver experiences. Penile erections while driving in military convoys. That's 'hard-ons' for the infantry, 'a curl' for the Cavalry, a 'span' for the sappers. The gunners call it a 'bag-charge'; I have heard the Intelligence, Dental and Education Corps don't do erections; that's very sad, imagine going through life without an erection.

Consider the impact factors. The military vehicles are being driven by young virile men. On exercise or ranges or operations the soldiers are generally without female company. Travelling along for hours on end, in slow moving vehicles, slightly vibrating vehicles, full testicles and fuelled by impure thoughts or erotic memories the inevitable happens. Convoy Lob or is it Convoy Cock?

Driving Centurions on concrete or tarmac roads was particularly stimulating. Not through any fetish for fifty tons of steel armour, nor for the throb of a 27,000cc Merlin engine. It was because of a simple case of moving along in second gear with the long steel central gearstick resting on and methodically and gently vibrating against your inner left thigh, and full testicles. At low speeds the steel on concrete created vibration coupled with warmth and tiredness was an erotically compelling experience. So, the best terminology is Lob or Cock? I think I'm a 'Lob' man, myself! Its more manly.

Character building? Hell yes!

<u>MOJOS</u>

Occasionally when having to move particularly long distances the tanks and ARV's would be carried on tank transporter lorries. The Mighty Antar. These huge powerful lorries were crewed by the misplaced persons organisation MSO.

Following the end of the second world war many displaced persons who were former residents of the Soviet Union, or from nations in Eastern Europe and the Balkans recently taken over by Communists, had no wish to return. Some had collaborated with the Germans and could expect little mercy. But even those forcibly taken by the Germans would still be suspects in the eyes of the Communist authorities. Political opponents of the Communists also feared going home. Many of those who did return were jailed or executed in countries like Poland and Yugoslavia. The British, in their zone of occupation, formed some of these people into the Civil Mixed Watchman Service. They were tasked with guard duties in the camps set up to deal with the tide of humanity moving through Germany. The British also established the Civilian Mixed Labour Organisation to undertake reconstruction work. In 1959, both organisations were

merged into the Mixed Service Organisation (MSO), which would continue to work for the BAOR for many years. MSO units had a British Army commanding officer and senior non-commissioned officers overseeing a multi-national rank and file.

There is nothing more disconcerting that sitting in the middle seat of a three seat Mighty Antar with a non-English speaking Eastern European Pole or Turk both of whom are smoking camel-shit-flavoured fags for a ten- or twelve-hour journey with the erection of all erections and you are unable to do anything about it but fidget. It's even worse when the Mojo's (Slang name for MSO's) decide to change seats and you must stand and move in the confined space whilst trying to conceal a tent pole in your trousers.

Character building. Hell yes!

A Poem

Back In the Day it Was Different

Back in the day it was different.
No war no sand and no grit
Only the cold wet clinging
Of the North German mud and shit

Back in the day it was different
The Tiffy the head of our clan
And a wizened old artisan Sergeant
Making sure we stuck to our plan

Back in the day it was different.
Our war was a Soltau Scheme
The 434 was a barrow
Filled with the Black Hand team

Back in the day it was different
The Cent was the ARV supreme
Crewed with a couple of fitters

Completing the Recy Mechs team

Back in the day it was different
Working till the moon was high
Changing a pack in the darkness
Tightening the last bolt with a sigh

Back in the day it was different
Cooking a choice 'all in'
Wolfing it down with an oily spoon
And sharing a grateful grin

Back in the day it was different
Guzzling strong army char
In a green plastic mug or a Dixie
The most welcome of drinks by far

Back in the day it was different
When the tools were laid down for the night
We'd gather round the warmest of smokers
And put the world to right

Back in the day it was different
Stand-to for the first frozen light
Lying out flat in the 'Ulu'
Seeing off the last of the night

Back in the day it was different
Breakfast was always the name
But no matter which way you cooked it
It always tasted the same

Back in the day it was different
When Endex was called on the net
The troops were always homeward
The REME were still breaking sweat

Back in the day it was different
Always last back to the park
But never a downhearted moment
Always a cheerful lark

Back in the day it was different
Sorting the wagons and kit

REME – The Magnificent Bastards

Exchanging tales of black humour
The established squaddie wit

Back in the day it was different
We'd meet in the mess for some beers
So here's to our skills and our colleagues
And here's to the REME so cheers.

Back in the day it was different
Or was it?

<u>Civilian Population (Civ-Pop) at Tin City</u>

The 13/18th Hussars would be, as a regiment, posted to Northern Ireland. They would be replaced by the 14/20th Kings Hussars. I was to stay in Germany with the incoming regiment. In preparation for their duty in NI the 13/18th had to undergo considerable specialist training for their upcoming tour of duty. I was to have some small part in this training, but little did I know it would be the first of many, many steps in the counter terrorism world for me.

The tanks were checked over, inspected, and parked in hangars. The roads and alleyways of Hohne camp took on the persona of Northern Ireland as NI training for the regiment began in earnest. There were soldiers carrying rifles all over the place. Foot patrols, mobile patrols, vehicle check points, stop searches, area searches and many other new skills were being practiced.

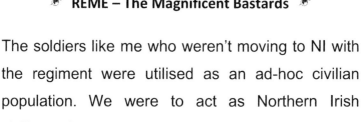

The soldiers like me who weren't moving to NI with the regiment were utilised as an ad-hoc civilian population. We were to act as Northern Irish civilians. We were searched, checked over, ushered in one direction or another and generally made to be compliant with the wishes of the training security forces to be.

We found ourselves carrying makeshift bombs down leafy lanes in the middle of the night. Trying to lay bombs close to bases and patrol points, we conducted sniper attacks using blank ammunition.

The best fun of all was the mock riots which we pushed to the extreme. All the while the regiment honed its internal security skills. It was great fun.

The NI training concluded with a fortnight long exercise at a Killimurphy or 'Tin City' which was a mock Northern Irish Town built in a rural area near Sennelager, a large German Town. I was employed at being Civ-pop (Civilian Population) for this exercise.

I and Nic Everitt another REME soldier and an instrument technician drove the many miles to Tin City in the Leyland Heavy Recovery Vehicle. It was probably the longest truck journey of my life. A big heavy truck with a 'crash' box and the speed of a 'stunned slug', terribly underpowered. All those miles on the Autobahn with the 'woofers' flying by; it was a nightmare. To crown it all we had a puncture and what seemed like hundreds of wheel-nuts and rim bolts had to be changed by hand. It took hours, but eventually we got the wheel changed and completed our journey. We were last to arrive as is traditionally the way of Recy Mechs.

At Tin City I was allocated a room in one of the houses. Comfortable it was not. Essentials only, but it looked the part. A fort, wriggly tin buildings and barricades, terraced houses, pubs, shops, detached and semi houses, a garage, bins, lampposts, everything you could possibly think of.

The regiment in training would treat it exactly as they would in NI. Everything was filmed and replayed and learnt from.

We, as the civilian population, tried our very best to be Northern Irish. We had priests, shopkeepers, vehicles, workers, rioters and even our own terrorists. We moved explosives and weapons around, laid bombs and proxy bombs, threw petrol bombs and house bricks wrapped in black tape. We had riots, charged barricades, slagged off and screamed at the soldiers; all to be as realistic as possible.

The fortnight over we returned to barracks and to the tanks at Hohne and the 13/18th Royal Hussars moved to Northern Ireland.

13/18 Rugby

There wasn't any. They had no rugby team. Bugger!

A PITCH AND SOME POSTS. NO BALL, NO PLAYERS. WHAT?

2nd Unit - 14th/20th Kings Hussars

My second posting was the 14/20th Kings Hussars they were a famous Lancashire recruited cavalry Regiment. At this time, they were composed of an Headquarter Squadron and four sabre squadrons each of sixteen chieftain main battle tanks.

I can honestly say without reservation the 14/20th Kings Hussars was the unit that gave my most enjoyable time in the army. My association with the regiment started off brilliantly and just got better. There were several reasons for this.

Significantly, it was not my first unit, and I will always be grateful to the 13/18th for the excellent first year I had with them. I had been made welcome, had a good boss in Roy Allan, excellent colleagues in Spud and Clutch, worked with ARV's been on exercise, been on the ranges, passed my JMC, upgraded to Class 2 Recy Mech. It was a fabulous foundation year to have under my belt prior to starting with the 14/20th.

Another thing was that the 14/20th were to be a four-sabre squadron regiment as opposed to three as were the 13/18th, This meant a new squadron being formed and they would require a new Recy Mech and your truly was in plum spot, and with great delight I took the offered job. I was a Craftsman in a full Corporal's post.

The new Squadron was 'D' Squadron, and it became known as 'Dirty D'. I understood the squadron was newly formed. Word on the ground was that all the squadron leaders were tasked with giving up a number their soldiers to form the core of the new squadron. Rationale dictates that if you can move somebody along you would move the least desirable, the most useless, the troublemakers and anybody else considered unworthy. Well as far as I was concerned 'what a brilliant strategy'; 'D' Squadron was fantastic. A superb gathering of real tough soldiers, experienced and proper!

Character building? Hell yes!

S/Sgt Dennis Jones

In addition to the new squadron and my new post, Roy Allan moved on because with the extra tanks his now enhanced position warranted a S/Sgt's grade; enter S/Sgt Dennis Jones. Dennis was the epitome of what I was aspiring to be. No nonsense, straight talking, hugely experienced and ultra-practical, probably the best senior Recy Mech I met in twelve years. He was a foundation of knowledge, gave very relevant advice and was keen and enthusiastic in helping me along. At this new stage in my career, he was the perfect Recy Mech supervisor. I would often visit his office with a recovery query. This visit would last hours, and he would regale me with recovery and army stories and sound advice. If I kept the Char going Dennis would keep educating me. I learnt a great deal from him. Thank you.

D Squadron Fitter Troop

I finally get my own squadron. How chuffed am I?

The Tiffy was Jim Adamson, a former commando gunner who had transferred to REME to become an Artificer. He was a good man. The Artisan Sergeant was George Jackson, time served and knew everything there was to know about repairing tanks. If George called you 'Sailor', you were fucked all over in deep shit. Occasionally there was friction between the new Commando Tiffy and the sage artisan Sgt, but it was always quickly resolved. Jim was the boss and that was the end of it, but I know he valued George's input and experience. We jelled quickly in the troop as we spent a lot of time together and being a newly formed troop in a newly formed squadron, we had something to prove!

My accommodation changed also, and I moved into 'D' Squadrons block. It was refurbished accommodation. I had my own room, furniture, and carpet. Also in the same block were two other REME guys Bryan Dyas and Tom Carlisle. 14th/20th guys in the block were Phil "Quassie' Baldwin (a Londoner with a Lancashire regiment?) known for his good looks. Billy (BFBS) Whittle, Mac McMullin, Bob Jones who kept getting bust in rank and a South African trooper who's name I have forgotten but he was the second laziest man I have met in my life. How sad that you get remembered for being lazy!

A Real Recovery Job

So, what is a real tank recovery job like?

You learn quick in the army. Excellent training, superb supervisors, and supportive units. The tanks would be on 'The 'Ulu" training. Moving day and night, fighting battles, supporting infantry, covering operations, the full gambit of tank work.

It may be at night in complete darkness, unknown terrain, lousy wet muddy ground pitted with drops and rises, trees and boulders. Other vehicles, fifty ton plus, will be moving under tactical conditions. There may be an Nuclear, Biological or Chemical (NBC) scenario, and everybody is in protective suits and respirators.

At night in the darkness, chieftain tank engines sound low and deep. They have a very distinctive rumble and pitch as they travel the rev scale with the drivers kicking the gears up and down; the gear changer is a pedal. Mellow at low revs and howling at high, it's impossible to tell what direction the sound is coming from. When the tanks are moving, stay in or on your vehicles. I often mused that I was lucky not to be on the ground in a trench or crewing a soft-skinned-vehicle on such occasions. The tanks, might war beasts that they are, wouldn't stop for anything; nor should they.

You will have either parked at a strategic point and 'cammed' over or you may be following behind you squadron, quite close but not close enough to be in front. You will be listening in to the squadron radio net taking great interest as to how the scheme is progressing. You may have a beer (not many during this point) but more likely 'char'. Meals are cooked, books read, kit cleaned, but always ready to move instantly.

Then a call comes over the radio that a tank is in trouble. It may just have broken down, or thrown a track in the sand or mud, or turned over with crew inside, or driven into soft ground or any number of calamities. What I do know, is that armoured regiments are excellent at their jobs, with no nonsense quality experienced soldiers and they won't be calling me unless they absolutely must.

What I do know from experience is that what I am told has happened over the radio, won't be the whole story and all the conditions I need to know to affect my job properly can only be adduced by me at the scene.

We clarify the situation tactically with the squadron HQ. It's an exciting time and my crew are hyped. Job on! Everything that isn't stashed is rapidly done so, we are prepared for this eventuality. We get a grid reference and a quick tactical situation.

Here is a hypothetical scenario -

It's night-time darkness and shit weather, at grid ref 123 456 Callsign 44 Chieftain Main Battle Tank belonging to D Sqdn (the 4th Squadron 4th Troop) commanded by an officer, normally a Lieutenant has 'fallen' of the side of a Royal Engineer Bridge Crossing which has been laid by a Chieftain Armoured Vehicle Laying Bridge (AVLB) (this army originality is getting to me). The stricken tank is blocking the bridge.

We make our way as quickly as possible under tactical conditions, no light in complete darkness, to the scene. We stop our ARV about a hundred or two hundred yards away. I must go forward on foot to carry out my reconnaissance. I need to check the ground (no good me getting stuck) and the approach. I speak to the senior soldier at the scene. He may be tank crew or a sapper with the bridging party. I ask what is the tactical situation? How did the episode happen? and what's ongoing? I also need to know the urgency of the job.

I am told it's a tactical advance to contact. One troop of four tanks has already crossed and this bridge crossing, for the benefit of the exercise, is the only way forward for the other tanks. The remainder of the squadron are waiting to cross. I can hear nearby tank engines, but I can't see them its complete darkness.

I examine the scene of the tank. The tank callsign 44 has slipped off the side of the bridge. One track is still on the bridge and the track has come off the final drive and hooked itself onto the metal bridge. The track is as tight as a bowstring; I can hear it singing, fifty tons or more of tension. Thankfully there are no human casualties, but that's not always the case.

My urgent priority is to clear the bridge for the tank advance to continue. This is a very high-pressure situation.

These are my priorities.

- Clear the bridge (which means removing the displaced tank track) without damaging the bridge.
- Recover the tank to good ground (Which probably means winching it away from the gully at the side of the bridge).
- Repair the track so the tank can re-join the battle.

Here are my available resources –

- 1 Fully working Chieftain or Centurion Armoured Recovery Vehicle
- I Full set of Oxy Acetylene Cutting Equipment
- 1 L/Cpl Recovery Mechanic (me)
- 3 ARV Crew (an assortment of REME tradesmen)

- 3 or 4 Tank Crew
- Some Sappers.

My consideration: the track must be cut. Plastic Explosive would be the quickest, but I haven't any. So, its oxy acetylene gear of which I have plenty. It appears the tank is being held almost totally on its side by the track gripped to the bridge. If I cut the track the tank may roll over onto its roof in a more difficult recovery position. So, I must cut the track, stop the tank rolling over and then pull the tank to good ground to repair the track.

My plan.

I gather all available soldiers and quickly brief them. I tell them my plan and then give them instructions.

The Pull out requires a 2:1 pull, which is sixty tons of force. I need to position my ARV in the correct place so the recovery tackle can be laid while I am cutting the track. Two of my crewmen will position the ARV and lay out the recovery tackle from the instructions I give them. My third man will help me cut the track.

The tank crew and the sappers, using shovels (there were always plenty of shovels) will create a bund (earth bank) on the off side of the tank in a bid to reduce the distance it may fall. The shovelers will also dig soil away from the rear of the tank to lessen the resistance for when I pull it out; the spoil they dig away can be moved to the bund at the side. I warn them about the dangers of getting too close to the tank.

I give my instructions. Any questions? No. Let's get on, tactical (in darkness no lights) and urgent, very urgent!

The shovelers scurry away to gather shovels and get on with it. REME, sappers and tankies working together on a single urgent understood cause. Is there a better combination?

We drag the very heavy gas bottles close to the hooked track. I arrange for my REME assistant to hold up a canvas sheet to tactically obstruct the light from the flame and spark. When the torch is lit, I have enough light to work with. I've cut a few tracks previously on course and in practice. It's a very dangerous operation. I must lean right into the work area, tight up against the tank with my arms inside the track parameters. Fifty-ton longbow keeps running through my mind and I could be the arrow. Robin Hood never had to do this shit.

I light the torch. I am mindful of the shovelers on the other side and before I am any measure through the track, I will make sure they are clear. I start cutting the track from the inside out, the sparks shower downward extinguishing in the mud alongside the bridge. If the tracks should suddenly snap, given its massive tension, who knows what could happen?

I start drawing the cutting lance towards me. Leaning into the running gear of a fifty-ton tank, half over on its side, is a very lonely place. Loud hissing and a fountain of dancing sparks diving into the ground under the tank. I am mindful that despite the canvas cover, under which its quickly got very hot, our tactical situation may be light compromised. It can't be helped. I'm halfway through the track and it's taken about ten minutes. I daren't go any more until I know there are no troops close to the other side. Time to pause the cutting and check the bund.

The shovelers are working fast and furiously. They have moved a huge amount of earth. Nearly enough, I think. My assistant and I get stuck in with shovels. The more the merrier. Merrier! Is that the right word?

A further ten minutes of arduous earth moving, and I ask everybody to stand back I check the size and location of the bund. I check the newly dug channels at the rear of the tank. I'm satisfied, the bund is big enough to reduce the sideward fall of the tank and the back channels sufficient to lessen the angle and reduce the required force I must use to pull the tank up and out.

I tell everybody to stand back, and I return to cutting the track. I relight the lance and apply the hot, angry blue flame to the steel. The sparks shoot again. I'm slowly moving outwards and the amount of steel holding the track together is getting less and less. I lean back, I extend my arm as far as possible giving me whatever little extra distance I can get. I can smell cigarette smoke. The shovelers have earned it. Wouldn't mind a fag myself right now!

I sense more than feel the track is going. I hear a very low humming singing sort of noise then suddenly with a sharp WHACK! the track parts and the two ends fall and swing slowly. I fall back on the floor and drop the burning lance into the earth. The bridge moves and jerks up sharply about six inches, and the fifty ton fully laden tank casually rolls over no more than a foot but clears the bridge. Joy of joys the bund has worked. We quickly place the gas bottles and lance to one side along with the canvas.

The track has rolled cleanly off the back of the tank and the remainder is loosely draped over the top idler wheels. I cannot see anything that would obstruct it rolling off when I pull the stricken tank out backwards.

Another quick briefing for the benefit of the sappers and the tankies. My crew know the 'ropes' (excuse the pun there). I just need the sappers and tankies to move to a place of safety some distance away.

My crew have laid out a steel wire rope towards the tank and around a ninety-ton pulley block (of the same type I had lifted above my head at the behest of Roy Allan) which is secured to the tank with steel fastening and then back to the ARV where it is further attached.

We slowly drive the ARV away paying out the winch rope as we go. Far enough away from the stricken

tank to give us room for two things. Firstly, ground enough for the tank to occupy when it's pulled out, and secondly enough room so that when the winch is operated and the tension is taken up, the anchor blade on the ARV will have enough room to dig into the ground to stop the ARV moving forwards. Fingers crossed I've got it right!

We have enough room. The winch operator battens down, and I go around to check the tackle one more time. I am using a 'muted' torch' and I start giving signals to the winch operator. The engine revs on the ARV increase, the steel rope starts to tighten and rises slowly from the ground.

ALWYS WHEN ITS DARK, RAING AND YOUR'E KNACKERED

I've considered the weight of the tank, the damaged track, the firmness of the ground and how much we have lessened the degree of slope up which we have to winch the tank. The winch rope is looped around a ninety-ton pulley block and this configuration will give us about sixty tons of pull. We should be ok.

As the ropes become taught and the tackle set up rises, I stop the winch for the final time. I make a final check of the tackle layout before the full strain is taken-up, I make sure the pins fixing the tackle together remain in, I make sure the winch rope is firm on the wheel of the pulley block. I make sure wooden rollers placed under the winch rope to stop it digging in the dirt remain in place. I check the discarded track isn't going to snag the wheels. I make sure the pull of the tank will miss the sapper bridge. All looks good! Let's do this.

I start the winching signal. The revs pick up, once more the rope tightens' there's a quiet creaking of steel on steel.

I am standing midway between the ARV and the tank, it's the best place. The winch operator must see me, and I must see as much as I can of what's going on. I maintain the winch signal and all appears to be progressing as it should.

Slowly, very slowly the tension of the tackle increases. I see a small movement in the dark gloom near the tank then the movement stops. I look towards the ARV, and I can see it is moving slowly forward. The anchor blade at the of the ARV is extending and slowly digging into the firm ground. The ARV raises as the blade bites, now all the tackle is in the air. The revs on the ARV increase as the full weight of the tank comes on, nothing seems to happen, but one of two things will. Either I have miscalculated, and the weight of the pull required is too great for the tackle I have laid out and the safety cut-out will automatically operate, or the tank will come out.

Slowly the tanks edges towards me. It's working. It's not out yet but it's coming painfully slowly, inch by nervous inch. The rear plate on the tank is pushing a low wall of earth before it. The wooden rollers so placed to stop the ropes and pulley block fouling in the dirt, are run over, and all the tackle is high in the air. The toughest part of the pull is passed and now it's just minutes before the tank is on firm ground. The sappers are already checking their bridge and in minutes the remainder of the battle tanks are moving over the bridge running very close to my ARV and the single-track recovered tank. The battle goes on. So far, it's a job well, done but the recovery is not over yet.

We slacken the tackle, unhitch the tank, and stow the recovery gear away, including the gas bottles, in their rightful place on the ARV. Then using twenty-ton chains we drag out from the gully the track that I have cut with gas, and we secure it with the chains to the towing eyes on the front of the recovered chieftain.

I then hitch the chieftain to my ARV with steel towing bars. The tank crew remove the 'quill shafts' from the chieftain so it can be towed without engaging the gearbox and transmission. The tank crew and the ARV crew mount the ARV and off we go across 'The 'Ulu'' to find some hard standing where we can get on with replacing the broken track. Removing the damaged track links and replacing with new links and replacing the track back onto its idlers and drives. A well-loved military activity known as 'track-bashing'. The tank crew are well capable of getting on with the track-bashing and I and my crew check over out equipment, make sure we still have it, its serviceable and where it should be. Then it's back into the foray following the squadron. Medals on your chest Sylvest!

My example above is based on an actual recovery job I carried out with the 14/20th Kings Hussars. Of course, that job went well but it isn't always the case. Consider what could have gone wrong?

Such as I might have had no gas, or the gas had run out halfway through. The tank might have fallen from being hooked on the bridge at any time. The tank may have rolled over when the track was cut through. My calculations for the winch pull and type of layout might have been inaccurate. There may have been an interfering higher rank who thought he knew better but didn't (I have experienced this also).

Vehicle recovery is a dangerous job at any time. Armoured recovery more so and add to that the pressure of tactical operations such as darkness, tired or inexperienced crews, irate under-pressure commanders, and sheer operational demand it can be a tough day at the office.

Character building? Hell yes!

Hohne Anecdotes 2

Coldstream & REME

2nd Battalion of the Coldstream Guards arrived in Germany after spending a few years on ceremonial duties. The sort of thing I envisaged doing at the recruiting office in Cardiff. The army way at the time was to form 'Battle Groups'.

As I recall a battle group consisted of a Company of infantry, a troop of four tanks, and some support troops in the way of sappers and gunners and so on. So, in this instance it was a Coldstream's battle group and 'D' Sqdn 14/20th provided the tanks.

I was a Craftsman Recy Mech at the time and my ARV commander was a L/Cpl Gunfitter. Let's call him 'Gonzo'.

I remember this exercise for two reasons; the first of which was that it was the first time I exercised with 'Guards'. I was in for an eye-opener. I was under the impression the Guards were notoriously strict on discipline, and the Coldstream's proved to be no exception.

My first experience of this was during a mealtime. They had set up a centralised cooking station where the meal was cooked for the troops by Andy Caps Commandos (the ACC), who did their usual magic job. We were in line waiting to go into the mess tent for our meal and I was standing alongside one of our REME Corporals. We were waiting patiently in the Queue. Then out of the blue along comes this guards Captain, so old he was probably an ex-ranker, and tears a new asshole for the REME Corporal. The Corporal's heinous crime was that as a full Corporal, the guards equivalent of a Lance/Sergeant, he should have pushed in at the front of the queue and not waited with the lesser ranks. How dare he! The Corporal went to the front of the queue as I stood there bemused and minding my own business innocently looking away. Just in case.

The meal, as I recall, was good, stand up Andy Capp again, and as we exited the mess tent the kitchen staff had lined up on a table, three dixies full of hot water. On the front of the dixies, in order were three signs written on cardboard 'WASH', 'RINSE', 'STERILISE'. We were expected to dip our aluminium mess tins into the first 'Wash', then into the second 'Rinse' and finally into the 'Sterilise'. Looking at the water it all looked like dirty grey soup, and I thought any consideration of it being hygienic and effective was optimistic in the extreme. The old Captain was overseeing the event, it must have been his thing, mess duties or similar.

Suddenly he exploded, he went terrifyingly ballistic. A guardsman two or three places in front of me in the wash queue had missed the 'Rinse' dixie and gone straight to 'Sterilise' from 'Wash'. Ever was there a capital offence this was it. I thought REME and Hussar Sergeant Majors could bollock people. But this Coldstream Captain was 'Universe Class'. It resulted in the guilty guardsman being marched off at double quick time by a screaming Corporal and placed under close arrest in a nearby tent. For fucks sake, I'm in a loony bin! Trying to be as small and innocuous as possible I stealthed back to my ARV without making eye contact with anybody or doing anything that might result in me being jailed in the middle of 'The 'Ulu''. I passed near the tent in which the criminal guardsman had been imprisoned. The flap was open and I could see that he and one other Major criminal, probably a litter bug, were sitting handcuffed to a pole in the middle of the tent. Madhouse: it was a fringe side of the army I had not experienced.

DIXIES THREE – DO NOT PASS GO

Another interesting thing that happened on this battlegroup is that we were to do a tactical replen.

The Coldstream QM's department were to replenish us with essentials. Fuel, water, ammunition, rations and so on. They would park their vehicles including a fuel bowser alongside a particular route and we would drive through the replenishment (replen) area, and they would hand over what stores we required. I was driving a Centurion ARV which was a thirsty beast and devoured petrol like there was no tomorrow. The Coldstream's, new from ceremonial duties, were on a steep learning curve. Their fuel bowser carried diesel and the petrol they had was alongside in jerrycans in the back of a **Landr**over. As I pulled level with the QM vehicle I shouted out 'Petrol, two hundred gallons". I can see the look on his face now. He just could not grasp that something would take two hundred gallons. I think he had about sixty gallons for Landrovers and the like. Every day was a school day, for others, as well as me.

<u>Soltau Hoppers</u>

I remember driving my Centurion ARV (50-ton armoured recovery vehicle, used for towing and winching tanks) into a tactical night-time replen. The ARV had a 120-gallon petrol tank in the front. The plan was that I would drive slowly past the replen stalwarts (Stalwart, a six-wheeled all terrain load carrying vehicle) whose crew would pass the jerry cans full of fuel to the ARV crew who would be standing on the front of the ARV ready to receive them.

The ARV crew would then open the 'fuel hopper' provided, fit the filler hose onto the hopper and into the fuel tank. I recall the hopper could hold about three or four Jerry Cans at the same time. The Jerry cans were upended into the hopper and the petrol would flow freely out and through the hopper into the ARV 120-gallon tank.

One night it was torrentially pissing down with rain and in the dark and on the move with no lights, the hopper filler hose hadn't been tightly connected. Consequently, as the jerry cans were upended into the hopper and the petrol flowed through the hose into the front tank, a decent amount of it spilled onto the glacis plate on the front of the ARV and ran along the gully recess and onto my lap.

It was very dark and very wet and of course the smell of petrol was expected so my overalls saturating with petrol went unnoticed.

Unnoticed that is until a short while later, after leaving the replen area, I was driving along and decided to have a smoke. In those days I was a dab-hand with a Zippo lighter which I used to light using one hand by flipping the lid with my thumb and rolling the striker along my thighs whilst driving, and thus igniting the dependable lighter.

In this instance these were my petrol-soaked thighs. I zipped the zippo. Flames shot up, filling my drivers' compartment. I reacted as quickly as I could and I leant forward against my driver's hatch, thereby

stopping the flames from licking my face which was the only exposed part of me. I rubbed the flames down as best I could, but I was 'hot' to the touch. I stopped the ARV, slid out tight to my hatch and belly-flop dived into the wet mud of the "Ulu". Crisis over.

Character building? Hell yes!

Staring Down the Barrel 1

We were on a night move on Soltau; 14/20th Kings Hussars. D Sqdn, The Tiffy, Jim Adamson a former Commando Gunner, decided we would all drive different vehicles so we could all cross crew. Another member of the fitter section drove my ARV (not without instruction and a great deal of practice beforehand) and I was tasked with driving the 432 (bit of a toy car TBH).

So, I'm following the squadron tanks across the 'Ulu', total darkness, raining (wasn't it always). I'm the leading fitter section vehicle and I'm following what I think is the last tank. All I can see is the dim convoy lamps, which are low down dim white lamps at the bottom rear of military vehicles, and with the sloshing mud and wet it was very difficult to see anything. It was the usual case of carrying on and doing your best. I had been briefed the route was marked at intervals by red light - but I hadn't seen any.

After a while I lost sight of the last tank, so I ploughed on a bit faster. In my mind I was catching up. High in the distance I saw a red light. Thinking I had fallen a long way behind I booted the 432 on. Suddenly the red light elevated very, very quickly, looming out of the darkness straight towards my face, just feet away was a huge gun barrel. I hauled on both the steering tillers bring the 432 to an immediate halt. As I stopped just touching my face was the hard cold end of a 120mm barrel. Lucky, Lucky, Lucky Bastard was I.

My head, minus my body, could have been rolling around in the back of the 432.

The tank commander, knowing his convoy light was kaput, had elected to substitute it with his right-angled torch, on red filter, which he held facing backwards. It was a poor substitute. From my limited, low down, wet, muddy, tired position I thought it to be a way-marker. I had escaped decapitation by inches. One of my nine lives, I think.

Character building? Hell yes!

Gonzo - What a Twat!

My ARV commander, Gonzo, was a loud mouthed, obnoxious, small man of a L/Cpl He was petty and interfering, he knew everything and was chief-nark to anybody with more rank than him. Nevertheless, the army is the army, and he must be tolerated. We were parked in a wood line and having a brew when over the squadron radio I could hear that one of the tanks a mile or two away was on fire. Our illustrious short-arsed commander was nowhere to be seen, he'd was probably brown-nosing somewhere, but hadn't told us where he was going. I had several fire extinguishers on my ARV, and we could be with the burning tank in a few minutes. After looking for but failing to find Gonzo, using our initiative, we went with the extinguishers to assist the burning tank.

We got to the burning tank sharpish. The fire was in the engine compartment, they had used their extinguishers and those, together with the extra we had brought we put the fire out completely and no doubt saved the tank, if not from destruction, then certainly from further damage.

We were cleaning up the tank and preparing to tow it back for repair when one of the crew said I was wanted on the radio. It was our section 'Tiffy' demanding to know where I and my ARV was. I told him and he wanted to know on who's authority I had taken the ARV and he asked me where Gonzo was. I told him I didn't know. I was ordered to report to the Tiffy immediately on my return. Gonzo was of course shit-stirring, as was his normal way, he was sitting with the Tiffy at this time.

I returned to the Tiffy, complete with charred tank on tow and I pulled up directly alongside the Tiffy wagon. It was the first the Tiffy knew of the fire, first he knew that Gonzo had fucked-off without telling anybody where he was going, first he knew that we had saved the tank.

The Tiffy rounded on Gonzo and laid into him in a decent swearing and shouting Sergeant Major fashion. Gonzo had – absolved himself of responsibility, not told his crew where he was, misled the Tiffy, and had acted in a way that wasn't approved, certainly not approved by me. Prick! It was his last stint as ARV commander. I was well pleased and vindicated.

I was to meet Gonzo a few years later by which time he was a S/Sgt, but a leopard doesn't change his spots.

Harry the Bastard

Harry the Bastard joined us at the 14/20th LAD. He had been an RAF electrician and had left the RAF and joined the REME. More importantly for me, Harry the Bastard was an established REME Corps rugby player. Coming in at about six foot three inches and fifteen stone he was a sizeable unit. He was an uncompromising and tough second row forward and I was to learn much from him. He took me under his wing rugby wise and I will always be grateful for that.

The LAD entered the REME BAOR rugby 7's which was a prestigious REME rugby festival with many units fielding teams. I thought we were being a bit adventurous, nevertheless Harry the Bastard was adamant we should enter, as we only had two established rugby players on the unit, that was Harry the Bastard and myself. So, Harry the Bastard set about forming the team.

221

We had fast four hundred metres runners in Gaz Watson and Martin Rae, who would be our wingers. Our officer Mike Pearce was a stocky unit and had played rugby previously and the other players were the usual 'volunteer gladiators' who would have a go at anything (the army and REME have many Gladiators). Our simple game plan was to get the ball to either of our two wingers in as short an order as possible as we were confident, they could outrun anybody else. It was a simple plan which would no doubt prove effective except for our weak link which was me. I, a sixteen stone competent and experienced tighthead prop forward was to play at scrum half! What the fucking hell was Harry the Bastard thinking. I challenged him on this; I could prop, hook, throw in and do all the forward things and I was particularly good at having a wrestle. But scum half? Passing, positional play, putting in, long-pass, quick-pass, decision-making, kicking even! All Harry the Bastard replied to my query was 'You'll be fine Taff, just get on with it'.

I wasn't too sure. I didn't want to let anybody down. Off I went to speak with Dave 'Bulldog' Drummond, the exceptionally talented 14/20th scrum half. A proper scrum half, he had it all. He was fabulous to play with and in army terms I could compare him to the incomparable Sean Anders of REME Corps fame. Bulldog had a plan.

He decided I would be OK in open play and at line-outs, which were straight forward. However, he thought I could get a march on opposition scrum-halves in the close vicinity of the scrums themselves.

We got together a dozen or so of the regimental team and formed them into two teams and we set about practising 'Bulldog style', scrum-half work at the scrums. Bulldog's plan was straight forward. He knew my style of play at fifteens, and he decided that it was easier to adapt that to sevens, than to teach me scrum half skills. The armoury we practiced wasn't a million miles away from my normal game. At all times I had to be as close to my opposite player as possible, rumbustious, and pushing, elbows and knees. Stamp on his feet on every occasion. Push him over his own ball, push him into his own players. Catch his arms and pull his sleeves, interfere with his putting-in and with his passing. Hound and harry and bully him constantly. Constantly verbally abuse him, slag him, his family and his friends and his style, off at every opportunity. And, when I could get a tackle in, make it count. Hard and driven and into the ground. When I won the ball, I wasn't to be too concerned about passing it out I had to charge at and engage my opposite number as physically as possible with my sixteen stones (very heavy for a scrum half)

The objective was to put my opposite number off his game, to detract his concentration, to make him fear me. It worked.

It would not have worked if I had playing against a Drummond or an Anders, but I wasn't. The opposite scrum halves were at best mediocre or gladiatorial, meaning very enthusiastic but unskilled.

We had a fabulous day. Harry the Bastard won everything at the lineout. Mike Pearce and I blocked the midfield, I managed to play havoc with the scrum-halves. Our flying wingers scored all our tries. We came away with winners' medals which I still have to this day. Sixteen stone winning scrum-half; my arse.

Character building? Hell yes!

Karate Competition

'Harry the Bastard' was big and mean and he had a nasty streak when provoked. One afternoon a few of us REME chaps found ourselves 'on the lash' in a German pub. Also in the pub were a large group of German Infantrymen also on the lash. As the strong frothy German beer was consumed the bar got louder and louder. As is usual the banter evolved between the Germans and the brits. Football was usually the starting gambit followed by who has the best tanks and before you know it 'two world wars and a world cup' are in the conversation and things can get a bit iffy. This afternoon was no different. The banter had 'turned' and one of the Germans, drunk and loud, informed us that he was an ace karate fighter and that he was prepared to use his skill to sort us out. It was getting feisty, as usual, and nobody was backing down, certainly not the British Army (that's us). Step to the fore one Harry the Bastard.

Harry the Bastard informed the irate German Karate soldier (lets christen him Eric), that he too was an ace karate fighter and that his 'karate chop' was so hard he could smash through anything with his hands. Eric said that he had the hardest chop, much harder that Harry the Bastard's and that he could also chop through anything. Harry the Bastard suggested a competition and Eric agreed. I had no idea Harry the Bastard was an accomplished martial arts practitioner I was learning this man was skilled at everything!

They would start by chopping a broom handle in half. It was arranged for Harry the Bastard to go first and for Eric to follow. A broom was acquired, and I could see the handle was about an inch and a half thick. I didn't think anybody would be able to chop it in half with their hands, let alone two NATO squaddies full of beer. Matters were getting interesting.

Eric held the broom handle out in his hands with his palms facing upward. Harry the Bastard stood in front of his opponent slowly moving his hand up and down in a slow karate chop fashion, as a snooker player does before taking his shot. Harry the Bastard adjusted the height of the broom being held by Eric, moving it up and down under his proposed angle of chop. Harry the Bastard was unhappy with the height of the broom stating it was too high. He told Eric to get on his knees and hold the broom at a better height for Harry the Bastard's chop. Eric, appearing confident of his impending victory to be, got on his knees looking up at Harry the Bastard. Harry the Bastard adjusted the height until he was eventually satisfied. Harry the Bastard asked Eric if he was ready. 'Ja good' was the reply from Eric the smilingly confident opponent.

Harry the Bastard braced himself, motioned his chopping had backwards and forwards a few times, his shoulders' swaying with his motion. 'Ready?'. 'Ja'.

Suddenly Harry the Bastard lurched forward smashing his clenched fist solidly into the nose of the kneeling Eric laying him prostrate on the floor, the broom clattering to one side. There were a few seconds pause that lasted a good hour. Spontaneously the room erupted into a giant melee with fists and boots flailing wildly. Furniture was broken, glasses smashed. Harry the Bastard, gentleman that he was, stood astride the prone Eric, ensuring he came to no further arm. The melee died

away as the combatants slowly withdrew and I recall Harry the Bastard picking the groggy Eric up from the floor and placing him on a bar stool and putting a beer in front of him.

Summer Hours & Canoeing

During the summer the regiment practised summer hours. How good was this? We would start work at 7am following an early breakfast, of which mine was always bacon and baked beans. Work would finish at about 1pm. The afternoons were then free to do as we wished.

Mac McGahey was not only a highly entertaining individual, but he was also a fabulously motivated character, every day he would arrange for a couple of four-ton lorries to be made available for us.

We would load the lorries with food for BBQ's, beer for drinking, and canoes for fucking-about in. We'd then drive them off to some nearby water filled quarries.

These quarries were also very popular with the German civvies for swimming, water-sports, and sunbathing. I think Mac's choice of venue was influenced by the large preponderance of semi naked, large breasted, athletic looking German women who frequented the site and enjoyed beer and BBQ's.

Our canoeing standard of proficiency was shite. Fifty-ton tanks easy, a fibreglass or plastic canoe weighing and couple of stones was just impossible. We tried, oh how we tried!

I learnt the phrase 'Eskimo roll' where you are supposed to be able to overturn and right the canoe in one flowing movement using your body weight and a dexterous application with the paddle. Most of us, certainly including me, could only manage half an Eskimo roll at best. The problem with a half Eskimo roll is drowning!

Apparently, when you are under the water you are supposed to slap on the bottom of the overturned canoe if you are OK. But what if you're not OK after you have slapped! It could be a fucker. There was much swallowing of quarry water, dragging of heads and faces in the shallow bits, and all for the amusement of the Germans.

A HALF-ESKIMO ROLL - NOT GOOD AT ALL

The BBQs were fabulous, the Andy Capp did us proud with the generosity of rations (again, as they always did). The BBQ's themselves were upturned half fifty-five-gallon oil drums, welded onto a steel cradle by the LAD metalsmiths and fired by any flammable material we could find. There was always plenty of food and we would share with the civvies; particularly some of them!

Yellow Handbags of Herforder fame were always in abundance, dozens of them. Easy to carry, cheap to buy, easy to drink. Liquid currency. We always cleaned up after ourselves not wanting to spoil a good thing. Back to camp for early evening, ditch the rubbish from the lorries, return the canoes to store, shower to remove the sand and silt. Then repair to the NAAFI to brag about our outstanding Eskimo rolls, despite the fact I couldn't recall any successful ones then, nor can I now. Sometimes, those NAAFI evenings would extend, and we'd practise Eskimo rolls in the bar. Shambles!

Character building? Hell yes!

CANADA BATUS

BATUS is the British Army Training Unit at Suffield in Canada. British army units go there for realistic, live-firing training on the huge prairie plains. The troops stay at Camp Crowfoot where they prepare the resident 'kit' for exercise use. In our case its chieftain tanks and for me a Chieftain ARV. We are given maps and briefings, then rationed, and fuelled we set off for the exercises.

First thing I notice is its bloody hot in the day, dust, and sun. In the night its bloody freezing, just the stars, but bloody cold. The stars are a help to navigation, as is the sun but only for general direction purposes.

The terrain is featureless, map readers must be on their mettle reading every contour and ditch on the map. Just stay on top of it and always concentrate. This is very relevant to Recy Mechs who often travel alone. There's nobody else to follow or to blame. The area had previously been used for nuclear weapon testing. I wondered if things would glow in the dark. So, the battle commences.

The tanks move forward closely followed by us and mechanised infantry in armoured personnel carriers, on this initial phase it's a dry-run, no ammunition being used. The units are getting to know each other. The armoured reconnaissance unit are the 15th/19th Hussars, a Geordie unit. I can hear them on the radio but it's an accent I'm unfamiliar with. It'll take a bit of getting used to. Probably just as well I don't have to speak directly with them. There are lots of tanks, infantry, gunners, and sappers. Helicopters are all over the place. It's a proper job. We follow the battle, up and down hills, into ravines, across ditches and bridges. Ironing out and practising communications and tactics. It's a big job and the battle group needs to get it right before the live firing.

After the first phase its back to camp crowfoot. As usual the REME are last in because of dealing with broken down vehicles. The ARV is invariably last in

towing a chieftain casualty. The ARV was always towing Chieftain casualties.

In Camp Crowfoot we have showers and a cookhouse. The accommodation is basic but at least its dry. Unit bars pop up and there's a choice of two beers Labatt's Blue and Labatt's Red; original I thought, I can't tell the difference. I chat in one of the bars with members of the 'pan-diving' team. Halfway around the world to wash pans for the cookhouse. That's adventure in the extreme. It's a tough job, but somebody eh! There's a bit of servicing of the equipment going on, but mostly it's down time before the live exercise.

Battle Group Attack

It's very early in the morning, first light, and the battle group moves into position for the start of the live fire exercise. A Squadron 14th/20th Kings Hussars, who I am attached to, set off and the fitter troop, that's us, follow closely behind. Its dusty and for the first couple of miles there are well worn rough dirt roads to follow. They soon disappear and we're on the 'Ulu'.

The tanks adopt a battle formation closely followed by the mechanised infantry; it's an advance to contact. The radios get busy with chat, and we can feel the tension, this is getting serious. We maintain our position behind the tanks but close enough to be just with the infantry, keeping the tanks in sight.

The tanks move tactically, moving from bound to bound, finding cover, and seeking out good fire positions. Contact with the enemy is made, the tanks slow, moving tactically forward, the infantry following several hundred yards behind. On our ARV we have a grand view. The movement forward slows and suddenly there is a mighty roar above us. It's the Royal Artillery. Somebody ahead has called in artillery support, and they are giving it big style. God bless the gunners! The air is shaking and roaring as the big deadly projectiles whoosh overhead. It's scary, I've never had artillery fire overhead before. I hope the artillery nickname of 'The Drop-shorts' is highly unjustified. I'm not aware of anything falling short. We can't see the fall of the big guns, its far ahead and over the rise in front of us. What we can see and hear is the tanks going into action. We heard the orders coming over then net first and then they start to move. The tank crews are in their element, this is as close to an actual war as its going to get for them. They move from bound to bound, fire, and move, machine guns rattling, the infantry armoured personnel carriers have joined in. I hear on the net that some of the tanks are being hit from behind by infantry machine gun fire. No problem for the crews within but the kit stowed on the outside stowage bins is getting lacerated. There's a suspicion the infantry's doing it on purpose. I'm sure it's more than a suspicion. On the ARV we have a General-Purpose Machine Gun (GPMG) and a couple of thousand rounds of belted ammo. I've locked the GPMG it in a stowage bin. I have no intention whatsoever of getting involved in a firefight or of shooting the ammunition off; none. Following the tanks closely is enough. Smoke and dust are now kicking up and the smell of cordite is very strong and blowing back at us. Behind us I can see a mixture of tracked ambulances, command radio wagons, land rovers and stalwarts carrying fuel and ammunition. Everybody has a part to play, and everyone wants in on the act. There are Gazelles and Lynx helicopters flitting about in the air, whether they are the same ones or there are a lot of them I'm not sure, but they are low and fast.

This cacophony of sound and movement goes on for an hour or two. We don't cover a great deal of ground and so far, there is no work for the ARV. We've had a few brews, and the visual entertainment has been superb. Eventually this stage of the live firing comes to a stop and the battle group 'lagers' up. Its replen time. Ammunition and fuel are brought forward, BVs are put on, cookers are lit, and ration packs are opened. There are briefings and de-briefings. What went well and what not so. The Tiffy and artisan go around the tanks querying their state of repair, any problems? Any issues? Anything we can do for you? There's nothing for the ARV, we chat with the tank crews who are excited, and adrenalin fuelled. They all seem to be enjoying the action, they are slating the infantry, Fusiliers I think, for shooting up the stowage bins. There is talk of turning the main guns on the infantry if they keep fucking about, but its only banter. Watered, fuelled, and fed the Hussars are keen to get on with the battle. More of the same.

Giant Viper

As the advance progresses the battle group encounters a minefield and a path through for the attacking vehicles must be made. I watch the Royal Engineers move up to the front with their 'Giant Viper'. This was a new one for me. The Armoured Vehicle Royal Engineers (AVRE), pass through us. It's a Centurion demolition tank with a huge mortar instead of a gun its towing a purpose made trailer carrying the Giant Viper. The giant viper is a two-hundred-yard-long hose of explosives, attached to a rocket which is launched from the trailer. We have a good view of the Giant Viper being positioned being about four hundred yards behind on the lee of a bund.

With an almighty bang, the giant Viper smashes into the air, spiralling and spinning in an awkward kaleidoscope motion. There is a great orange flame jetting behind a trail of dirty grey smoke. We can clearly see the Giant Viper trailing out behind the rocket. Its dirty white or grey in colour, its thick enough to be seen from our position. The whooshing rocket sound gets louder and louder and eventually the rocket has flown its course and it crashes to the ground as does the giant Viper. There is an almighty bang as the two-hundred-yard-long hose of explosives explodes in a bright orange line generating a thick curtain of black smoke. What a spectacular event; well done the sappers!

GIANT VIPER AT REST

If it's done its job, there should be a six-yard-wide safe path through the minefield. It was meant to have detonated any mines in its path and any nearby mines would have been sympathetically detonated. Immediately the flame and smoke had cleared the AVRE drives through the cleared pathway pushing its front fitted 'mine-plough' to push any undetonated mines to the side of the cleared area.

There is now a two-hundred-meter path through the minefield and the lead tanks begin to move through. I realise this is a bottleneck danger and if a tank is rendered immobile in the narrow channel the safe path would be blocked and there would be problems. Clearly a task for REME Recovery here. I brief my crew for any eventuality, it wasn't something I had considered in depth previously. Speedy obstruction removal would be the name of the game. It would be the subject of a technical paper I would write a few years later.

The battle group moves on and the battle is won. The advance is successful. Replen and rest are the order of the remaining day.

Fucking Hell! It's Coming Our Way!

A further stage of the live training is fighting an orderly retreat. This time the shoe is on the other foot. The enemy are attacking, and our battle group are conducting a fighting withdrawal. It's the reverse of going forward. This time all the odds and sods vehicles, including us, are in the front leading the way. We fight back through the night; it appears to be going well.

At first light we cross over a Royal Engineer laid bridge (the sappers have been busy, tough boys those sappers), it's going to be a bridge crossing with a reserve demolition. Meaning after the good guys (that's us) have crossed the bridge, it's destroyed to deny the enemy use. Once gain the battle group must pass through a bottleneck, as they did on their advance through the minefield. It's an important and vulnerable point in any battle and will be the focus of all commanders and units while it's in operation. At the bridge crossing the ARV has an important role to play. It must be nearby and ready to immediately respond to any blockage that may deny the units access through the bottleneck; in this case a temporary steel bridge the width of a single tank and the length of two or three.

I park my ARV within about fifty yards of the bridge, just on the lee side of a low slope overlooking the bridge, taking us off the skyline. I have chains ready for quick towing and a 'nosing prop' ready for pushing. The nosing prop is a ten-inch square of wood about two yards long. There is a heavy steel cap on one end and metal handles on the sides. There is a metal indent on the front of the ARV in which the end fits. The prop used for pushing tanks short distances with the power of the ARV. It's a 'giant-spear', too big and heavy for anybody to ever throw.

I brief my crew as to how we're going to operate, who does what and how. Forget the niceties of more intricate recovery jobs this is all about keeping the route open at all costs. Urgency is the name of our game!

We have a panoramic view of the units moving back over the bridge. The tanks being the last vehicles fighting a retreat. We can see artillery falling in the distance and the barrage slowly moving back towards us. We have been told the battle plan is to get over the bridge, blow it, and then consolidate on our side. We were the front line.

The infantry and odds and sods pour over the bridge and move past us to the rear. The sappers at the bridge, combat engineers, are calling them forward, guiding them over the narrow ramp and sending them on their way. This is no place for the soft-hearted or hesitant; this is the British Army in action and the British Army stops for no one. Bring it on!

We are stationary, standing on the back of the ARV, in NBC kit, drinking a hot brew and watching it all happen before us; we are ready to move at moment's notice. The battle is getting closer, the noise louder, the smoke and dust thicker. Helicopters join the action.

Apparently, the Lynx helicopter is the fastest in the world and can fly upside down, armed with missiles and guns. A Lynx Helicopter was flying in our area and as the battle drew near and the last of the tanks were crossing the bridge, I saw one Lynx move closer. We had a grandstand view from the back of the ARV. The Lynx was about a hundred and fifty yards of to our right and about a hundred yards above. The sound from the Lynx was steady and loud, it was a fabulous sight and so close. Suddenly, because we didn't know it was coming, the Lynx fired a TOW wire guided missile, off in the direction of the enemy (there were scattered hard targets for the battle group to fire at). I looked to predict the target of the missile but couldn't see a likely target. I was watching the missile slowly arc to the left. I had heard these missiles were guided by the firers helmet. Apparently, he has a sighting system fitted and wherever he looked the missile was sure to go. Allegedly!

Sure to go - my arse! The missile continued to arc further to the left. I looked up at the Lynx, the chap in the front was violently shaking head back and fore, the missile continued to arc to the left running from right to left across our front. There were no targets there in that direction, something was amiss. The pilot continued to shake his head and the Lynx accelerated after the missile. I started to get an uneasy feeling; alarm bells started to ring and the hair on my neck began to bristle.

The missile continued to arc left, the Lynx went madly after it, the pilot continued to shake his head.

I looked again at the missile. FUCK ME! It was still arcing left and was clearly heading our way. Fucking hell boys. JUMP! We launched ourselves off the back of the ARV, brews up in the air, crashing to the prairie floor on each side of the ARV. We scattered in different directions. We had no clue where the missile would hit. It was however, COMING OUR WAY, and very, very quickly. It was terrifying. I knew those missiles could make a mess and we were in the way. Bollox!

FUCKING HELL - ITS COMING OUR WAY!

In the event the missile continued to arc and passed us by about a hundred yards distant, whistling speedily along on its mystery, deadly path. The Lynx undercutting the missiles ARC and passing close and low over us with a roar. The missile smashed into the ground with a dirty brown cloud of smoke and a bright flash of orange flame about four hundred yards away. That four hundred yards was too close; ruined our brew, we had to make another.

Character building? Hell yes!

The Fourth Part of a Circle

Sometime during the BATUS training I was towing a dead tank across the 'Ulu', and we came across another ARV from the Royal Scots Dragoon Guards. The Recy Mech had been towing a tank and he had jack-knifed on a quite steep slope and was stuck. The tank he was towing had a dozer blade on the front of it and he was towing the tank backwards. He was going down the steep slope, had sticked left, the dozer tank ran on, and that was it. Stuck fast. His ARV was over a ninety-degree slope, the fourth part of a circle, to the tank he was towing and the Chieftain ARV didn't have the guts to power itself out. The fact that it was a 'dozer' tank being towed made it even more difficult because the front of the tank where the dozer blade was fitted was inaccessible to attach towing equipment. The craftsman Recy Mech was challenged and had no clue as to how to get out of the situation. It would have been remiss of me not to help another Recy Mech.

I looked at the situation and it was difficult. My ARV had a casualty on the back and a quick tow was out of the question; I didn't want to be in the same position. I confirmed the engine on the towed dozer tank could be started and there was drive. The tank was being towed because of a coolant leak, yet to be repaired. So, I took the job over. My plan was to replace the quill shafts in the dozer tank so we would have 'drive'. We would use all our spare water and coolant to fill the dozer tank radiators. It would be OK for a short while and hopefully would not seize the engine. The driver of the dozer tank would drive it forward, up the steep bank, hopefully just enough to take the tight strain off the tow bars enabling somebody get in between the RSDG ARV and the towed Dozer tank, to release the quick release pins, drop the tow bars thus enabling the RSDG ARV to drive away across the slope thereby resetting the situation.

There was danger for the person who would have to stand between the revving RSDG ARV and the dozer tank. Who was that person going to be? Well, it was my plan! Bollox!

I briefed the RSDG ARV driver to watch for the dismounted signal from one of my crew to drive forward when uncoupled from the tow bars. He told me his handbrake wasn't too good. Fuck!

I briefed the dozer tank driver that he had to keep the revs on and drive forward loosening the tension on the tow bars; whatever he does he must keep the revs on! I would have to drop the tow bars completely or they would dig into the ground going back down the hill and we would be none the better off.

So having explained the plan to everybody, clarified they knew what to do we filled the dozer tank with water and coolant, and fired up the engine. I grabbed a 'tool Recy Mech' used for removing quick release pins, and as the engines revved, I got into the triangle of the tow bars and set to my urgent and dangerous work.

The dozer tank was on max revs, and I was stood directly in line with the blasting, filth spewing exhausts. Hot, breath, stealing diesel fumes crashed over me, searing and gaseous. Behind me the diesel fumes for the RSDG ARV spewed from another direction. I couldn't stay in this situation for long, the least time the better, this was very dangerous. With all my strength and speed, I unlocked, twisted released the front pin enabling the RSDG ARV to drive off. He did so under direction and the front apex of the tow bars dropped to the floor. The dozer tank continued to spew fumes at top revs. I was mindful that only the revs were stopping the dozer tank from rolling back over me, and if he did so the dozer blade on the front of the tank would probably spread me into the prairies like jam. I managed to release the tow pins, dropped the bars to the floor and jumped clear just as the dozer tank rolled involuntarily backwards. I watched it run backwards down the hill. I could see the frightened face on the driver as he wildly ratcheted the handbrake, trying to slow or stop the tank. It careered for about a hundred yards to the bottom of the slope, rolling slowly to a see-sawing halt in the bottom of the fold.

Job done. But it was risky and dangerous. I'd calculated the risk, worked out the possible dangers and my plan was to jump clear if I had the slightest inclination or warning that the dozer was going to roll back. On reflection it was the most dangerous situation I was in on any recovery job with the tanks. I was at the top of my game, we were in the 'Ulu', it had to be done. I'm still waiting for the yellow handbag.

Character building? Hell yes!

<u>Casevac</u>

Tim Gill, a gun fitter, was one of my BATUS ARV crew. A good crewman, he made an excellent brew and didn't shy away from the graft involved with tank recovery. One night we are driving across the prairies on a night move. I was driving and I was, as always, mindful of the comfort of my crew. Ray Stopinski had taught me well and I had plenty of real-life practice since. I tried to be as smooth a driver as possible. Tactical night deriving is dangerous and in total darkness your eyes adjust and gather as much light as possible. It's amazing how much we can see. Even so, some things throw you. For example, level areas of dry dust can look like water, and water like dry dust. It can be particularly difficult on unknown or previously untraversed new ground. Ruts and ditches can't always be seen and are an ever-present hazard.

This night I was moving along at an average and safe speed when there was an almighty bang as we hit a ditch and crashed into it. I heard a piercing scream through the live 'mic' from atop. I quickly stopped the ARV and climbed up to join the crew. Tim Gill had been sitting on the roof of the ARV with his legs dangling in the third-man hatch. The hatch was held open with a steel catch and the jolt had thrown the hatch closed and it had crashed across Tim's knees with great force. He was in a right mess screaming with pain. It was agonising. We're in the middle of nowhere with a serious issue. We laid him back on the ARV, tried to comfort him and called for a casualty evacuation (Casevac). We had a rough idea where we were and passed our grid location over the radio. It took about three hours for the ambulance to find us, they had got lost along the way; it was easy to do so. Tim was stretchered off in the ambulance.

While he was lying there the black squaddie humour kicked. While he chain-smoked and we brewed, he'd probably dislocated both knees. He was told he had no use for his new boots, or all his exercise fags as he was getting evacuated. We could eat his food. He had no need for his watch, or anything else of value where he was going. He's lying there, in agony, laughing like a drain. What a strange lot we were.

In the daylight we examined the hatch bolt. It had been eaten almost clean through by rust. It was a BATUS ARV, every ARV I had after that I checked for such things.

Character building? Hell yes!

BATUS Anecdote

Rattlesnake Games

Somebody has run over a rattlesnake killing it dead; it's a souvenir. Outside one of the huts there is a small table, and four or five troopers are playing cards. Another trooper has discovered that if you rub a belt of machine-gun ammunition against itself it sounds like a rattlesnake's rattle. The same trooper also discovers that if you feed the body of a dead rattle snake over a card players shoulder headfirst, at the same time your nearby mate rattles an ammunition belt, you can bring a game of cards to a very abrupt end. Accompanied by the tipping over of a table, the scattering of cards and a huge amount of profanity and threats. Very entertaining for us watching!

Character building? Hell yes!

POKER ANYONE

Most Memorable Drink

We had been out on the Canadian 'Ulu' for days, it was non-stop working, towing, winching, moving, setting up camp and taking camp down. Our rations were very bland, and we were down to pilchards in tomato sauce a well-known shite meal. All we had to drink was brackish water and we were well overdue a replen.

Driving across the 'Ulu' we came across a '434 Barrow' coming out of Camp Crowfoot with a replacement 'pack'. The lads on the barrow had with them a yellow plastic barrel filled to the brim with 'Grape Juice' and ice.

The generous crew offered us a drink; I had never tasted anything like it before or since. It was sweet and very cold. It was like liquid magic on our parched throats. We became instant 'grape-juice' addicts. Gulping with greed we must have done half the barrel in a few seconds. No drink has ever even come close to that occasion, no doubt impacted by our previous few days of meagre beverage options.

FINE GRAPE JUICE

Operation Banner West Belfast

The 14/20th were rostered to do an emergency tour of Northern Ireland as were all Major units in the 70's such was the demand on manpower. The regiment had toured NI previously as a cavalry regiment crewing armoured cars and conducting reconnaissance and escort duties. This time however was different, they were the first cavalry regiment to be deployed in a full infantry battalion role in a 'hard-area'. It was going to be West Belfast, right in the thick of the troubles. The REME LAD consisting of about 150 soldiers would supply some troops to the regiment for the tour of duty and others would remain behind to service and repair the tanks and other equipment.

REME Brick Commander

I was chosen (is that the right word) to stay behind in Germany. Huh! I wasn't having any of that. Many of my REME mates were going and besides I now had a lot of friends in the regiment who were going also. At the first opportunity I was knocking on the EME's (Captain. in charge or the REME attached personnel) door. The conversation went something like this –

> *'Yes Cpl Rees (I was a L/Cpl)'?*
> *'Sir I want to go to NI with the regiment'.*
> *'Why'?*
> *'All my mates are going; I don't want to be left behind'.*
> *'Good, a volunteer is better than ten pressed men'.*

That was it. That briefest conversations placed me on a path to one of the most exciting years I was to serve in twelve, and on a journey of experiences that would stand me in good stead forever.

Very soon I paraded with 4th Troop D Squadron, I was given my own 'brick' to command, my new name was to be callsign 44E. A brick is a half section of four soldiers commanded by an NCO or officer. In my case 44E meant fourth squadron, fourth troop and the E was the sixth brick. That was me: last in the line as the most junior of the NCO's.

There were twenty-four of us in the troop. Three of whom were REME soldiers, my mate Glenn Ewen a tank mechanic, Chris Lombard an electrician, and myself a Recovery Mechanic. Now we were all there going to be infantrymen.

All the others in the troop were 14/20 KH proper. The troop leader was Lt Peter Garbutt call sign 44, the troop Sergeant Sgt Al Beveridge call sign 44A. among the other brick commanders were Mac Hutch, Mac McGahey. Lots of Mac's around I thought!

The troopers allocated to my callsign throughout the tour were, Andy Bevis, Geoff Sherrat, Joe McCormack, Pete Woolston and Robbo. Top men without exception. All slightly older than me except for Pete "Woolly' Woolston who joined us direct from basic training. He did however have a driving licence. Designated as our brick driver he was going to be on a very steep learning curve, very steep indeed. I did threaten to shoot him on one occasion; I didn't mean it Woolly, honest!

They are five in number because of some slight movement due to leave, courses, and compassionate matters. Also, during the tour and training occasionally other members of the troop would vary and exchange amongst the 'bricks' for the same pressures.

It was a fabulous troop of soldiers. Peter Garbutt was a motivated officer; keen and energetic he had a willingness and positivity that infected us all. He was prepared to go the extra distance for us and in turn us for him. I felt very welcomed despite my different cap badge; I know the three of us REME soldiers did.

Al Beveridge was the troop Sergeant, wise and experienced, he was studying social matters at the Open University and Bernadette Devlin, a prominent republican activist, was on his course; he took delight in telling us about this time after time.

Mac Hutch was the composite soldier. During the tour he was to probably save mine and some others lives.

Mac McGahey had a superb and constant sense of humour. Never one to waste an erection even if he woke in a room with twelve other soldiers, at least he didn't share it around.

The troop bonded, soldierly and socially. It was a good omen and we mixed well.

NI Training

The first thing we had to do was to write our 'Wills'. I didn't have a great deal in the way of possessions, just an analogue electric alarm-clock with an in-built radio I had bought from the NAAFI shop, and my blue-faced 'Timex' watch. I was poor, military poor that is, which meant rich in friends, adventure, and experiences, but I owned literally nothing of any value. Our pay was crap, it always was.

We were issued NI kit. Self-Loading Rifles (SLR's) and rifle slings, two magazines each, Flak jackets, NI boots which were higher than DMS, NI black gloves with a weighty pad across the knuckle area, Federal Riot Guns like single barrel shotguns, Long Wooden Batons (Baseball bats) for snatch-squad duty and instant retribution, Motorola radios for the brick commanders, plastic-cuffs, and torches. Tribal Maps of our Territorial Area of Operational Responsibility (TAOR) mine was Andersonstown. I would come to know it like the back of my hand. The important Northern Ireland Operational Aide Memoire. A pocket sized dark green plastic folder containing army instructions for just about everything we would encounter in the province. I still have mine. Within were cards giving instructions about –

- *Instruction for opening fire in Northern Ireland. The famous 'Yellow Card'. (This was the all-important one and we learned it off by heart).*

- *Instructions for accidentally crossing the border.*
- *Operating a Shrike Exploder*
- *Engagement with PVC Baton Rounds*
- *Engagement with M79 Grenade launcher*
- *Dealing with terrorist ambush, bombs, and booby traps.*
- *Instructions for making arrests.*
- *Tasking of tracker and search dogs*
- *Instructor for Projector Area Defence Pad*
- *Rules for handling IR Torch*
- Rules of engagement for Special Water Dispenser

(I haven't remembered all these I've just revisited the Aide Memoire).

We had much to learn. Above and beyond the procedural matters we had to learn to be active-duty soldiers in Northern Ireland. It's a different world to Cold War Fighting with main battle tanks. So, we set about with a will.

The practical pre-tour training was overseen by the Northern Ireland Training and Advisory Team (NITAT). These were well experienced soldiers from all different regiments who had seen a great deal of service in Northern Ireland. They were professional in the extreme. Also attached to us for training purposes was a platoon of Royal Fusiliers who had recently completed a tour. Foot patrolling was to be our daily bread and butter.

The fusiliers gave us a demonstration, then we went about it ourselves under their guidance and correction. They were very good and impressed us greatly.

It started with how to carry our rifles. The sling was used as a lead with the rear clamp on the rifle used, but the other end of the sling fastened around our wrist. In the event of us becoming a casualty our rifles would remain attached to us. Then it was four man 'brick' training.

The idea is for the four men to move along working as one to maintain all around observation, take full advantage of all possible cover and to support each other mutually always. This was practiced at different speeds, in all weathers, across urban, rural, and semi-rural terrain. Patrolling a terraced street was different to leafy avenue, or an industrial site or a shopping area. Lots of pedestrians made it different also, they could provide cover or be a hazard. It was the same with vehicular traffic, busy or otherwise.

Once a single 'brick' got the hang of it we would put two bricks to work together, utilising their learnt individual skill and then mutually support other and multiple bricks right up to whole troops supporting other whole troops. It became second nature. I didn't know there were so many ways to hold a rifle.

Shooting response and accuracy was a big thing. We spent days and days on the ranges. Zeroing (making accurate) the rifles, practising shooting, and reaction times. Still targets, moving targets, long range, then short range, then very short range, then long range again. I was right-handed but I discovered I was also a decent left-handed shot. Again, and again and again we practised. We got good at it, our accuracy and response times improved daily.

Radio communication was already a proven and honed skill to the tank soldiers. Our control room Corporals Johnny Morris, Ron Warren and John Wood were on our cases constantly. If we messed up or didn't follow procedure they were on our case, and rightly so. They were consummate professionals, top men and I learnt much from them.

Searching cars, searching people was a trade in hand job for us in the province. We practiced and practiced, stopping cars, stopping people, we had our own civ-pop who were very enthusiastic, as was I when doing the same for the 13/18RH. While the search was carried out those not searching would provide cover, the other bricks would move in, checks would be made over the radios. It became a well-oiled essential procedure.

We learnt mobile patrolling in open-topped land-rovers. It wasn't a case of just driving around. Distances to other military vehicles was important. Don't sit in a stationary vehicle, de-bus and quickly. Find some cover, look out, keep an eye on the commander, respond quickly. Always look outwards. Always keep your rifle ready for the shoulder.

Search Team

Searching houses, buildings and areas, large vehicles (buses) was the job of a trained search team. Each troop formed a search team. The team consisted of a team commander, in our case Mac Hutch, a 2i/c and Scribe, in our case me, and two or three teams of two soldiers to do the searching. We were trained by the Royal Engineers who were absolute experts at such matters. There were risk levels of search High, Medium and Low. We did

Medium and Low and the sappers High. However, we trained to do high risk searches also. High risk meant there was high probability of booby-traps or explosive detonation. Where's the fun in that?

Essentially, if there were people in the building or area we wanted to search, we entered through a door as they did. Then conducted the search.

If there was nobody there, we entered by unconventional means, through a wall, window, or roof or other non-existent access point. Also, we never touched anything personally without moving it with inert means beforehand. Everything was pulled by a hook and rope from a safe distance, or weight was dropped on it from a small scaffold. Everything we touched was 'disturbed' by us first. We worked very thoroughly and very, very slowly. We didn't want to miss anything and certainly not spring or initiate anything that might go bang. We learnt about booby-traps, switches, detonators, and lots of other evil dark-art and nasty things.

My job as 'scribe' was to identify and record details of everything, and everybody about the search, and within the premises, confirm who they were and what they were doing there. I was to try and gather as much intelligence as possible. I would carry out 'P' checks on everybody. At the outset of the search, I would, along with the homeowner or senior occupant conduct a 'damage check' throughout the property. I would conduct the same damage check at the conclusion of the search. If we had damaged the property, and we often did, and if there was no 'find', then the army would make good the damage i.e., ripped up floorboards, opened wall cavities and the like. If we had a 'find' such as weapons, explosives, ammunition, or any other nefarious material, then – too bad.

Some clever sapper soldier, named Winthrop (he might have been a 'pirate treasure hunter' in an earlier life), came up with a theory of how to find things. There were, as I recall, a couple of elements to it.

Consider you have information that something is hidden in a huge field, but you don't know where in the field -

Firstly, put yourself in the position of being the person hiding the object in the field and go look in the place or places you would consider a suitable place to hide your object.

Secondly, if you are hiding something you wouldn't just hide it anywhere, you will be hiding it to retrieve it later, otherwise you would just throw it away. You will need to know where it is, so you will have to identify and remember markers that will guide you to where you have hidden your object. Or to guide a third person if you must pass the location instructions on.

> *Consider – 'the object is buried in the field'.*
> *Compared to – 'the object is buried in the field under a large flat stone in the hedge ten yards to the right of the single oak tree on the north border of the field'.*

In practice, look at the field, look to identify markers and then to identify possible hiding places. Or reverse engineer the process; hide the object and look for markers to guide to the location.

Riot Training

We practised for riots with a fit and ready civ-pop at 'Tin City'. We also had a few minor riots around the tank Park areas. Shield training, baton charges and so on were all part of the remit. I had great fun being a member of a snatch-squad.

The snatch squad consisted of four soldiers. Two armed with baseball bats, I was one of the two, a third soldier armed with a Federal Riot Gun (FRG, rubber bullet gun) and the fourth armed with an SLR. The standard operating procedure would be that the troop commander on the ground would, in the event of a riot, identify the front-line riot leaders. The troop soldiers would, on command, fire a volley of baton rounds at the target, the soldiers' shields would part and the snatch squad, with all the lightning and aggressive speed they could muster, charge towards the, hopefully now prone, target led by the two baton wielders. Closely followed by the riot gun carrier prepared to give it some business at close quarters, and the rifle carrying soldier bringing up the rear in case it all went 'tits-up'.

The baton men would grab the target and drag him or her back behind the troop line whilst being given cover by the baton gun and rifle man. Well, that was the theory!

Our final element of Northern Ireland training was the full experience at Tin City in Sennelager. I knew the Tin-City from being civ-pop, being a brick commander was a whole new world. We put the patrolling, searching, rioting all into practice. We were filmed and debriefed, it was very detailed, minutely critical, and very valuable.

I personally found the Close Quarter Battle Range (CQBR) very useful. We patrolled in this urban area using reduced powered live ammunition rounds in our rifles. The bullets were hard plastic but still went off with a serious whack! The CQBR tested observations, reaction times, response times, return fire accuracy, almost the real deal. Trooper 'Dirty Harry' was particularly adept at responding to and identifying targets very accurately and quickly. We were ready to depart for the province.

Character building? Hell yes!

Chopper Skills

Part of the NI training is transportation of troops by helicopter. Helicopter training was novel to me, but I was very much looking forward to it. On the allocated day we arrived in a designated field where we met an RAF chap; the RAF are always 'Chaps'. He was going to brief us on what we would be required to do.

Essentially, we formed up before entering the helicopter. Approached from a particular angle, so that the crew could see us, didn't move towards the helicopter until we were given the thumbs up by the air crew. We had to be mindful of ground angles because the rotors were at varying heights from the ground.

Peter Garbutt our troop leader briefed us. There was going to be a PUMA coming for us to practice the business on. My job was to be first on the helicopter and to adopt a position directly behind the pilot. Peter Garbutt would be last on after ensuring everybody else had got on; he would also be first off. I was to ensure everybody got off, nobody was to be left behind and I was to physically manhandle off anybody who didn't want to go, no problem. Everybody always went.

The PUMA arrives. It's a chunky helicopter and can carry about twelve troops. It hovers around in radio contact with the RAF Chap, the PUMA lands, the crew get out, there are three of them; a pilot, second pilot and a load master. We introduce and chat and the crew show us around their aircraft. We are all impressed. No doubt they, the air crew, would be impressed with our tanks.

With the PUMA stationary and switched off, on the ground, we have a couple of dry runs. We have two columns of soldiers at two o'clock and ten o'clock from the front of the aircraft. We can see the pilots and the Load Master from our position. I am at the front of the first column, Peter Garbutt is at the rear of the second, the rest of the troop are in-between us. We get the OK from the crew and we run in and on the PUMA. The idea is to be as quick and efficient as possible; this applies both to embarking and disembarking. The least time on the ground the better, both from an action and surveillance perspective.

I run to the open side door, it's not easy. I'm wearing a flak jacket and carrying a rifle and radio, along with ammunition and other NI accoutrements. No headgear. I jump into the body of the PUMA, there is a narrow doorway behind the pilots and that is my place. The rest of the troop follow closely behind quickly filling the aircraft. The troop leader is last on, and the pilot gets the nod from the crew master.

Next, is getting off. Still stationary with engines switched off we get the go from the crew master. Peter Garbutt explodes out of the side door with his usual gusto. The troops follow and I am last man out having ensured there is nobody left on the PUMA who should have got out. Hitting the ground outside we deploy in a semi-circle around the PUMA, facing out, weapons raised covering in a defensive arc. At this point the aircraft would leave, and we would commence patrol, or search, or support or whatever out task was.

We practiced the dry run a few times, it wasn't difficult, repetitive if anything. Next would be a proper run. Engines running, PUMA to take off, fly around a bit and then land and we would disembark. With the loudest engines in the world running, crushing down wash, unable to hear each other, grass and dust stingingly swirling up and around it's an entirely new endeavour.

We stand off to the sides and deploy ready to embark exactly as we had been taught. The pilot winds up his motors and takes off. The noise at our proximity is deafening, the down wash is alarming. The PUMA flies over us and away. We watch it circle at a distance. We look at each other, nodding assurances and giving the thumbs up. This is a first for us, let's get it right.

The PUMA returns, quite quickly and steeply, and lands exactly bang on where it should. The air crewman gives me the thumbs up and shouting at the lads behind me to move, I run to the open side door. I clamber on the deck of the aircraft and stand near the narrow doorway directly behind the pilots; I have an excellent view of the controls of the aircraft and out of the front screen. The troops quickly file in and plant themselves into the narrow canvas rack seats on either side. Peter Garbutt sits nearest the open door and gives me a thumbs up; I thumb back.

The sound increases mightily as the giant rotors grab air and wash it down, the PUMA clawing itself upwards. The PUMA starts to shake and vibrate, at the same time there is a discernible sway and we're up and away off the ground.

Speech is impossible. Non-verbal nods and thumbs are the only communication. It's exciting watching the ground fall away and from my prime spot its fascinating watching the pilots work as they literally throw the PIUMA around the in the sky.

Time to land and we shallow dive to our landing mark, the PUMA gentles onto the ground and in a flash the troops are off and I'm following. I spring out about twenty yards and join the rest of the troop in a pre-planned defensive arc. The PUMA repeats the taking off process and is soon gone from sight and sound. We practice this about four or five times. Each time the take-off and landings are the same, but the pilots noticeably make the actual flight more agitating. Tighter turns, steeper climbs and dives, greater variations in height and speed. It's a regular roller coaster of a ride, yet the 'coup de grace' is to come.

Having now become proficient at the regular troops on and off there is an intention to up the anti-slightly. We are going to go for a take-off under simulated attack, and we are going to hover the aircraft to disembark.

Take off under fire. We get on the PUMA in double quick time, even before we are all on board the engines are winding up to a greater pitch, the noise is deafening, and the wash seems to have reached an impossible level. The PUMA jerks violently into the air, I cling firmly to the sides of the small internal door, and I am swaying with the movements as we thump, thump upwards. Suddenly we appear to be many feet off the ground, then with the pilot looking at my worried face and smiling (he has a sense of humour, but at my expense) he dips the PUMA straight down towards the ground. Oh fuck! The craft accelerates and I think we are going straight in; then with enormous power the PUMA moves forward and accelerates sharply away from the area. The PUMA, its crew, and a dozen troops are swiftly accelerating forward at a downward facing angle. My relief is tenable, I'm probably going to live after all! I look at the others, I think we all had the same adrenalin rush. We get thrown around the air, left, right, up, and down, back on the roller coaster. It's time to disembark at the hover. This was going to be interesting.

We come into our designated landing spot, but this time much quicker. The 'G' forces are apparent. The PUMA hovers and one or two feet off the ground. The sound is deafening, no hope for words. The aircraft is vibrating harshly, and the crew master gives Peter Garbutt the nod and out he goes. Dutifully, as last man, I watch the troops exit and disappear from my sight. The down wash and noise continue. What I don't know on this my first hovering exit is that every time a person exits a hovering helicopter the load is less and the helicopter 'goes up' a little bit, maybe six inches or a foot. That's fine and no issue. But it goes up another little bit with the next egress, and the next, and the next and so on. All those little six inches or a foot add up and by the time it's my turn they have accumulated into about ten or twelve feet. I haven't been looking outside, or even judging the height to which we had sneakily ascended. I had been looking inside the aircraft at the troops disembarking in an exciting adrenalin driven rush. I was shouting and encouraging them out and I'm tight close against the last trooper heading towards the door.

Suddenly the door is there, I'm going out of it, the ground is miles away (ten foot probably) and added to the drop is the fact that a hovering aircraft produces massive down wash compared to one on the ground. The gravity of the fall, the extra mighty push from the wash – I was off. Bowled along, fully out of control, like a leaf in the wind. My wrist strapped rifle dragging along behind, no direction, no focus, in a deafening noise and tornado downwind. I must have travelled many yards banging my head, my arse, twisted arms, and legs. I would know better the next time. Those RAF helicopter boys are clever with a sense of humour.

Character building? Hell yes!

Little did I know at the time, but I would qualify as an RAF helicopter handler a few years later and I would be the soldier responsible for training 'troops on and off'.

Hohne Anecdotes 3

Pokey for Princess Anne

The Colonel of the Regiment was Princess Anne. She was very popular and had a long history with the regiment. She was to visit us during our NI Training and the regiment would be very pleased to see her. The regiment went into full royal visit mode and planning was surveyed in every detail.

It was planned she would visit every squadron and every troop, each of which would be doing a particular activity relevant to our upcoming tour. Fourth troop D Squadron, my troop, were designated with doing 'pokey drill'.

Pokey drill was something we practiced every morning. It involved exercises using our arms outstretched with rifles. Arms above heads with rifles, arms out to the side with rifle and holding them there. Eventually the seven-pound rifle gets heavier and heavier until it's impossible to hold any longer.

POKEY DRILL

So, we regally poshed and scrubbed for the royal visit. We were to wear NI boots, highly polished, lightweight green trousers with stable belt and a red PT vest. Our rifles were to be sling-less and immaculately clean, of which we achieved. We were briefed that should Princess Anne speak to us we were to address her as Ma'am and nothing else, and that our answers should be short, polite, and respectful. Furthermore, if she asked us what we were doing it was under no circumstances to be called 'Pokey Drill', it was to be 'Rifle Exercises to Strengthen the Arms'.

The Royal party arrive; it's a warm day and we are in a semi-circle carrying out 'Rifle Exercises to Strengthen the Arms' around the semi-circle walks the Princess and her entourage. She chats to one or two, walks straight past me and stops in front of Joe McCormack who is to my left, huffing, puffing, and his spectacles dripping with sweat.

'Good afternoon' says the Princess, 'what are you doing'? she asked Joe.

'Pokey Drill Ma'am'; replied Joe in his best Irish brogue, a man of few words but on this occasion he excelled.

Well, the troops and I were entertained. The Commanding officer less so and the RSM was whistling out of his ears. Peter Garbutt was just shaking his head probably contemplating a career elsewhere.

The Royal looked a little bemused, I thought she might converse further with Joe, her lips pursed as if to speak but she probably thought better of it, paused, stared at him for a few seconds and walked on. Followed by the officer entourage with only the RSM looking back at Joe with a 'You're going to be well fucked son', look on his face. But nothing ever came of it which pleased us all. Top man Joe! Did us proud.

West Belfast

Andersonstown the Camp

October 1978, we fly into Aldergrove airport, Belfast, in a RAF VC10, its full. We get loaded onto army lorries (it always seems to be lorries). We have all our kit with us including rifles, but no ammunition is issued yet. We have an escort from the unit we are taking over from who were 1st Battalion the Queens Regiment. D Squadron, Black D that is, are headed for Glassmullin Camp, Andersonstown.

Between August 1969 and July 2007 1,441 military personnel died because of operations in Northern Ireland. In nineteen seventy-eight, thirty-four soldiers were killed in action in Northern Ireland: in nineteen seventy-nine, seventy. Our officers had told us beforehand that the regiment expected to lose six men and one officer if the averages continued. It was sobering information.

The dozen or so miles drive from the airfield to Glassmullin camp, (hereafter called the camp) took about an hour. The four tonners we were in had a tight job being driven through the 'wriggly tin' fencing and around the concrete bollards of the entrance.

The camp covered about an acre, bang in the middle of Andersonstown and surrounded on three sides by houses and a grassed area at the rear leading to a parade of shops. The wriggly tin (corrugated steel sheets), stood about twelve feet high around the entire circumference. At each corner and at the front of the camp were concrete sangars, with observation slots and gun positions. The camp had come under terrorist attack on many, many occasions. Every time shots were fired through the wriggly tin a yellow circle was painted inside around the bullet hole. Practically the entire inside wriggly tin of the camp was yellow. For fucks sake! What have we come to?

Inside the camp was a control room, briefing room, barrack rooms and some ancillary buildings for the intelligence section and the Royal Ulster Constabulary (RUC) detachment. The largest, and most popular, building was the cookhouse.

We slept one, two or three, to a room depending on your luck. It was sparse accommodation. A metal bed and spring, a metal locker, a metal small bedside locker. That was it. There was a corridor and a TV room situated at the bottom of each barrack with a few chairs in it. Every building was surrounded by a two-foot-high blast wall which were supposed to give some cover from mortar attack. The camp had been mortared numerous times previously.

The cookhouse was open 24/7 and the chefs, once again, did a fabulous job. There was always a giant pile of fresh eggs alongside a hotplate and a bottle of cooking oil. Stacks of army bread, often of dubious freshness, were always accompanying. I cannot eat an egg to this day without thinking of Andy Bevis of the 14th/20th. He loved eggs, fried, and ate millions of them, but he always cut around the yoke, removing the white and ate the yolk whole. Sometimes he would dribble the yolk and wipe it with his sleeve. The image is with me forever, Andy was a member of my 'brick', and a real good soldier.

Belfast Work Methodology

The squadron had four sabre troops and a HQ troop. Fourth Troop, of which I was a member, was a sabre troop. Each troop took it in turns to carry out the different styles of duty for two days at a time foot patrol, mobile patrol, Quick Reaction Force (QRF), Guard Duty.

Foot Patrolling

I think I enjoyed the foot patrolling most of all. The troop would be instructed to meet at the briefing room at a designated time. The NCO leading the patrol would have attended a pre-patrol briefing at the control room, given by a squadron officer or member of the intelligence cell. No patrol ever went out without good reason, there was always an objective even if it was no more that being a military profile in a particular area or providing close support for another brick. There was always a reason, it was unit policy, and a good one.

We would check ourselves before we assembled for brick commanders' inspection; proper clothing, batons, maps, first aid dressing, pen, aide memoires, clean rifles, rifle straps, ammunition. Then it was move to the briefing room, get inspected outside by the brick NCO's then into the briefing room. Maps on the wall, thick with fag smoke, green plastic mugs of char and the briefing would commence. A few questions and clarifications, and more intense discussion with the brick commanders and the troop leader or Sergeant and of to the loading bay.

Rifle strapped to wrist, muzzles pointing into the bay of sand and fag ends, clear the rifle to make sure there is nothing in it, no ammo up the spout. Safety catches to safe, magazine on, rear sight up and set at 100 yards. Ready to go. As the tour progressed, unofficially we changed our procedure to make sure there was a round 'up the spout'. This would ensure a second or two quicker responses in the event of a contact. The official issue was twenty rounds per man, a full magazine. However, many of the troopers would carry an extra two rounds, acquired from range days, which they felt gave them a little leeway in the event of a cock-up such as a negligent discharge or some other blameworthy misdemeanour.

Joe and Taff after a sharp run-in.

First Foot Patrol

I remember my first patrol. It was a tense yet exciting time. All the training, all the practice, all the fuck-ups and all the good things and now this was it. We were going out the front gate, turning right and heading off from there. Terrorists know one certain thing about the military, they know exactly where they will be when entering or leaving the camp and it's a good place for them to snipe of bomb. It's dangerous, fucking dangerous!

I speak to my boys, encouragement, remember the drills, where we are going, hard targeting, covering arcs, covering each other, non-verbal communications (hand signals), move fast, move low, trust only ourselves, use cover, above all eyes and ears outward and open, rifles to the shoulder.

I'd seen pictures of the outside of the camp, I'd looked at maps, and I'd arrived in complete darkness the night before. I'd climbed into one of the sangars and peeked through an observation slot, but it was a limited view. I was going into the unknown.

We are the first foot patrol of the squadron, and my brick is the first brick out and I'm going to be first of my brick through the gate. We gather at the gate, the second and third bricks will follow at some minutes of intervals. The sangar guards are briefed we are patrolling, and they will give top-cover from the sangars. There are a few minutes before we go, time to think; shit!

My mind racing over, nice clear day with excellent visibility – good for a sniper. Good for a sniper; for fucks sake! We had been told we could expect to lose six, I could be the first. What if there's a bomb planted out there? Where's my field dressing; I check for it. I look around at the lads, I think we all have the same thoughts. It's the first time for all of us. We nod, acknowledge smile, mouthed 'OK"? nod again. I look at my watch. Seconds to go. I watch the second-hand creep around, the word 'TIMEX' on my watch filling my vision. The hand lands upright, a quick look and nod and with a big suck-in of air I'm off.

I hurl myself as fast as I can towards the gate, the guard drops the chain barrier and I'm through the wriggly tin and onto the street. I'm going as fast as I can. My rifle is swaying powerfully from side to side as I zigzag across the tarmac road, my mouth is dry and I'm sucking and blowing air. I have about fifty yards to cover and I 'm going for a record, a world speed record. 'Good day for a sniper', is going over and over in my mind, keep going, faster yet!

I'm looking for cover, a good place to go to ground. Many patrols have come out of that gate before me, and done the same thing, charged out, looking for cover, looking for a safe place. What if I take cover on the same place? Where somebody else took cover! Where the terrorist saw my predecessor take cover, and they know soldiers use that place for cover and they've put a bomb there they can detonate remotely. What if? Or they've lined a sniper on it with a clear line of sight on this excellent day for a snipe. What if? I glance behind as I speedily zig-zag on, the lads are with me, no doubt thinking the same what ifs. What if? that bin, that drain, that car, that lamp-post, that gap between the houses, that slightly parted curtain…what if? Oh, for fucks sake!

I keep my running speed at full throttle, but my brain starts to rationalise. I've sprinted about fifty yards, I'm still alive, not blown up, not shot, not anything. I find some cover and go to ground; my brick does the same. I try to make myself as small as possible. I check the position the boys have taken, all looking for the best cover, maintaining our shape, outward looking, covering arcs, scanning over rifle sight, rifles in the shoulder moving with our line of vision. I make eye contact with each of them nod, smile, well done. I look back at the sanger, I see movement trough the slit, our top cover is there and alert. We have done our first bit, holding our first bit of ground. I'm expecting the next brick to come through us and hold further along the road, then another. Then we leapfrog through them and so on.

The next brick shows. I watch them sharply close and then pass through us. It's as new and scary to them as it is to us, same thought for them as for us. The brick commander Mac McGahey, arrows past, and we exchange curt nods. So far so good. They go to ground thirty or forty yards ahead. We adjust our positions, the arc where they are is now covered by them, there are more of us on the ground mutually supporting each other. A moment later a third express brick flies through, Mac Hutch (there's a lot of Mac's around here) same first, same thought, same nod. They go to ground. We and the second brick adjust. It comes to us naturally, we've practised enough.

First task over. We have successfully put three bricks on the ground, twelve men, having exited the camp according to plan without incident and safely. For the rest of the tour, we displayed the same level of expertise, the same diligence, the same discipline. This was a good regiment, with good leaders and good men. We had trained hard, the first cavalry regiment in a full infantry role in a hard area. There was a lot to prove and the REME attached weren't letting anybody down.

Character building? Hell yes!

Mobile Patrolling

We carried out mobile patrols in open land rovers, driver, and Commander in the front seats, two further brick members in the back. We normally patrolled as pairs of vehicles and our main work was snap Vehicle Check Points (VCP's), and the quick moving of foot patrols from one area to another.

Drive discipline was an important thing, not too close together to make too big a target, using larger civilian vehicles for cover. Mobile patrol duty was ok unless it rained or was cold and windy when the elements made it bloody wet and freezing; snow was the worst of all, guaranteed wet and cold.

When not actually on patrol we were at liberty to get a brew and watch TV. We remained in full kit for any necessary eventuality.

Quick Reaction Force

This was probably the cushiest duty in the province. Inside, warm, regular food, plenty of tea, television, sleep. We only responded to incidents. There would be twelve of us, three vehicles on duty at any one time, revved up and ready to go at an instants notice. Sleep with your boots on.

We were crashed out often to support foot or mobile patrols, that found themselves involved in incidents that sprung up out of nowhere. Cordon duties and bomb incidents was a regular chore. I recall one incident where many vehicles had been high-jacked throughout the area and we found ourselves on cordon duty at Stockman's Lane and its junction with the motorway, it was about 8:30 am, rush hour. Our orders were to close the roundabout as there was a suspected device in a lorry on the other side of the roundabout. The general Belfast public were going about their business, mostly travelling to work. We were stopping them doing so. They were well used to interference in their routines and could be quite blasé about things.

> "Sorry, you can't come through this way, there is a bomb". Followed by a stock collection of replies; take your pick –

- "I'll run past it".
- "it's OK it's one of ours".
- "But I have to get the kids to school".
- "It's not due to go off for another hour".
- "You're always fucking us about".
- "Whose fucking your wife?"
- 'Fuck off home you Brit bastard".

On this occasion I was stood in the road redirecting traffic and a large van comes along. It was a fridge van belonging to a fish wholesaler. There were sliding doors at the front of the van, both of which were open. The van stops alongside me I'm on the passenger side. The driver speaks to me first –

> *'There's a bomb'*
>
> *'I know as long as you don't go past this point, you'll be ok'.*
>
> *'No, there's a bomb',*
>
> *'I know, don't go past this roundabout and you'll be ok'.*
>
> *'No, there's a bomb in this van'.*
>
> *'What! What do you mean?'*
>
> *'Two men, they've got my mate and they put a bomb in here and they told me to drive it to the police station'.*
>
> *'For fucks sake, right move the van up the slip road onto the motorway', it was the only clear area nearby. With that the driver started shaking and fumbling for a gear. He was*

shitting himself. I began feeling very laxative myself. I jumped onto the footwell of the vehicle. I spoke with him firmly and calmly.

'It'll be Ok, take your time, put it in gear and drive up the slip road. Do it now'. The driver manages to get it in gear, we move through our cordon and up onto the slip road I could not see into the back of the van, where I had assumed the bomb was.

'Where did they put the bomb?' I asked.

'Under the seat in front of you' he replied. I looked under the seat and there was a wooden box about ten inches squares. For fucks sake I thought! How shitty was this?

'Ok that's far enough, stop, handbrake on, switch it off, get out'. He did so, very hurriedly, and he and I ran as fast as we could back down the slip road.

We extended the cordon. Called in Felix (Explosive Ordnance Disposal (EOD, Bomb Disposal)) and after a few hours the matter was dealt with. The IRA had taken to stopping commercial vehicles, lorries, and vans, taking one of the workers as a hostage, placing a 'bomb' on the vehicle and telling the driver to park the vehicle at a given place where it would cause the most disruption. Police stations, fire stations, military bases and Major road junctions were prime spots. The security forces would react accordingly, clearing the areas, putting in cordons and so on. Half a dozen of these at the same time would bring Belfast to a standstill, as it did on this occasion. The fish van bomb was a proxy, a hoax, everything there except for a viable explosive device.

I reflected on my actions in getting on the van knowing there was a possible bomb on board. It was dangerous and risky, I'd assumed as the instructions were to take it to the police station, there was some time available. At that time, I was a young JNCO, and I was bullet proof, we all thought we were. It was the seventies, I was in West Belfast, there was a serious shooting and bombing war going on. Fuck it! Would I do it today? No way.

Character building? Hell yes!

Guard Duty

This was where we crewed the sangars, manned the front and rear gates, carried out area cleaning, swept the yards, emptied the bins, cooked, and ate loads of egg-banjos and drank buckets of char. We provided two bricks to Andersonstown RUC Station and escorted the cleaners in and out of camp in Saracen Armoured Cars (PIGS).

We also provided the guard for Musgrove Park Hospital. There was a military wing there for wounded and ill soldiers and a secure ward for injured terrorists. We manned sangers and patrolled the hospital grounds. It was an onerous guard duty and not very exciting but at least we could get some sleep, and lots of egg-banjos.

L/Cpl Taff Rees Guard Commander at Glassmullin. Just inside front gate.

One day, I was second in command of the guard at the hospital. There had been a terrorist attack on the Grenadier Guards at Crossmaglen near the border. A foot patrol had been ambushed by IRA gunmen in a sandbagged protected van. Three of the young Guardsmen had been shot and killed and their bodies were brought to Musgrave by helicopter. I together with others helped to take the bodies off the helicopter and onto transport to the hospital morgue. Their names were Graham Duggan, Kevin Johnson, and Glen Ling. It was a solemn respectful duty. I think of those three young soldiers often, Rest In Peace gentlemen. Northern Ireland is a shitty place.

<u>Andersonstown RUC Station</u>

This building had the unenviable reputation of being the most attacked building in the world. The station faced onto a large roundabout at the junction of the falls Road and Andersonstown road, it faced toward Belfast city Centre and overlooked the Ulster Bus Depot and the entrance to Milltown Cemetery. During our troops spell of guard duty two bricks would be despatched to guard the police station. There were two gates, but only one used at a time. A sanger overlooking the falls road and we also operated the 'Vengeful' system from within the station. 'Vengeful' was a computer system into which we would input the registration numbers of cars being stop-checked by the troops on the ground. If there was information on the car, we would pass it back to the patrol.

There was a permanent RUC presence, it was after all a police station.

One evening I am the guard commander and Robbo is on duty in the sager. He contacts me on the intercom and asks me to join him sharpish. I can tell from the timbre of his voice something is up. I grab my rifle and flak jacket and rush outside. There is a man hammering at the wriggly tin gates, he is the watchman from the Ulster Bus Depot across the roundabout. We open the gate and bring him into the yard. He is visibly shaken and stammering incoherently. We try to calm him down. He tells us he was at his security lodge at the bus depot when two armed men forced their way in. He was held at gunpoint by one of them and the other placed, they said, twenty incendiary bombs, in the and around the depot and on the buses. They had then told him to run to the police station and report it, and here he was. They hadn't given him any timings. I asked Robbo if he had seen anything, he had not. I was presented with a quandary. Uppermost in my mind was why had they told him to report it here. They must have known he would, but why tell him to do so. Was it a come on? If we responded straight to the depot, which was only a short distance away, was there a bomb planted enroute? Was there a sniper watching the gates through telescopic sights even as we talked. I told Robbo to grip the watchman and keep him close. I got the rest of the guys to get their gear on and standby.

I got on the radio to the command room at Glassmullin, I recall Johnny Morris was the operator I spoke with, either him or any other controller would have been fine, they were all at the top of their game. I explained the situation to John. We would have to respond to the incident, it was confirmed by the watchman. There was a cordon to be put on for safety of the public, it was a busy pedestrian and vehicular traffic area, and there was a pub in very close proximity to the entrance to the depot and a row of terraced houses alongside. Directly opposite was the entrance to the Milltown Cemetery. We also had to maintain security at the police station. No way did I have enough soldiers. John and I discussed the situation as he wanted more information, he would get more troops down to us a soon as possible. I left two soldiers in the police station, one on the gate and one in the sanger. I took the others out the reverse door of the station onto the Falls Road (It was the Glen Road gate we had mostly used). We hard-targeted out with me dragging the watchman along. An issue I was mindful of was that over the years there had many incidents and attacks at the police station and the troops within had run out as we were doing, hard targeting and going for cover. The IRA would know this and may have laid bombs or booby traps at those natural cover points. So, its 'eyes wide open' looking for anything suspicious or unnatural. I bundled the watchman along; he was crapping it!

Almost immediately the Quick Reaction Force were on the scene, Troopers from the Queens Dragoon Guards (The Welsh Cavalry Regiment), who were on attachment with D Squadron and made up our third troop. Good men all. For normal duties in Germany back on the tanks, they would have been our armoured reconnaissance unit using Scimitar and Scorpion fast light tanks. I also knew the QDG from playing rugby against them, they were a good rugby side, Welsh mun!

The S/Sgt from the QDG took command of the scene. He came over to where I was covering with the watchman, asked me for all the information I had, queried a few things with the watchman and then start directing the operation. He was fab and quickly got things in order. Soldiers appeared from everywhere, fire-engines appeared from everywhere, bomb disposal arrived. The military police turned up; the Colonels rover team arrived. There was a Major walking around in slippers smoking a pipe. Revellers from the pub on the Glen Road were gathering at the front of the pub on the pavement. A newspaper reporter arrived and started asking me questions; he got no answers and became quite persistent; eventually I told him to 'Fuck Off' and he did.

The incendiaries with the depot had started going off, but they didn't have a lot of explosive clout. They were muffled little puffs of flame. Initially, relatively harmless if they were found quickly and extinguished, the danger would be if they weren't found quickly and started a serious fire. The fire service and bomb disposal seemed to be coping well. I remained in my cover spot close to the Milltown Cemetery entrance opposite the bus station. The watchman had been purloined by bomb disposal because of his knowledge of the bus depot.

THE MOST ATTACKED BUILDING IN THE WORLD FALLS RD TO THE LEFT-GLEN RD TO THE RIGHT

Suddenly a shout went out 'Sniper'. The word was repeated like wildfire. I have never seen panic set in so quickly. Everybody just dove for cover, soldiers, firemen, civilians, the reporter, everyone. I hadn't heard anything over my radio. I hadn't heard any shots fired, I had no clue if there was or was not. I thought why we would get a warning of a sniper; surely the first we would know would be the arrival of bullets. I seemed to be aloof to the situation, it wasn't making any sense to me.

I scanned around, keeping low cover, told my guys to do the same, 'keep your arcs, eyes looking out, rifles to the shoulder. Nothing. It was deathly quiet with the most still of feelings. There was an expectation something serious was going to happen. It was in the air; the expectation was immense. Nothing happened. Not a sausage.

It was a lesson in surreal inactivity manifested from absolutely nothing. I have not forgotten.

On another occasion I was on duty in the police station. I was operating the vengeful computer. The sanger occupant starts yelling down the intercom. Here we go again. A flatbed coal lorry has been parked right outside the Falls Road gate. The driver's mate has been taken at gunpoint and the driver is told to park the lorry against the police station and he's done so. We evacuate the station with the same quandry. Are there bombs planted or snipers in place, or both. The position of the lorry brings the Falls and Glen roads to a standstill, effectively freezing West Belfast. We deploy and take cover around the area, evacuating houses, pubs, and shops. Felix turns up with his team. He is a Sergeant, but I call him "Sir". He has my respect. He sets about defusing the object placed amongst the coal sacks on the back of the lorry. It takes hours, some rifle shots, a few blasts with a shotgun and some minor controlled explosions. It's a hoax, designed along with many other hoaxes at the same time to bring Belfast to a standstill. It works.

Belfast Analogy

I enjoyed the tour of Belfast very much. It was the proper soldiering of the day, and I was fortunate to be attached to a very good regiment. The 14th/20th Kings Hussars had excellent leadership at all levels and outstanding troopers. They had all taken the job in hand seriously and competently. Despite the pessimistic pre-tour casualty projection there were no fatalities and I'm sure West Belfast was in a better place when they left.

The regiments attitude to the public was civilised and respectful and I think this paid dividend.

I know that when speaking with the public on a one-to-one basis they were generally very amenable and supportive despite the area having a strong republican population.

I observed on many occasions that people's attitude to us would change when they were no longer alone with us. It would go from amenable and courteous to either complete silence or downright abuse. It depended on who was watching, even amongst families. They were a population in fear.

Belfast Anecdotes

What's that Brown Stain?

The Sun newspaper used to run coupon collecting scheme during the seventies. If you bought the paper, you could cut out some coupons and send them off. When so many coupons were accumulated (enough papers had been sold), the Sun would send a television to Northern Ireland for the troops. There were TV's everywhere, and in all fairness they were welcome.

Eventually, the army in the province were inundated with TV's so the Sun turned its attention to saunas. There was one at our Glassmullin camp.

It was a low-quality wooden box, with a wooden door and a solitary plastic window on the one side. The 'coals' were heated by electricity and rested in a metal cradle on the floor. The water bucket, containing a tin ladle, sat alongside the coals. Ladling water onto the hot coals produced the steam.

There was a single slatted bench seat on which two people could sit comfortably and three at a squeeze. I used it once, but only the once.

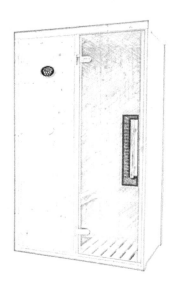

WHATS THAT BROWN STAIN?

I had entered the sauna naked except for a towel around my waist, I laid the towel on the wooden slatted bench. Switched on the heater for the coals, I waited until it got hot enough and began ladling cold water over the coals. It worked; clouds of hot steam quickly filled the small cabin and I quietly sat there sweating away. I decided that the sauna did nothing for me and it wasn't my thing and I've never had one since.

I gathered up my towel and noticed a brown stain on the slates of the bench upon which I had been sitting. I didn't know what it was. I wrapped my towel around my waist, I switched the heater off, replenished the water and went about my duties.

That evening I was talking with one of the RUC officers who was permanently stationed at the camp. The subject of the sauna came up and I queried with him what the brown stain on the slatted seat was. He went on to tell me a member of a previous infantry unit was using the sauna some time past. The infantryman had sat directly on the slatted bench seat without using a towel. He was sat there enjoying the sauna and because he had no towel his testicles had settled through the gap in the slatted bench and were dangling below the bench. At this time a mortar attack had took place on the camp with the bombs falling very close to the sauna. The infanteer, on hearing the bombs explode had dived for cover outside the sauna and close by the mortar blast walls. Unknowingly, he had left his testicles behind, ripping them off in his hurry to get to cover. The RUC officer went on to tell me that the soldier didn't realise what had happened until he went back into the shower after the short attack and saw the blood-stained slatted bench, below which, on the floor were his testicles. Nope, no saunas for me!

Sauna promoting? Hell no!

Character building? Hell yes!

DIRTY 'D' The Black Flag

The 14th/20th Kings Hussars regimental badge was a Prussian eagle with wings extended, and in the claws are held an orb and a mace. There is a crown on the head of the eagle. From a distance the badge is very similar in shape to that of the Special Air Service, a winged dagger. The troopers wore the regimental badge, made from dark cloth, on their berets. I know there was some speculation amongst the civilian population that we were an SAS unit. We did everything we could do dispel the rumours and I think we were successful. We didn't fancy the idea of being labelled an SAS unit and having to deal with all the extra attention such a unit would attract from the IRA and others.

At Glassmullin camp 'D' Squadron proudly flew the regimental flag from a flagpole inside and against the wriggly tin about ten yards to the right of the front gate. D squadrons colour was black, and so was the squadron flag. Within a white circle in the centre of the black flag was a black version of the SAS winged dagger lookalike Prussian Eagle.

BLACK'D'

I was guard commander, and I was looking at the flag fluttering in the breeze atop the flagpole, against the wriggly tin. I followed the line of the flagpole down and saw where the flagpole concealed all the yellow paint behind it which were the indication of bullet holes created by terrorist gunfire previously. I realised that were I a terrorist, with a view to killing a soldier, all I would have to do was wait at a significant position outside the camp where I could see the flag. As soon as the flag started to lower all I would have to do is fire a burst of automatic fire at the base of the wriggly tin directly below the flag. There would be a good chance I would hit the soldier lowering the flag. To make it an even more precious terrorist target, the flag was lowered and raised at the same time every day.

As it happened the squadron leader Maj. David Coombes, an excellent officer by the way, was nearby and I told him of my concern explaining my rationale. He immediately agreed with me and told me to tell the guard commander to take the flag down. I was the guard commander! The flag was normally lowered at six o'clock and that time was approaching. I wasn't going to lower it anywhere close to six o'clock.

I told the trooper on the gate to ensure nobody touches the flag. Went to our search team store and got a length of thin rope that we used for 'pulling' on searches. At about eight pm I went to the bottom of the flag rope and without moving it I tied the extra rope onto the end of the flag rope and then untied the flag rope from the cleat on the pole. Stepping off to the side a goodly way I then lowered the flag, which would be for the last time in the camp, it would not be flown again. There was no gunfire as the flag came down, no large calibre machine gun bullets ripping into any soldier, no casualty. Nothing.

I was feeling trepidation as I lowered the flag, no doubt because of the danger scenario I had built in my head. However, it was a real danger, a tangible risk. I was thinking in this manner in no small part to my training, and to the level of professionalism and consideration than was emanating from being part of such a professional unit.

Character building? Hell yes!

Bass Brewery Fire

The IRA placed incendiary bombs in the Bass Brewery on the Glen Road in Andersonstown. I believe it was something to do with the brewery not paying protection money. The incendiary's exploded setting the warehouse, which was absolutely rammed with all manner of booze for the impending Christmas period, well alight. The fire service responded to fight the large fire, as did the police and army to give cover to the fire fighters. It was a Major emergency services operation.

In addition to the incendiary's the terrorists had also placed grenades within the warehouse with the intention of them being detonated by the fire therefore making the fighting of the fire even more dangerous. One of these grenades exploded close to 'Fireman Wesley Orr', who was sadly killed by the blast. It was a very morose fire service that eventually extinguished the fire with the aid of Felix and cover from the army. I remember being at the scene, I had never seen such a mess, hoses, barrels, bottles, crates, all soaking wet and just lying all over. The air was acrid and thick wafts of steam and smoke pervaded everywhere. No order or shape, a total chaotic shamble.

The powers that be, whoever they were, decided that none of the stock was fit for human consumption and it was all to be destroyed; tons of it. Much of it was bottles of spirits with charred labels, or they only smelt of smoke. Nothing serious enough to put anybody off drinking it but not perfect enough for general sale. Lorries were brought in and loaded with the bottles of spirits and beer; they were driven to the tip under escort from us. We were told that we had to smash all bottles to ensure none were taken full and intact from the tip. Well, I'm qualified to say you can only smash so many bottles before you get well pissed off with it; we smashed thousands, but they kept coming. In the end we gave up and the lorries just tipped their loads. The good folk of Andersonstown and the wider West Belfast got wind of this booze bonanza and they descended like flies on shit onto the tip and the bottles. They came from all angles, through fences, over gates across refuge heaps, there was no stopping them. They had bags and boxes which they filled to overflowing. The impending Christmas was going to be boozy and free, and it was.

I can add, with some authority, that many troopers went home carrying four or five bottles of charred Bacardi or whisky in their bags. Nevertheless, it was a tragic episode if a little unusual.

Dirty Harry

On one of our 'mobile patrol' stints of duty a group of about eight of us were watching a rugby international on the TV it was a big match England v Wales. The TV was old, it had been donated by the Sun newspaper, and placed on a table in the accommodation rest room. The aerial was atop the TV and had to be strategically placed to get a good signal. We sat around watching the game when

'Dirty Harry', one of the troopers, but not of my brick, came in and sat down to watch the game. The place he sat in caused the TV picture to go fuzzy; it was very distracting knowing how good the picture had been. We asked 'Dirty Harry' to move but he refused to do so. I think he thought we were winding him up, he hadn't seen how good the picture had been. We asked him again, once more he refused. So, Neil Brennan, one of the troopers, and myself explained and asked him to move his position, but he wasn't having it. Frustrated with the fuzzy picture, Neil and I grabbed Dirty Harry and threw him out of the room. He wasn't happy. We shut the door, the picture improved, and we continued to enjoy the game. Minutes later we could hear footsteps hurrying along the wooden corridor outside, no problem. However, we then heard the distinctive double click of metal on metal as an SLR was cocked. Very quickly we realised 'Dirty Harry', he had that name for a reason, had 'lost it'. He was coming for us with his rifle. Fuck! Mark Hamilton, Neil Brennan, Glenn Ewen, and I jumped up and held the door shut. We had our feet at the bottom of both sides, and we stood out of direct line of the door and off to the side. We were expecting high velocity rounds to come through the door at any minute. This was very worrying, the other lads who weren't near the door had dived out the back door and through the windows. No bullets came through the door. Instead, we heard scuffling and raised voices in the corridor outside.

Mac Hutch, one of the brick commanders had been sitting in his room when he saw Dirty Harry, run past in one direction, and then run back the other carrying and cocking his rifle. Mac reacted superbly quickly and pounced on Dirty Harry disarming him and unloaded the rifle. Peering through the door we saw the end of the intervention. Dirty Harry was lying on the floor, red faced and huffing, puffing, and wriggling, while Mac calmly sat on top of him examining and unloading his rifle. The highly charged situation had been defused by an alert and responsive soldier. Thanks Mac, very much appreciated even to this day. Who knows what would have happened without the decisive intervention; it could have been disastrous.

The incident was probably a testimony to the continuous strain and danger we were facing, it had only taken a minor incident like that for things to boil over. Dirty Harry had been stressed, he was sent before the MO and given some leave. Besides, for future reference he could sit wherever he wanted, watching any channel he cared to!

Character building? Hell yes!

Short Fat Wobbling REME Wallah

After returning from Northern Ireland following our successful tour the 14th/20th held a few returning parades. The Hussars weren't the best at marching at any time but when you have the whole regiment trying to keep in step it was very challenging. I was happily marching along with the fourth troop of D Squadron; we were the last troop in the line of marchers. Squadron Sergeant Major John 'Johnny

Rotten' Rushton was the man in charge of our bit, and he was trying his best. I'm going along with everybody else and suddenly, very loudly I heard –

> *"You. Corporal Rees, you short, fat, wobbling REME Wallah! Get a grip and sort yourself out!"*
>
> *He was addressing me!*
> *He called me a short fat wobbling REME wallah! The cheek of it. How wrong was he?*
>
> *Short? I'm not short, I'm five foot eleven inches.*
> *Fat? I'm not fat, I'm just a little rotund.*
> *Wobbling? I wasn't wobbling, I just had a pleasant ambling relaxed gait.*
>
> *'Yes Sir' I replied bracing up and displaying extra gusto and enthusiasm.*

Leaving the 14/20KH

The 14/20KH were fabulous, I had after all tried to transfer to the regiment, (I was a protected trade in REME), but it was now time for the REME to move me on. Postings normally lasted three years. I was posted to 27 Command Workshop at Warminster but on leaving the 14/20th I was to attend my 1st Class Upgrader course at SEME Bordon, before reporting to Warminster.

14/20th Rugby

The 14/20th Had a wonderful rugby team with some great characters in it. Skip Rae and Ginge Mayall were the team Skippers when I was attached. Lash Hansel as hooker, Austin Honeyman as prop. An exceptionally talented Dave 'Bulldog' Drummond at scrum half. Trev Jones, Pat McNulty, fabulous players all. Dave Low wasn't just an excellent cook. Dave Lee was a competitive handful for anybody Mick Geraghty was a constant. We played regularly in Germany and even got to the army cup quarter finals whilst in Northern Ireland and only didn't get further because we were on an emergency tour and countering terrorism took precedence. Priorities eh!

After match festivities were compelling and thoroughly enjoyable, sing-songs were the norm and Ginge Mayall always started off with a song entitled 'The Battle of Selby Bridge'. I'd never heard it before joining the 14/20th and I've not heard of it since.

This is the song; the lyrics are brilliant -

The Battle of Selby Bridge were fought on the forty-fourth of March.
The King's Cross Fusiliers turned out. They marched as stiff as starch.
They marched as far as Bolton Brow and the enemy hove in sight,
And they called us generals nasty names and challenged us to fight.

CHORUS: We were amongst them. We were amongst them.
We slished and we slashed, and we slaughtered and we slew
Till the air for miles around were blue.
For an hour and a quarter, we held the foe at bay.
There were only two were left that day, and we were amongst them.

At break of day down Copley way, we went to fight the foe.
Our good scout Billy Higgins come to tell the tale of woe.
He said the enemy had advanced, so we retired pell-mell.
They shouted to surrender but we shouted, "Go to 'ell".

The enemy then retired into the wilds of Shipley Glen.
The switchback were invaded by an 'undred thousand men.

They hung their wounded out to dry across the aerial flight,
And they stuffed their guts wi' monkey-nuts and challenged us to fight.

We chased the enemy round the town till their stockings all fell down,
From Cavering Slacks to Boulder Clough and to Norland Town.
We came across a public house and there we raised a cheer,
For in that cellar we did find an hundred casks of beer.

FINAL CHORUS: We were amongst them.
We were amongst them.
We supped and we drank and we drained and we drew
'Till the air for miles around were pheeeeew!
For an hour and a quarter, we put that beer away.
There were only two carried home that day, and we were amongst them.

1ˢᵗ Class Course

A 'Bastards' of Recy Mechs

What do you call a collective of Recy Mechs 'A Bastards' that's what. Upon arriving in the UK, I didn't own a car. The first one that presented itself to me was an Austin FX4 London Taxi with about a million miles on the clock. KYU574D. I paid £200 cash for it. It was a runner. The central partition and fare-meter had been removed so effectively there was a driver's seat and a rear seat and about an acre of space in the middle, of which I would make future good use. The 'Taxi' light on the roof was still operating. There was enough room, if a little cosy, for a rugby team and a canoe.

Soon after taking ownership, it developed an injector air input issue (it shouldn't have one) which often resulted with me wielding spanners under the bonnet effecting a temporary repair.

Ever was there a collection of rogues that gathered for a Class 1 Recy Mech Course, Kev Boulton, Bob Smith, Graham 'Hoppy' Hopkins, Tony 'Clutch' Patterson and a few marginally milder souls. As opposed to the initial course where we knew very little if anything, a Recy Mech 'two to one' course is a whole new ball game. We were all NCO's having undergone trade and military training. My time had been spent with tanks and as a Section Commander in Belfast. The experiences of my fellow upgraders were similar, we were the real deal, and we knew it.

The recovery element of the course, if passed, would qualify us to become supervisors in the trade, something which most of us had been doing practically for a few years, I had certainly been doing so as a full Corporal. Moreover, we were the current practitioners at the job, and it showed on our coursework, the format of which was familiar to us all. Split into crews, wheeled and track jobs, dump crews' demolition, driving and towing skills. We'd been doing it tactically, and to a professional level.

The instructors knew this and gave us the respect that goes with our endeavours, they had after all been there and done it. They were good and we all passed the course.

Bordon Anecdotes 2

The recovery on the course went as expected, however, with the enormous personalities on the course anything could happen, and it did.

On this course is where I met Kev Boulton, a giant of a man and a REME legend (not leg-end). Clutch I knew from the 13th/18th Royal Hussars, Hoppy I knew from Recy Mech basic, JMC and three to two upgraders. We formed a recovery crew which was talented, experienced, and highly competent with a ton or so of mischief stirred in for good measure. We worked well for each other, and it was great fun.

We were also talented in socialising and adventures to the extent that being on a SEME course would allow.

<u>A Dangerous Place to Piss</u>

Hoppy had a small Army Green Ford Escort. It was the same model as the army used, same parts, same fuel, same everything! I can't think why he had it. One evening on the course he and I decided to visit his hometown of Cinderford in the Forest of Dean in this green Escort. We were travelling along the M4, it was a shitty, dirty evening, dark and drizzly. His windscreen washers ran out of liquid and seeing anything through the screen was impossible. We were driving blind along the M4. Hoppy pulled over to the hard shoulder, where his plan of action was for both of us to climb on the engine bay of the car and piss into the washer bottle. On the hard shoulder, vehicles passing at 70mph, visibility zero, raining, dark. Yep, we did it, pissed in the washer bottle and on we went.

<u>Apple Core Teeth</u>

On arriving at his hometown, Hoppy decides the first stop is the White Horse Pub in the Forest. Hoppy parks the car and I go in first, he has told me he'd like a scrumpy, pint of. No problem.

I walk into the bar and there are about ten men of varying ages sitting there, each of them has a pint of what is obviously scrumpy in front of them. They are unsmiling, severe looking men. I nod at them go to the bar and order two pints of Scrumpy. As they arrive Hoppy walks into the bar and he smiles his toothless smile at them, they all know him, and smile back.

Not one of them has got a tooth in his head! Not one. The scrumpy has done its corrosive work on them; its apple core teeth. Where the sugar rots the enamel off. Very unexpected and disconcerting. Note to self, very little scrumpy.

Another course night out and we are in a pub not too far from camp. In come some Londoners, a little bit cocky and loud as is their way, one of them is quite a lump, a big strong man. There is bit of banter between them and us which culminates in an arm-wrestling contest between the cockney lump and Kev Boulton. They were both very big, very strong men. Unfortunately, the table on which the contest took place was not a lump, neither was it big and strong!

Finally, course over I need to report to Warminster. The injectors on my taxi have given up and I need a tow. Enter Kev with his Volvo estate. He's a top man and he tows me all the way to Warminster from Bordon. Ever was a taxi towed faster, we scorched along the A303. New class One Recy Mech Corporal arrives at the workshop being towed in a London Taxi. Welcome to Warminster.

Character building? Hell yes!

3rd Unit - 27 Command Workshop, Warminster

It's a UK posting to Warminster in Wiltshire. No doubt it's the cushiest posting of my twelve years. The main unit is the command workshop which carries out Major repairs and modifications to all kinds of military equipment's. Most of the six hundred workers are civilians.

The military element is small consisting of about thirty soldiers who worked out of a small workshop at Battlesbury Barracks which is occupied by the Infantry Demonstration Battalion (IDB). The REME soldiers are effectively a Light Aid Detachment (LAD) for the IDB. The unit is managed by Sgt Dick Hone, a Geordie, and a very competent Sergeant. He is holding a post that would normally be held by an Artificer or similar. He was awarded the BEM for his excellent work. Well done Dick.

Infantry Demonstration Battalion (IDB)

The IDB as well as being the commander UK Land Forces' Special Reserve Battalion provides manpower and mechanised Infantry resources for the School of Infantry which runs year-round courses for army Officers and NCO's.

Uniquely, the IDB is a composite battalion composed of about twelve soldiers from every battalion in the British Army. The rumour has it that the IDB is where Battalion Commanders send their "ne'er'-do-wells", incompetents, malcontents, and anybody else they want to get rid of. Allegedly the battalion was full of troublemakers. There was every type of cap badge and uniform, different traditions, different drills, and marching speeds. A mixing of traditions and customs. It was fantastic. In my view it was an eclectic mix of interesting and diverse personalities. Each had different stories to tell from different experiences all over the world. Different practices to

346

exhibit and display and I learnt a great deal from this fine gathering of men.

The Commanding Officer was from the Welsh Guards. There was a Scots company, an Irish Company, and an English & Welsh company.

The only blight during my three years there was when we were all confined to barracks for two weeks while the camp was searched for some weapons that had been stolen from the armoury. A Royal Highland fusilier, who was a bit of a nutcase, was eventually found to be responsible, it was a very beery two weeks. The WRAC contingent with whom we shared the barracks were raucous and very entertaining. Soldiers should steal more weapons.

Battalion parades were fabulously fascinating things with all the different uniforms and hats on display coupled with the different marching speeds. The marching phases and parades were very entertaining with some contingents moving faster or slower than others. The hurried quirky trot of the

Light Infantry compared to the regally sedate ambiance of the guards. As REME we generally were observers of such things which suited us well.

Army Driving Instructor.

I get sent to the Army School of Motor Transport at Beverley in Yorkshire. I'm a capable HGV 1 driver and I have been Recy Meching for about five years, albeit mostly heavy armour. It is an all arms course and there are about ten of us on it, two to a vehicle. The instructors are all Sergeants from the Royal Corps of Transport (RCT (Rickshaws, Cabs, and Taxis)). Essentially, we drive around the North all day being sure to follow the highway code, and the direction of the instructors. It's a tough course to pass and only about four of us are successful.

It was a notable course for me for only one reason. There was a rugby player playing for Hull Rugby league at the time, I can't recall his surname, but his first name was Ken.

I noticed when I was out and about driving the army lorries that lots of people would wave and shout greetings at me. It transpires that this Ken and I are so similar looking we could have been separated at birth. I saw photos of him, and the likeness was uncanny.

Of course, when out and about I tried to take full advantage of this but my Yorkshire accent fell far short and my Welsh valley lilt was no substitute. Nevertheless, an interesting time and an HGV instructors' certificate to boot.

Motorbike Licence

Having completed my HGV instructors' course, I began teaching people to drive. The army had its own examiners and Sgt Wally McAleavy of the Light Infantry was the resident examiner at the IDB.

I had taught a soldier to drive a Landrover and his test was booked with Wally. I arrived with the Landrover at the allotted time and place and Wally arrived on his Honda 250cc motorcycle. The candidate for the test didn't show.

Wally asked me if I could ride a motorcycle, I said I could but hadn't passed my test. Rather than lose the time Wally suggested I ride his motorcycle around the town, and he would follow and assess me in the Landrover.

That's what we did, and I successfully passed my test after about a fifteen-minute ride.

By virtue of me being a qualified army driving instructor I was from that moment of passing, a qualified motorcycle instructor. Only twenty minutes riding and I could formally teach it by virtue of the driving instructors course giving me accreditation to instruct for any licence group I held. Thanks Sgt Wally of the Light Infantry, you're a top man.

<u>EPC & APC(A)</u>

At Warminster the unit put me forward for my Education for Promotion Certificate (EPC), which I would need along with a Senior Military Certificate (SMC) to qualify for promotion to Sergeant. So, I attend the course which consisted of four subjects: 'Military Calculations' (Maths), 'Military Communications', (English), 'Army in the Contemporary World', (Current Affairs) and 'Military Management' (Management). I passed all four subjects easily enough. The unit decided shortly after that I should be sent on the Advanced level course EPC(A), which is a qualification required to be promoted to Warrant Officer, and me still a very young Corporal. I passed the EPC(A). They must have thought highly of me, and I was pleased with my progress. However, little did I know that by virtue of my having passed EPC(A) it would, at a future unit, put me in career changing conflict with an envious, small minded, senior rank who was unable to pass the exam despite numerous attempts.

<u>SMC</u>

An early thing the unit did was to send me on my Senior Military Certificate Course (SMC) at the training Battalion and Depot REME at Arborfield. The same garrison town at which I had done my Basic Military Training (BMC) five or six years before. At this point I was a full Corporal, I had about five years in, had been on active service and I was again in the land of shouting and swearing. The thing about the SMC course is they have you by the balls. You need the Course for promotion, and you are at the point where you must make a fist of it because it's a career making course. A must have.

Our Course formed and there were about fifty or sixty Corporals on it. I knew a few of the attendees, but the staff were all unknown to me. It was bullshit city and there was nothing anybody on the Course could do to change it. Having been in fully operational armoured units with massively experienced soldiers and leaders I thought the outlook at the depot to be a tad petty. There were lots of running about, bed blocks, bull nights, kit inspections, drill, field exercise. The usual gambit of military stuff. I think the RD staff had been over it many, many times and they were good at drill and shouting and the like. Bulled boots, polished brasses, parades.

There was a military maturity about the course members that was absent from the RD staff. The members, all Corporals mostly came from first line teeth arm units and had undergone experiences like me. They had been 'soldiering' in the real world and not in the false manufactured environment of depots and parade squares. Some of those depot soldiers needed to get out into the real army. I didn't learn anything on the course that I wasn't already doing proficiently at unit. But it had to be done. One of the course instructors, a gobshite Corporal, found himself at a BAOR workshop soon after where he was dished his just desserts for thieving from soldiers' lockers. Good enough for him.

There were a couple of notable things on my SMC that I remember.

Firstly, I met Ginge Warne, who became a good friend of mine, he could bull boots like nobody I ever knew. Like glass, absolute perfection. I never, ever, bulled boots on my ARV's. Ginge was to become the model for the REME soldier statue some years later. He transferred to RD and became an instructor, and in his later years became 'The Locksmith of Kabul', there's a book title there. A top man.

Secondly, at the depot there were a series of ammunition bunkers buried below ground in a row. They were earth covered and formed a series of hurdles over which the courses, in our case in full battle kit, had to scramble over. It had been raining and the earth was soggy, and very, very slippery. We could not get any traction whatsoever. We clawed and pulled and pushed at the ground with absolutely no progress whatsoever. We were at it for what seemed like hours. Eventually the staff called us off.

We had been unsuccessful, ripped uniforms, mud-soaked kit needing to be clean the next morning, torn fingernails, we were absolutely knackered, exhausted. Alas we had to stay up half the night cleaning our kit.

Character building? Hell yes! But for all the wrong reasons.

Other than those two things it was a necessary evil.

To The Eternal Memory of those Members of The Corps of Royal Electrical and Mechanical Engineers who Lost Their Lives on Active Service'

Warminster Anecdotes

<u>The Masons Arms</u>

The best pub in the world is in Warminster. It's named the Masons Arms and is located on the high street. The landlord's name is Fred Scott. He is in his sixties, has an unruly bush of grey buffy hair, thick rimmed spectacles, and a clipped grey moustache. He wears sleeveless cardigans buttoned all the way up over a striped grey and white long-sleeved shirt. He is a gentleman and pleasant, polite, and helpful. The only nod to entertainment is Radio Four playing quietly from an ancient transistor radio on a corner of the bar. Near the radio is a cake-plate over which sits a glass dome. Stacked inside the glass dome are ham salad sandwiches made by Fred's wife Phillis. Don't' eat any until you've had four or five pints; by then they will be fresher and tastier.

The jewel in Fred's crown is his beer. He keeps the finest HB Best Bitter in the land, probably the world.

Rich and creamy, the perfect temperature, the perfect head, a tulip glass. It's the sort of beer for which you crave after a hard day's work or a successful difficult endeavour and for which you deserve a reward. So, you order your reward and watch as Fred masterfully pull your ale. He does it so well, and places it on the bar in front of you. You deserve this.

It's so good to not drink it right off. It's best just to stand there and stare at the pint, anticipating its smoothness, and body. As you stare, unspeaking, your thirst increases, you know you deserve this, you know that waiting will escalate your enjoyment. It's worth hanging on.

The full ale settles, you raise it and intend to sip slowly. That first taste is so good your sip moves into a swallow and continues into a gulp and then a second. When you put the glass down you are slightly surprised to see the glass threequarters or

almost empty. How did that happen? It happens every time!

The bar area is quite small and if you are in the bar, you are in the conversation. The world is put to rights over some fine beer. On one evening I was chatting with an old boy whose company I enjoyed. He was knowledgeable and interesting, and I listened to him with great interest. The next time I saw him he was in a Major's uniform instruction on my EPC(A) Course. A slight nod of recognition and that was it; there's a big rank distance between a Corporal and a Major. Back in the Masons, no difference a complete gentleman.

Warminster was a fabulous town with fabulous people.

I am not a young girl!

I am instructed to take a Volvo EKA recovery wagon to Bovington Camp, home of the Royal Armoured Corps, to show it off at a display to be held there. Apparently, dignitaries from many different countries will be in attendance and us Brits are showing off our best kit with the hope of international sales. I'm accompanied by Pike, a man of temperate indecision and thirst a proud West Country Man, and fellow Recy Mech. We drive down to Bovington and get lodged in some transit accommodation; we are ready for our part in the display.

The next morning, I wake up and I'm feeling like shit. I'm running a temperature, aching all over and in the most debilitating stomach pain. Things are not good. I report to the Medical Reception Station (MRS), where I see a Medical Officer (MO). He clearly knows I am ill, but he is unable to make a diagnosis. So, I get bedded down in a ward there. I have a miserable painful night. Not only am I kept awake by my pain and discomfort but there is another admission on the night of a person who has had a clear kicking and is bandaged up like an Egyptian mummy.

I wake in the morning and turn my head to the fellow in the bed near to me. He is groaning and clearly in pain. He turns his head towards me. His head is fully bandaged with slits for eyes, nose, and mouth. He groans and says, 'Hello Taff, how you keeping mate, long time no see'? I have no clue who it is, it's not Pike, he should be with the Volvo at the display. Transpires its 'Ox Murphy' who I knew from my time with the 14th/20th Kings Hussars. He had been in an altercation in the NAAFI in Bovington camp and had come off second best. By some way by the looks of him. I'm too ill to get involved a conversation and I drift off to sleep.

I get moved to a larger general hospital. I am in serious pain, and I am given sedatives and intravenous pain killers and I move in and out of

consciousness. The doctors are unable to diagnose my illness. I have the most awful stomach cramps and I have come out in huge red blotch sores all over my stomach, legs and back. I'm in a mess. The doctors are considering explorative surgery and I'm not looking forward to it. It's the doctors and surgeons' uncertainty that is worrying me between bouts of consciousness and agony. As a last resort the doctors send for a dermatologist to examine me. The dermatologist arrives and looks at the sores about my body and thinks I have what looks like Henoch Schoenlein Purpura (HSP), a quick blood and urine test and it's confirmed.

The symptoms mainly affect four areas of the body and can come and go for several weeks or even months in some cases: the symptoms are-

- *A purple-red rash, which does not turn white when pressed.*
- *Rash can turn into ulcers.*
- *The rash is usually over the backs of the limbs, especially the legs, which can also be swollen.*

- *Tummy aches and pains which can be severe and occasionally result in blood in the stool.*
- *Painful and swollen joints can occur due to inflammation, usually affecting the knees and ankles.*
- *Protein and blood may be found in the urine due to inflammation in the kidneys.*

I had every symptom, all aggravated by my age. HSP is normally the reserves of girls between the ages of two and eleven, not fifteen stone rugby playing REME Recy Mechs. No wonder the doctors were perplexed. Medication was proscribed and I was to stay in hospital until fit enough to return to my unit at Warminster. The rest did me good and I was reading Kipling at the time, and I was moved to put pen to paper to write a poem about my situation. I decided to write it in Kiplingesque fashion. I was quite pleased with my endeavour, it's called - 'Like a Fittin Squaddie Should', by way of explanation Raj was the hospital porter who brought the food to the ward, and Wales were playing France at rugby the following Saturday. Here it is –

<u>Like a Fittin Squaddie Should</u>

'Like a Fittin Squaddie Should'

A' lying here in hospital,
not feeling very good
I'm not crappin' proper,
like a fitting squaddie should
The rash is on me feet,
and half around me back
The drip is in me arm,
and the pain is hard to hack

My gut is turning over
as montezumas aim
An no matter how I move me'sel;
the pain is jus the same
The doc is fairly puzzled,
he ain't seen this afore
He turns and muses deeply,
as he exits through the door

Rank red pish on porcelain,
leaning on a strut
A rusty blunt bayonet uppered,
hard and deep in my gut
Nil by mouth no solids,
only water to dribble down
Cramps again and gut-ache
causing the sisters to frown

Nothing again for you sir,
Says Raj as he passes by
I can taste the sickly aroma,

of his hospital corn-beef pie
We need more blood says staff,
as she sharps another vein
I'm all done in resistin',
and the cramps attack again

Two square by two we're barracked,
none of us are clout
But we've all got optimism,
we'll all be better out
For three hurt days I've lain here,
in drug induced respite
Still there is no answer,
an I carries me some fright

This rash is a constant query,
the cramping pain the same
More saline and drug infusion,
Into the same ol' vein
Enter the dermatology,
'strewth I know what is this'
HSP is the problem
'But your age is far, far amiss'.

She gives me a brief explanation,
the surgeon he has to stay
No knife or a lance to inspect me,
in the 'good ol' military way
The consultant knows what I've suffered;
my god, tis a rare old thing
You should be young and a female,
with all the ailments you bring

Overdue I feel some movement,
whilst straddling the porcelain crown

REME – The Magnificent Bastards

'Look out' on the Channel Ferry, f
or flotsam of stinking brown.
Perchance I'm getting a furlough,
on Friday Wales attack France
I've got a seat in the stand there,
and maybe we're in with a chance

My stag in the pain was unwelcome,
the care that I had did me good
So, it's back to the slog and the grind,
like a fitting squaddie should

Tyrone Rees

<u>Thirsty Pike</u>

While I'm recovering in hospital, I've assumed Pike is showing off the Volvo EKA at the RAC demonstration. Not a bit of it, he has made a intemperate decision.

Pike has decided to go for a beer, and the best place, as far as Pike is concerned is his local pub, which is OK, but it's in Plymouth which is one hundred and ten miles away. So how was he to get there? Well in a Volvo EKA of course. What do you do when you get to the pub which is in a narrow street? You park the twenty ton plus Volvo EKA on the pavement so that vehicles and pedestrians can get past on the road, but not the pavement. Having been so considerate for the local populace what do you do then? Well, obviously, you go in the pub and get rat-arsed.

You must admire his pluck; it was a good effort.

My only involvement is, when I get discharged from hospital and returned to unit, to get interviewed by Captain. Jim Brown, our OC. Obviously I know nothing about Pike's actions or motivations, and I'm cleared of any involvement. The Captain tells me Pike is to be charged and he asks me for the value of the diesel used on a run to Plymouth and return. I have no idea and I grasp £20 out of the air. Pike gets a fine and that's the end of it.

<u>Gored by a Bull</u>

At one point I'm managing the workshop as a Recy Mech Corporal. Just a figurehead really, the tradesmen got on with their regular stuff and I with mine. It involves calling the role at parade and not much else. One morning one of the guys is absent from parade. Let's call him Tug. Tug was normally of jovial disposition and a West Country Man from a nearby large town. He played second row at the School of Infantry Rugby Club and was a decent unit level player. From farming stock, he stood about six foot four inches had huge bushy sideboards and a very sociable character. One morning on noting Tug's absence from parade I wasn't too concerned, he lived locally and was prone to often turning up late having been working on the family farm. This day he phones in and tells me he's been working on the farm and that over the weekend his father had been gored by a bull and was in a bad way. Not only was he concerned for his father, but the running of the farm fell to him.

NASTY BULL

Ok I told him, no problem with being away, stick with your dad and the farm and keep me informed of things. I let the Captain. know and carried on with my duties. About three days later Tug phones in again stating his father condition is unimproved. No problem I replied, take the time you need. I asked if I or the unit could do anything, but there wasn't other than give time off I assumed. The following Monday Tug phones in again. He tells me his father situation is worsening, and there's lots to be done on the farm, that he's under pressure and finding things very difficult. I tell him to take the week, and to phone in the next Monday. I update the Captain. who agrees.

The following Monday I get a phone call from Tug; his father has passed away from his 'goring' injury. Oh no. I pass on my condolences, tell him to take all the time he needs. To phone in the following week and to keep the unit updated. I inform the Captain. of this sad news and he informs me to order flowers for condolence to be delivered to Tug's mother at the family farm. No problem. I get the flowers and as it's not too far away I elect to deliver the flowers myself.

I arrive at the farmyard in an army Landrover and carrying the huge bunch of flowers I knock on the farmhouse. Tug's mother answers. I pass the flowers to her telling her I and all the unit are sorry for her grievous loss, and what a tragedy it is. 'What loss?' she asked as she was joined by Tug's dad at the doorway, who was looking the picture of health and not a 'gore' hole insight.

It transpired they hadn't seen Tug for weeks and his 'goring' story was pure bullshit (see what I did there?). Tug had fallen in love with a woman he had met, lust had overtaken him, he'd left his wife and moved in with the new one. I admired his gall.

The Captain. wasn't too happy, and he was on Tug's case from then on making life miserable for him. Very quickly Tug's marriage fell apart, and he bought himself out of the army. On his last day we loaded his married quarter contents onto the back of a four tonner and delivered them to his new house.

Returning from dropping his belongings off we were in the back of the four-tonner sweeping it out and I found some photographs on the floor of the lorry, they must have fallen from the load of Tug's furniture. There was Tug, all six foot plus of him, sideboards, and hairy chest, reposing in garter belt, black stockings, and high heels. He was prostrate on a bed with his naked wife astride him, and other poses. He was very flexible for such a big man; they looked such a happy couple. Well suited to each other. Invariably the photos found themselves pinned to the workshop notice board. The comments about which were mostly related to Tug's wife rather than Tug himself. He was a good man and I hope he did well in life, the sad thing was that he was a big loss to the rugby team.

<u>Big Lizzie Prowls</u>

Being a soldier is a dangerous occupation. There's wars and dangerous training, operations, and tactical manoeuvres and so on. There is nothing more dangerous than being a young soldier on the lash in Warminster town, particularly in the Bath Arms.

Picture the scene. You are a young soldier say eighteen or nineteen years old and you are out with your mates. You have a few beers in the NAAFi and then a few more, and then out of camp to the town moving from pub to pub having a few beers in each hostelry. You are not an experienced drinker and after seven or eight beers you feel bloated and even a little sicky. Nevertheless, soldier on and a few Bacardi and Cokes are easier to drink and most welcome. Eventually, well pissed, you enter the infamous 'Bath Arms' in the middle of town. You go to the bar to order a few last drinks. The evening is coming to an end, or so you think.

Sitting menacingly and alert in a dark corner, drinking slowly from a pint pot is 'Big Lizzie'. She has a second full pint pot on the table in front of her as she orders beers two at a time. She is a very, very big woman. Probably thirty or forty years of age, maybe older, it's hard to tell. Her hair is a greasy, streaky, and black, tied back with a dirty bow. Her eyes sit atop saggy dark bags, and her broad pug nose looks out of place, offset slightly to one side. A sheen of beer froth arches her top lip which synchronises with her three ever widening chins. She has a wide mouth with chubby pale lips. She is wearing a flowered summer dress which shows every fold of her ample girth. There is no discernible body shape, just mass. Her bingo wings hang loosely and wobble every time she lifts a pot to her lips for ale. Lizzie fills her chair, her broad girth overlapping the narrow arms. Her expansive thighs tightly forced together by the chair sides. Her legs, seen from the knees down are blotched red and her ankles, as fat and podgy as her knees, give the impression her legs are on upside down. She is wearing dirty white slip-on sandals probably about size eleven or even twelve.

Elizabeth

Lizzie is well known to older soldiers and well known in the town. There is a nearby house on the side of which some wag or previous victim has painted in huge white letter 'BIG LIZZIE – VIRGIN'. Big Lizzie is predatory, and her hunting ground is the 'Bath Arms' near closing time, and her defenceless prey is young very drunk soldiers. It's open season on young drunk squaddies, it's always open season, as

far as Big Lizzie is concerned. 'Big Lizzie' is hunting tonight!

You are in her sights; she can smell you. As you lean against the bar for support you sway slightly, sipping your much too strong, at this stage of the night, drink. Big Lizzie knows this. She empties her second beer in one and heaving herself from the chair slowly walks the long way around the room, stalking, to get near your blind side. She's worked out the less you see of her the more advantageous it is for her. She can smell you, she is closing in.

Older more experienced soldiers can see what's happening, they have either seen it or experienced it before. They say nothing and don't intervene. It's a school day, a rite of passage, it's growing up. Besides they are amused and entertained and will have another target for their piss-taking in the days to come.

Big Lizzie asks the young soldier to buy her a drink. He, looking at her through the thickest of hazy beer

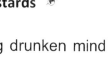

goggles, agrees to do so. His erring drunken mind thinks he's onto a good thing, he's pulled a decent bird. Big Lizzie has chosen well; she's an artist.

They leave the bar together his arm clasped, very tightly indeed, by Big Lizzie who leads the way. They are both happy but Big Lizzie is the happiest. The older soldiers cheer as they leave.

About mid-morning the next day, the young soldier, feeling as rough as dog-shit, is walking back through the town centre to camp, not knowing his face is covered in menstrual blood. He struggles to remember the details of the night and as each part-memory surfaces he winces and explores self-denial. The shock of his bestial-like escapade is still maturing. As he nears the barracks, he has a decision to make; he must either man up and take ownership or lie for the rest of his life.

Character building. Hell yes!

Pete Must Piss

Living in Battlesbury Barracks at Warminster was no problem, us twenty or so REME soldiers had a corridor to ourselves. There was a WRAC contingent on the floor above us, there were infantry elements on the other four corridors. We REME guys had a block inspection every Friday morning, so it was block-jobs every Thursday evening. I was the block NCO, and I managed the block-job rota and made sure the block was ready for inspection every Friday. Keeping on top of it was easy and straightforward.

For a while the barrack block was being renovated and we had to evacuate the ground floor and move up to the second floor for a temporary period. It was a round-robin affair for the entire barracks. The floor layout was the same as ours on the ground floor.

Following our regular Thursday night block jobs, which continued as normal, we would stroll into Warminster to the Masons Arms for a few beers.

On our return, and because we had cleaned the block earlier in the evening, we would refrain from using the ablutions as much as possible. It was normal practice for a group of us to return from the pub together, grab a Chinese on the way back and gather in the TV lounge for a bit of TV prior to bed. All the Chinese wrappings went out the window for the last block job prior to inspection which was outside area cleaning. It saved getting the bins dirty. It was likewise with the toilets which had been cleaned, the lads would urinate outside in the nearby undergrowth rather than use the toilet block.

One warm summer evening we returned from the pub, with our Chinese on our laps we sat watching a Donna Summer concert and the windows to the TV room were wide open.

One of our armourers, a very likeable young man named Happy Pete, decided he needed to piss and with his usual vigour he launched himself through the window to piss on the grass area outside.

The remainder of us just sat there staring at the window through which Happy Pete had so athletically and gracefully exited. He had clean forgotten we had moved for renovations and were on the second floor. How we laughed. Our sides were aching.

He was in plaster for weeks and weeks. We couldn't help but laugh every time we saw him. Blimey, I'm even laughing now as I write this.

Character building. Hell Yes!

Longleat to Ascension Island Hash Run

Early every Friday afternoon the REME soldiers, other than the sick, lame, and lazy would have to go on a 'hash' run in the grounds around Longleat (where the lions live). Two of the men would be designated to collect a few sacks of sawdust from the main workshop woodwork shop and their job was to go off early to the area and lay a sawdust trail for the others to follow. At any junction on the route a pile of sawdust was placed on the floor. Then trails of sawdust were placed leading off in different directions but only one of the trails, the one with extra piles of sawdust was the correct route. this meant that the first runners at the scene may have to spend time going down false trails and a consequence of this was that often the slower runners would be in the front.

One day I was tasked with another soldier, I think it was Tich Latham an armourer, to lay the trail. We set off to the area early in a Landrover with our sawdust and off we went to lay the trail knowing a lorryful of troops would be along within the hour to follow our trail. It had been raining heavily and the ground was very, very wet.

The ground was heavy going and about a mile into the trail there was a shallow valley like depression off to our right. The depression had filled with water and running perpendicular through the water was a stock fence of only which the tops of the fence posts could be seen. The posts stood about four foot high, and the very cold water was about six inches less. We laid a sawdust junction at the side of the field and while Tich laid out the proper route I laid a bogus trail along three or four of the exposed fence post tops. It looked for or the world as if the trail led across the lake to the other side of the depression. We finished laying our trail and waited for the lorry full of soldiers to arrive which they did in due course.

Accompanied by the usual 'slagging off' of to us trail layers the hashers set off along the route. Tich and I followed behind as was the custom bringing up the rear and destroying our sawdust pile behind us.

There was a technician Sergeant in the unit who was famous for his whinging, grumpiness', and all-round lack of a sense of humour. He was a heavy-smoking, short podgy man and running was not his forte. Let's call, him 'Sgt Grumpy'. Due to the vagaries of the hash run, Sgt Grumpy was about third arriving at our junction marker near the water filled depression.

Tich and I were close enough to watch him stand at the junction marker, look around in complete disgust, and see the disagreement on his face as Sgt Grumpy realised the only option to him was to wade out along the submerged fence line to see if it was the correct path. In all fairness he did so, and once the very cold water was above his waist, he heard the shouts from other runners identifying the correct route. Sgt Grumpy turned and waded out of the water. He was wet cold and furious. Tich and I were rolling on the floor laughing, we couldn't help ourselves. It suddenly dawned on Sgt Grumpy that he had been 'had' though it could have been anyone of the others. He wasn't happy one bit. He gave up on the run and walked back, pouting, and cursing all the while, to where the truck was waiting to return to the unit at the completion of the run. When Tich and I joined him at the truck sometime later he made it clear we were going to pay for our mischief and we were a pair of twats, or worse.

Sgt Grumpy tried to give us an unpleasant time over the next few months, he was always on our case. Niggling annoying things such as fatigue parties and other onerous tasks. It was becoming a bind.

Roll on a few months. Sgt Grumpy had not forgotten and was still vengeful. I had copped a duty as duty orderly officer. Unusual for a Corporal but the unit was small and with no commissioned officers the senior ranks and senior Corporals took it in turns. The duty lasted a week and was a sleeping duty. There was a bunk in the main workshop along with single ablutions and a telephone. It was boring.

One night about 3am I'm sleeping in the bed and the phone rings for the first time I had ever known. The conversation goes like this-

> *'Orderly Officer, Corporal Rees speaking sir'.*
> *'This is Major Smith (name made-up) at Headquarters United Kingdom Land Forces I want to speak with the orderly officer'?*
> *'Sir, I am the orderly officer'.*
> *'You said you were a Corporal'.*

'Yes Sir', I went on to explain the circumstances of the unit.

'Very well Corporal I need a Fridge Mechanic to be deployed to the Ascension Islands immediately'.

I replied incredulously 'A fridge mechanic for immediate deployment'?

'Yes, there's' a bloody war on you know', he said rather condescendingly. The Falklands matter was gaining momentum.

I pondered, a fridge mechanic? a fridge mechanic?

'Well Corporal'? said the Major.

'I do believe we only have one soldier who is good with fridges sir, a Sgt Grumpy', I replied.

'Thank you, Corporal,'. And he hung up on me.

For some reason a signal arrived at the unit later in the morning deploying Sgt Grumpy to Ascension Island. To this day I have heard no more. I wonder if the deployment contributed to building his character!

That episode was the first of my two contributions to the Falklands War.

The second was that I oversaw transport for the procurement of wood and other items for the construction of huge wooden boxes that were being made at the workshop. All manner of 'kit' was placed in the boxes; from helicopters to nuts and bolts and thousands of other military necessities. We drove thousands of miles, worked tirelessly throughout the nights and at weekends to meet task force deadlines. I learn that everything the workshop produces was safely stowed on a ship called 'The Atlantic Conveyor'!

Pissing Down at Fremington Camp

Off we went for our annual REME military training camp at Fremington Camp in North Devon. Spiders once more. These spiders were the worse I ever stayed in, good for bonfires and rats only. It wasn't a particularly noteworthy time but there are some incidents worth recording. Also, there were some female soldiers with us from the Women's Royal Army Corps (WRAC). I don't know where they came from or why, but they were there for part of the time.

Welcome to Fremington Camp; first things first, in good army fashion, we started with a Basic Fitness Test (BFT), one and a half miles squadded run in fifteen minutes, followed by a return one and a half miles best effort and in any case under eleven and a half minutes. Wearing the heavy DMS leather and rubber boots took the fun out of it.

The first night we were in barracks and there was, in the middle of the night, a fire alarm. We rolled out of bed and formed up on the square as per fire instructions. Uneventful except for one of the Sergeants who turned out in his Dickensian night wear complete with sleeping cap. All he was missing was a candle on a small tin holder.

We did some canoeing, oddly again, none of us were accomplished canoeists. The memorable thing about this was that the small estuary in which we canoed was just downriver from a 'tannery'. The water tasted of dead animals and had a definite orange tinge to it. Horrible.

Abseiling was on the menu and over cliffs we went. I didn't mind abseiling; I wasn't the most enthusiastic, but I was competent enough. One abseil event is memorable to me for one very unusual reason. Not because of the great height involved, not for any great element of danger, not for the stunning North Devon scenery not for any real good reason.

I had been over the cliff edge a few times on this day and I had climbed back to the top where the instructor, a S/Sgt whose name I can't remember was briefing a few of these women soldiers on what to do. None of them had abseiled previously and there was a lot of trepidation. I watched the first few go over very cautiously, but they went, and they went well. The third girl over was a stone or three heavier than the first few and she seemed to carry more trepidation, even fear, of going over. She was harnessed-up by the S/sgt and coaxed on her way. The S/Sgt paying out the rope slowly, as she leaned backwards and stepped off the cliff. Ever so slowly she paid out the rope and very timidly she started to descend the sheer rock face. It was a goodly height, perhaps a hundred feet or so. About thirty feet down she froze. And with terror in her voice screamed up the cliff face that she couldn't move and was terrified. Despite all the coaxing from the S/Sgt she wasn't going anywhere.

The S/Sgt became frustrated with his inability to get her to move, so he asked me (I was the only one there, there were better abseilers than I), to go down alongside her and see if I could help. I agreed to do so. I harnessed myself to another rope and over I went.

I drew level with her and looking in her face it was clear she was very afraid. Almost crying. I, hanging ponderously alongside, tried to calm her. She was in no danger of falling as she was well lashed to the safety rope and if she wouldn't go down of her own accord the only option was to pull her up back over the cliff edge. That would be the last and most difficult course of action, she was a big girl. I agreed with her that I would go down just below her and place her feet on any suitable places and the S/Sgt above would belay her very slowly until we got her to the ground. She agreed to this, and I shouted up to the S/Sgt what we were going to do, he agreed. So, I dropped to her feet height, and we slowly started to 'step' her down. It was going along fine, and soon we were halfway down. I was below her and placing her feet, one at a time, against the cliff wall. I suddenly felt her start to shake violently, and she started to cry and sob telling me she couldn't do it. Her shaking became more and more violent, and I realised her fear was rising and things would become more difficult.

I was contemplating the 'getting a grip' of her option when I felt rain falling on me. I thought unusual it was a fine day and the rain was very warm. Most odd. I looked up, the girl had light coloured grey tracksuit trousers on, and I could see a dark patch rapidly expanding from her crotch area. She was pissing herself. She was pissing from fear, and she was pissing directly on my head. Now I have known soldiers who would have revelled in this sort of thing, some Recy Mechs even, but it wasn't my inclination. Not hanging halfway down a sheer cliff face, with a terrified sobbing woman hanging just over my head. I was dancing on the rope, dodging what seemed gallons of the warm wet stuff.

That was it. I took a firm hand with her, grabbed her by her scruff and shouted up to the S/Sgt to belay as quickly as he could. We banged and bumped to the bottom in double-quick time. She bleated, and sobbed, and hollered for the minute or so it took to get her to the cliff base. On arrival at the bottom, she collapsed to the floor, ignoring me and others and just curled in a ball. A WRAC Sergeant came along and took care of her.

I felt very sorry for her. How embarrassing it must have been. She was in a position she could not control, and which had overwhelmed her. Awfully for her, she had pissed all over a relative stranger.

Some of the watching soldiers were highly entertained, I understand squaddie humour, but told them to shut the fuck up anyway. The WRAC's and the girl in question were with us till the end of the exercise, but I never spoke with her, nor her with me. Embarrassed I suppose. I hope she got over it.

On the penultimate day of Fremington camp the powers that be decided the troops, unfortunately including me, were to go on a thirty-six-mile route march along the North Devon coastline. Junior ranks only, no Sergeants or officers, not that we had many. Thirty-six miles, with weapons and battle kit, and no build up training for it. I knew it was going to be shit and it was.

It was a very hot day. The roads were tarmac and heavy on the feet. Flat roads would have been bad enough but if you're not going steeply down on the North Devon coast then you are going steeply up. There were no way points, no food or water stops just a straight thirty-six-mile slog. It went on forever.

To make it worse I was designated to carry a radio. It hissed and buzzed in my ear for the whole thirty-six. Not one miserable message to receive or give: pointless. My seven-pound rifle weight twenty-seven by the end. My feet were ridiculously sore, and I couldn't walk on them the following day – so painful.

There should have been build-up route marches, there should have been water and food replenishment, there should have been way-point tasks, there should have been radio activity. There was nothing but a pointless slog. Clearly put together by somebody who had never done anything similar, somebody without intelligence, somebody who wanted to inflict, somebody who clearly wasn't going to do it themselves.

Whoever planned that stupid slog should have been pissed on and thrown off a cliff.

Character building? Hell yes!

Best Bollocking Ever

As a Corporal the only duties I carried out were workshop orderly officer and rarely, very rarely, I would be second in charge of the guard at the School of Infantry. The guard commander was always a Sergeant, normally off a senior Brecon Infantry Commanders course, and the guard themselves were nominally infantrymen from the School or the IDB. So, on this duty all goes well, it was my job to see the 'stags' change and that was it. The guard was done, no issue. Relieved by the Regimental Police, off I went to my room at Battlesbury barracks where I could get a shower and a few hours kip before reporting to the workshop at about midday; it was a cushy unit.

The ASM at the unit was named Bruce Forsyth. He was a top man and he and I formed the unit hammer-throwing team. He was very good, and I was better with sledges. Nevertheless, we got on well. I was called to his office in the main workshop. I sauntered

into his office in my usual casual way, he was sitting at his desk. I noticed another person, a Scotsman in a kilt, who I did not recognise, sitting on a low chair off to my right. Bruce smiled at me, asked how I was doing in his normal friendly manner and introduced the gentleman on my right as Mr Berry, RSM of The Black Watch, a very old and proud Scottish Infantry Regiment. Bruce told me Mr Berry would like to have a chat with me before he left the room leaving Mr Berry and I alone.

I was unsure what this was all about. Mr Berry stood up, silently he adjusted his kilt, placed his Scots Hat complete with Red Hackle on his head, grasped his pace stick firmly in his right hand marched to in front of me, stamped his feet in the old 1-23-1 way and stood motionless staring at me.

I began to feel distinctly uneasy, pulled my feet together and slid into a position of attention. I knew some good old traditional military flak was heading straight towards me. Then Mr Berry embarked on the finest bollocking of my twelve-year career.

Screaming like a lunatic at about an inch distance Scots manufactured spittle spraying my face, unpleasant warm fetid breath wafting over me. I was informed in the loudest and highest pitched foul torrent of filthy expletives that I was fucking useless, too shit to be a soldier, that I should be jailed, that I was unfit to wear the Queens uniform, that I should be bust of my rank, that I should have died at birth, that I should be made an example of, and on and on it went, for what seemed like an aeon.

His last scream at me was – 'TWENTY FUCKING EXTRAS" - and he marched out of the office stamping his feet as hard as he possible could. He didn't even close the door behind him. I looked through the glass paned wall behind me and I could see about ten of the civilian workshop men just standing staring open mouthed. I had been well bollocked, 'premiership level', but in good army fashion I didn't know what the bollocking was for. Nor did I know where the twenty extras would be. A bit confused and a bit shaken I turned to leave the ASM's office when Bruce walked back in. 'Coffee'? He asked with a smile!

4TH BOLLOCKING – PREMIERSHIP

Over a mug of coffee with a civilised un-shouting, pleasant Artificer Sergeant Major and my Hammer/ Sledge Throwing partner, I learned that the previous night the armoury at the School of Infantry had been left unlocked by the duty arms storeman and the felony had been discovered by the Regimental Police. The Sgt guard commander was bust to Corporal, the arms storeman was jailed, and I had twenty. I didn't do the twenty, Bruce saw to that. He was amused and he had agreed the course of action with Mr Berry. Would I like to meet Mr Berry again? No thanks.

Character building? Hell yes!

Warminster Rugby

Rugby was plentiful at Warminster. I played for Warminster RFC for a season. They were a great social side based at the 'Bunch of Grapes" pub in the town centre. There was a fair mix of civilians and soldiers in the team, and we all got on well. Frank Leatherbarrow of the Irish Guards and Graham Cory Trevorrow of the Coldstream's made up an abrasive, formidable and very sizeable second row. We were a reasonably successful side and played against all the Wiltshire towns in the area. The military influence in the club was tangible. Consequently, the Warminster RFC club benefitted immensely from the use of military amenities by way of pitches, changing rooms and cookhouse food. It was a very convivial agreement.

In addition to the town rugby, I organised and Captained the School of Infantry rugby team who played every Wednesday. The strength of the side varied from week to week depending what young officers were on courses at the school, sometimes we were very strong and at other times ...well, not so strong.

Elderly Scots Gent – My Arse

The School of Infantry team used to meet at midday at the Infantry Demonstration Battalion guardroom. I would then book transport, sort the side out, pick players, allocate kit, and so on. One day an elderly Scots gent, that's elderly in army terms, he was probably in his late thirties, approached me while we were arranging at the guardroom.

He asked me if I was Taff Rees and I replied in the affirmative. He asked me if there was any chance of a game that afternoon. I asked his position; he said prop and I made a quick assessment and formed the opinion he was far too old for rugby; he'd never keep up and we could do without him. I told him to hang around, my regular players would get in first and if there was a space, he could probably sub. He agreed, and he sat there quietly. As it transpired, we

needed an extra front row player so with a little reservation I told him he was in for the full game; a huge smile broke across his face.

I recall it was an away game against one of the regular infantry battalions at Bulford Camp. The old Scots prop of whom I had stereotyped as too old, and well beyond his best played an absolute blinder. He had it all pure rugby nous, fitness, strength, skills he had everything, and had it in spades.

I was well impressed and chatting with him in the bar later discovered his name was Dave 'Jock' Geddes. He was I believe originally Royal Army Pay Corps but transferred into the Royal Regiment of Wales just to play more rugby. He was a class act and a great guy. The RRW were fortunate to have such a player.

Lesson learned by me as a relatively new Rugby Captain, never, ever, judge a book by its cover.

Playing at Warminster was fine, but the lure of Welsh Valley Rugby was ever stronger. One weekend while

I was at home (we did not work weekends except for the rare duty at Warminster), I was in my local rugby club Rhigos RFC, and they needed a player, and I was asked if I would like a game. I borrowed some kit and played in the first XV and it was good fun. After the game the club Captain, Howard Williams, asked me if I was available for the following Saturday. I gave it short consideration, told him I was too far away (ninety-six miles, a two-hour drive), to train regularly but I could make most Saturdays. That was it, I was a first team regular from then on. Rhigos in that era were a fabulous side. They had reformed a year or two before under the guidance of none other than Mr Dai Morris, the 'Shadow' himself. Thirty-four Welsh caps and a living rugby legend. Most of the players had played at decent levels and as a village side we punched well above our weight, taking on much bigger clubs and scalping a few ground records along the way.

At about this time I found myself at Arborfield playing in a REME Corps trial. It was up to this point the highest level of army rugby that I played. The REME CORPS rugby was much stronger than Warminster more akin to Rhigos, though a different style and ethos.

First REME CORPS Game

After attending a REME Corps trial match I was successful in being selected for the Corps side in an upcoming game against Sandhurst officer training college.

I didn't know any of the REME Corps players, I had just turned twenty-one and they all seemed to be a lot older than me. We gathered at Sandhurst, and I wore the Corps strip for the first time. Red shirt with REME badge and black shorts, red, blue, and yellow socks the REME colours.

For some reason, probably through my relatively young service I had a notion the Sandhurst Officers would be gentleman and play a very public-school type of rugby. On reflection I didn't know what public

school type rugby was. I was playing on the tight side, and I learned that the officer against whom I would be propping had been involved in the England setup somewhere along the way, not a full cap, but youth or seconds. First scrum and the gentleman officer against whom I'm propping takes it upon himself to gouge my eyes. I was slightly taken aback; this is the sort of thing I'd encountered at Ynysybwl RFC or Treorchy RFC back in the valleys. I was taken aback not because of the gouging act, or the violence of the event, but because in my mind he was supposed to be a gentleman and hadn't acted like one. It was no big deal and he got as good as he gave and quite a bit more.

So, my first Corps game, I had played decently, got well around the pitch and importantly I managed to put the pressure on my opposite number and I, that'll be me, was successful in taking two against the head. We won the game.

Following the game there was drinks and food in a cricket pavilion type building alongside the pitch. It was very pucker. The environment was new to me, lots of high-ranking brass and even the beer was drunk from half pint pots with handles.

HANDLED HALVES - HOW PUBLIC SCHOOL IS THIS?

I sat quietly without speaking to anyone. Near me was our hooker and team Captain Wayne 'Taff' Cullen from Pontypridd way. I listened to him tell a Brigadier, I didn't know who the Brigadier was, how he had personally taken two against the head despite the best efforts of the opposition. Taff Cullen was a decent player, and I would play alongside him many times, but those were my 'two', I had done all the work from haranguing the scrum half, pressure and lowering of my opposing number, stopping the hooker from signalling to the scrum half when to put the ball and striking and winning the fifty-fifty ball. It was my first 'Corps' game. They were my two and my credit was being claimed elsewhere. Every day is a school day. The only consolation was a Colonel, I didn't know who he was, I think REME, came and chatted with me and complimented me on my game. It became clear you had to play a good game off as well as on the field. I would never be any good at 'off the field' playing. No matter, I had played for the REME Corps side and would do so many more times both in the UK and mostly in BAOR.

A memorable hard game at this time for the REME CORPS was versus London New Zealand (or London All Blacks as they liked to be called). It was the era of 'rucking' meaning everything above grass

height was kicked to death. I recall it was an exceptionally hot day, the ground was very hard as was the New Zealand style of rugby. Tony Anthwhistle scored a fab try for us. It was a memorable tough game, thoroughly enjoyable.

Warminster for three years was fabulous, a cushy unit, rugby on Wednesdays for the REME Corps or the School of Infantry RFC, Rhigos RFC on Saturdays. It couldn't be better.

Whilst at Warminster my good friend Steve Ogarra, a very formidable Widnes No 8, joined the unit and when I moved my rugby playing to Rhigos he came along also, playing alongside Dai Morris in the back row. Steve earned himself a solid reputation at Rhigos as an uncompromising No. 8 and was well liked by all.

4th Unit - 3rd Battalion the Queens Regiment

The 3rd Battalion the Queens Regiment was London recruited. It was a mechanised infantry battalion with its main equipment being the 432 Armoured Personnel Carrier (APC). It also is one of the first units to be issued with the Warrior Armoured Fighting Vehicle.

I'm posted to the 3 Queens LAD, stationed at Bad Fallingbostel. I knew the area reasonably well as I'd spent three years at Hohne which was about thirty miles away around the concrete range road which I had travelled many times, often with 'convoy lob' towing tanks and backloading military vehicles for repair and modification.

I was to manage the small Recovery section and the LAD motor transport. The OC was a REME Captain named Tony Anthwhistle. I'd played Corps rugby with him in the UK. He was a decent second row and a decent officer.

I had a separate small workshop containing our AEC recovery wagon and we had stores for all the motor transport essentials, jerry cans, flags, jacks, camouflage nets and so on.

Gary Penman was the Craftsman Recy Mech a likeable character who was ably managed by his wife Yvonne. 'Rem' was our driver.

The battalion was one of the first to be equipped with Warrior, an armoured fighting vehicle, and they still had a sizeable collection of 432 Armoured Personnel Carriers. The battalion was London recruited and they were very, very strong on boxing, good on football and sometimes enthusiastic about rugby.

Tragically, just after receiving the first Warrior, and prior to my arrival, the battalion had lost an officer in an accident inside a vehicle hangar. The officer was inside the vehicle command seat when the driver moved the Warrior forward out of the hangar and the officers head was caught between a low ceiling beam and the upright commander's cupola-hatch. A very expensive and tragic fatal lesson learnt.

Recovery within the unit didn't present the more frequent and hardy jobs I was used to with main battle tanks. Most recoveries were managed with a six-wheel drive AEC Wrecker and steel towbars or tow ropes. Track and wheel bashing was also much lighter.

What I did find particularly irksome was putting camouflage nets on the AEC. The AEC is quite a large vehicle and requires a large camouflage net. Moreover, the AEC has lots of bits that stick out of it which the cam-net would catch on. Wet or snow-covered cam net removal is a total arse pain. Oh, for a farmer's barn or factory shed to park in on exercise.

The LAD had its own bar in the basement of one of the barrack blocks. It was typical of LAD bars. Managed by a few volunteers we had some fab evenings in there. We also performed some

Christmas shows. The usual totally amateur military production which are only funny if you're in the unit and know the characters portraying or being portrayed. All military shows are fabulous, and all are more fabulous the more drink is drunk. The cost of the drink and fags was ridiculously low and there was always plenty.

One of the company commanders called me to his office one day and asked me to help with the battalion rugby team. They had a few decent players, mostly officers, but the rank and file were more football. I arranged a rugby match game between the REME LAD and the battalion. This would give a clue as to where we stood. I was a known rugby player in the LAD and there was a Cornishman named Bob Tregellis. He was a fabulous hooker, one of the best I played with in the army. He deserved much more army representative recognition than he ever got. I hope he went on to do well.

I supplemented the LAD team with a few ringers from 7 Armoured Workshop, who were a full Major REME unit and had a very strong rugby team. Take a bow Tony Hibbert, Phil Hope, and a few others. It was a fab game and resulted in a tight win for the battalion. We had a rugby dinner in the evening, the sort of thing the Army and Rugby does so well. I was sitting alongside officers from the battalion, and they were absolutely gentlemen. It was probably the first officer company I had enjoyed since joining.

One Wednesday sports afternoon the LAD were ordered out for a march. Full equipment, uniform, webbing, back packs, radios, section, and individual weapons, the whole full shamonka. Our water bottles were checked for fullness and all our required kit had to be present. Respirators were also required.

Off we went around the range-road. Hard concrete road with undulating slopes and hills. One hundred metres at the double, one hundred metres at the march, repeated endlessly. Respirators on and off

and on again. For eight miles. It was tough, hard going, shin splitting, hot dry and dusty with passing tanks and convoys chucking it all up in our faces. If we did it every day, then fair enough. But it was normally a three-mile run. The worst part of all was returning into camp and there were the infantry guys, the actual people whose job all this tough military stuff was, playing netball and having barbecues. Lucky bastards.

They jeered and whooped and piss-took with great joy. Can't say I blame them; we would probably have done the same.

Not long after this I was approached by a couple of fine gentlemen (If you can call REME Corps rugby players gentlemen) from 7 Armoured Workshop and invited for a discreet coffee with the Commanding Officer of the REME unit. Essentially, I was asked, in the nicest possible way, if I would consider a transfer to 7 Armoured Workshop: a Major all REME unit and famed for its quality of rugby. The Commanding

Officer Lt Col Rawlings was looking to bolster his rugby team and the addition of a REME Corps level front row forward would be most welcome. That would be me!

I mulled it over for a couple of days before deciding to make the move. Little did I know it would lead to the longest posting of my army career. The REME Captain, Tony Anthistle wasn't much impressed that I was leaving, but he would arrive at 7 shortly after to take up the post of Adjutant. He was a very good rugby player but chose not to play at 7. I only spent nine months with the Queens.

5th Unit - 7 Armoured Workshop

I WAS A 'DESERT RAT' - NEVER WAS I EVER IN A DESERT!

The armoured workshops provide second line support to the first line units. It's full of REME tradesmen. The recovery section has a lot of recovery vehicles and Recy Mechs. At a first line unit the Recy Mech is a valued tradesman's, invaluable to his unit and trusted to keep his vehicle and equipment operationally fit for purpose. He is appreciated and respected, particularly when operational or on active duty. At second line large REME workshops all this collective respect and value goes straight out the window.

There is seldom enough work to keep the Recy Mechs busy. There is a long standing saying that the REME are like manure. When they are spread around, they are useful and do a good job, and when they are together, they are just a pile of shit.

In large workshops Recy Mechs spend much of their time sweeping floors, painting vehicles, carrying out equipment checks. They spend a lot of time doing nothing. The senior ranks, Sergeants and staff Sergeants are in abundance and rather than being a recovery 'God' in, say a tank regiment, they are just a one in many, all competing for the boss's favour and their next promotion. Some so far up the bosses arse they could see their predecessors' feet. I knew very few Recy senior ranks that ever did any recovery when they were in a workshop. It was all left to the Corporals.

The workshop management was out of touch with the shop floor, the senior ranks had no more to do than chase another promotion and suck up to the

Recy Mech Warrant Officer (WORM). It was a pitiful place. As a measure of supporting my opinion, there were a lot of very experienced full Corporal Recy Mechs at 7 Armoured and not one of them, in the five years I was there, was promoted to Sergeant.

I guess it was the way the recovery unit was managed. How could people, the same qualifications, the same experience be so good at first line units and then devolve to utter tardiness and disarray at large workshops. I could give many examples of crapness, but I won't enjoy writing it nor will I embarrass people who may still be around.

Things got so bad, so untrusting and so disrespectful, in the Recy section, that the officer Lt Taylor assembled all the Recy Mechs together for what he called a 'Persian Parliament'. He explained that we could all speak freely and air our grievances and concerns and there would be no repercussions. The problem was all the issues lay with the senior ranks and how most of them treated the troops very badly. Those same senior ranks were in the meeting and if we aired a grievance, they would know who it was, and they were of the ilk there would be repercussions and undoubtably more of the same. I remember looking across the room at two senior and very competent Scots Corporals Shuggy and Willy, and we all shook our heads slightly; not a word was coming from us. There was no trust.

There was a Warrant Officer who displayed absolute favouritism to a very few, at the expense of others, it was very unfair. Unfair on those missing out on normal deserved due favour and unfair on those being shown favouritism because of the flak they then had to take from the rest of the troops. There was a Sergeant who would screw it up and then run to the Warrant Officer and blame junior ranks; the Warrant Officer would then shit all over the junior ranks. There was another Sergeant who hid vehicles and equipment's out of petty nastiness, or because he thought it funny, then when the blokes fell short because of the absence of gear he would deny it

leaving the guys in the shit. It was a rancid working environment.

Thank God for Kev Boulton and Jim McDonald the only two decent senior ranks there.

On this short and unsavoury subject on a personal level, I had issues with a S/Sgt who had a serious drink problem that he hid well. He needed EPC (A) for promotion. I had passed it as a Corporal, and he couldn't handle it. My passing it was nothing to do with him, and his failure to pass it was nothing to do with me. He was on my case about it often, frequent snide remarks and comments. He never did pass it. I had written a substantial technical paper entitled "REME Recovery Participation at Royal Engineered Reserve Demolitions and Bridge Crossings". It was based on my own experiences and considerations'. I had to submit it for approval to the S/Sgt who was my line manager. After submitting it I returned to his office to check he had forwarded it, I didn't trust him. He wasn't there, but my work was in the bin. I'm

convinced to this day it was all above him and beyond his level of competence and within his level of petty envy. Twat!

I rescued it from the bin and circumvented him and gave it to an officer who submitted it through proper channels to the 'Army Technical Suggestions and Awards Committee', where such suggestions went.

I received the following reply from Brigadier Webber-

> *'The committee were impressed by your approach to the problem. And recognised the technical initiative you have displayed and the trouble you have taken in developing it'.*

I was consequently awarded a substantial sum of money for my initiative, and an endorsement on my record of service. Remember, he, who was envious of my EPC(A), who I knew was as secret drinker, had binned it. Twat again!

For all the unnecessary shit at 7 the blokes were fantastic, and I made many lifelong friends. The young Recy Mechs posted in were keen and eager to learn, they were fortunate to have decent Recy Mech Corporals to put them right and show the way. Willy, Shuggy, Les, Glen were all well experienced and very good at their trade and I know many of the youngsters went on to full and successful careers.

Instructing at 7

I found myself as an instructor at 7 working on Samsons Pride a three to two upgrader course for craftsmen Recy Mechs, it was held in the 'Ulu' at Soltau. I intended for my group to do well, it was a matter of personal pride, it always was. I would help them as much as I could, and hopefully we could get 'best crew'. It was up to the individual students to get best Recy Mech, no doubt being on the best crew would help.

I had a decent crew to work with, Ian Macdonald was noteworthy, but they all put lots of effort in, the dump crew weren't getting the better of us. I personally held the Recy Mech senior ranks in poor esteem as they weren't quality men. While driving up to the exercise area I was the passenger in a Leyland Wrecker and as such I had a vantage seat. In the cab with me was the driver, a course member, and Ken Smallacombe an Australian REME Recy Mech Sgt who was on an attachment with us. Ken was a decent enough guy, we chatted often, and I know he was perplexed by the senior rank antics. Apparently, it wouldn't be allowed back in Oz. A second recovery wrecker was following with student crew aboard.

As we were travelling along, I saw a car that had come off the road and had overturned. I caused the Leyland to stop, ran down to the car and I could see a person inside. I reached through the broken window, touched the man and he was stone cold dead. There was beer scattered around and a strong smell of drink. I called the crew down from the wrecker. I formed a line and conducted a near area search, somebody might have struggled from the vehicle; best to be safe. I sent another soldier along to call the civilian police. the police arrived and we had to give a few statements there and then. All in all, we were delayed for an hour. When cleared by the German police we continued to our training area.

On arriving at the training area, the Warrant Officer called me over and asked why we were late. I explained the situation and for my efforts I got a Major bollocking.

5TH BOLLOCKING – FOR FUCKS SAKE WHAT WAS I SUPPOOSED TO DO?

For fucks sake! What was I supposed to do? Ignore the body? Just continue to drive by. Ignore the German police and tell them to go to hell? I couldn't win. By any measure I had done the right thing and got a bollocking. If it was a one off, no issue, but it was typical of the attitude of the people running the Recy Section.

It had been a tough day on the course, and we were told that the chefs, god bless em', had prepared food and it was being brought out in dixies. Hot food would be fab, we were working in snow and ice. The crews were wet and tired and hot food and drink makes the difference. The land rover arrives being driven by two of the Recy Mech Sergeants. They have got the blokes in a queue to receive their hot food. The back of the Landrover is thrown open and there is only one dixie of hot food. There is however a pile of ration boxes which the senior ranks take delight in throwing to the floor at the feet of the crews. The senior ranks then, in front of the wet and very cold crews, proceed to eat the hot food.

Arseholes. There was no need for it; none. It wasn't that the food was in ration boxes, it was that hot food was promised, wasn't delivered and that the twats revelled in the situation, feasting in front of the lads. I had seen similar obnoxious behaviour by RD staff on my SMC course. What was the point of it. Small minded people revelling in their own spite and inadequacy. I never ever treated people like shit!

I could immediately see the crew's heads were down, they had worked hard and didn't deserve this drivel. I took my crew to one side and told them we were having a feast. I got them to build a table from gangplanks and anchor pins. We 'bow' ties from oily rags, cook the rations with as much care and presentation as possible and took turns to waiter serve each other in the finest style. We played it up 'putting on the ritz'. Morale was recovered. I know some of the crews had a humour loss over it and morale hit the deck. That group of senior ranks, were tossers, not all of them, but the majority;

Leadership? My arse!

More instruction duty at 7. They decided to run Armoured Fighting Vehicle courses. Myself and Glyn Mountjoy, a top soldier, and CORPS rugby player, were on the first one. We helped devise and advised on the course as we went along until we had something tangible to teach. It was the usual stuff for armoured vehicles. Driving, supply, map reading, camouflage, radio skill all bread and butter to us. Thereafter I was an instructor on the course that the usual Sergeants had claimed the credit for putting together. My arse again!

I was getting pissed off with the army. I was at the top of the tree in my trade and soldiering wise. I couldn't be any more qualified, in fact I was in some way overqualified. From a REME soldiering perspective I had successfully done everything, and I was having to put up with the petty antics of a group of low-quality senior ranks. My view was that if you carry rank, at any level, then use the rank to support the troops; teach, train, support, cajole, encourage and endeavour to get them to do their best. Above all leadership and importantly leading by example. Just lead for fucks sake! I just didn't want to be like them. My attention was being drawn back to considering a police career.

Map Reading

The Corporal instructors on Samsons Pride were allocated different recovery subjects to teach to the students prior to moving to the practical phase. I was allocated recovery theory and map reading. Recovery theory is straight forward Recy Mech maths, formulas to work out 'pull' requirements. No issue!

Military map-reading is much more diverse. A lot of Recy Mechs and other soldiers didn't get the full value of understanding of how much work could be saved by being skilfully adept at map reading a vitally important skill. Recy Mechs need to have solid map reading ability, certainly the usual skills and

knowledge; an added crystal-ball is occasionally useful and should be issued as part of the recovery vehicle standard kit.

Often, the location of vehicles needing the Recy Mechs skill set is straight forward. It could be a six or eight figure grid reference, or a particular pub car park, or along a stretch of a main road between two towns. No problem, if not exact a short time searching may be fruitful.

Such clarity was regularly not the case. Often a location is 'somewhere between here and here!'. Or it was last seen about here! as a large greasy black thumb is pressed into a map, or 'Well this is where it was supposed to be!'.

The regular skills are useful, but we learn to study the map from the perspective of recovery. The lie of the ground, hills and undulations, water such as rivers, lakes, and marches. Railway tracks, woods, ravines, urban and industrial areas. All the different features require their methods of negotiation.

Add to the mix that your vehicle weighs at least fifty ton, maybe over a hundred if towing, enter a whole new ball game, driving in darkness on the "Ulu" ups the 'anti' even more-so. Stars are good, especially the North Star, direct left or right, towards or away from and you'll be on a known general course. While calculating from the North star enjoy the view of hundreds of satellites traversing the night sky, but don't try to follow them. The sun rises in the east and sets in the west. Moss grows on the north side of trees. Water runs downhill.

A twenty-ton bridge weight limit is what it says on the tin. Soft verges have been the demise of many a tank or heavy lorry journey. A low bridge or weight limitation may require a twenty-mile detour. A quarry or large building such as a barn or factory, are good places to hide vehicles. Better to know all these things at the outset. Bridging maps, terrain maps, ordnance survey maps are all useful, without common sense and experience they are nothing.

Consider this. You are driving your ARV on the 'Ulu', it's been raining as it always was, but its stopped and the night sky is clear. You are on a well-worn single tank track in a forest, tall trees either side of you. The water on the track has pooled deep, three or four feet is some places. You are towing a main battle tank and the tank crew as well as yours are atop the ARV. Other than the stars above you can see anything. You can hear the Commander in your headphones, and he is telling you he can't see anything either. The other sounds are the comforting assurance of the engine be it diesel, or petrol; the sloshing of the tank's tracks through water; I imagine it a bit like being at sea at night with the ship's bough slicing through waves.

How do you navigate? Well, you look up at the sky, hopefully seeing the stars. Your focus is on the slightly different darkness shade between the trees and the night sky. It's your only reference point and it needs concentrating on because it's easily lost. While you are looking almost directly up, you are not

looking down or where you are going. The water sloshes and your thoughts turn to; how deep? Is there a ravine? Will I see a change of course? Is there another 'blacked-out' tank stationary in the track?

Sometimes at night in the darkness, dry dirt reflects moonlight and looks like water. More than once I've stopped sharply (brakes permitting) much to the discomfort of my crew; hips jolted against armour and brews spilled. Foul mouthed people those recovery crews, with an excellent wide-ranging vocabulary of piercing profanities.

Character building? Hell yes!

Methods of Instruction

I get packed off to the Defence School of Languages at Beaconsfield to attend a Methods of Instruction course. It's an all-arms course and is about a fortnight long. The idea is to equip the attendees with rudimentary methods of instructing; if they understood the subject matter, they could teach it. I didn't know it at the time but the skills I learnt were to stand me in excellent stead for my entire career in the army and beyond. Probably the most useful course I attended in the military. The course assembled and most were infantry. There were also two WRAC ladies on the course.

The accommodation was old and had been used to accommodate Captured high ranking Nazi officers during the war. It had been a top-secret establishment. The school now taught many languages such as Russian, Chinese, Arabic, and anything else the army required. English was also taught there particularly to Gurkhas and other nationalities who had such a requirement.

Everybody knew the Gurkhas were present as the camp was pervaded throughout with the twenty-four-hour smell of Gurkha curry. In the cookhouse at one end of the hotplate was a huge cauldron in which the Gurkha food was cooked and served from. It continuously simmered away and as far as I could tell it was just added to. The Gurkhas ate from it for every meal, breakfast, lunch, and dinner. I bravely investigated the pot once and I saw fins, teeth, beaks, and feathers and possibly some scales all slowly swirling in a morass of different coloured liquids and pastes. I wasn't adventurous or brave enough to sample it. It was good fuel as the Gurkhas were constantly running everywhere.

The course instructor was a Major Thomas from a county infantry Regiment. He was an absolute gentleman. He had earned the Military Cross as a Lieutenant commanding his battalion mortar platoon in Korea. Apparently, the Chinese were attacking in their thousands, and despite overwhelming odds, the battalion had beaten off the attack; he had played a crucial role in the action directing mortar fire. Sometimes during the course, he would lapse a little in his concentration and look off into the distance. We assumed he was looking across that Korean landscape, bless him!

On the last Thursday of the course, we all agreed to meet in the bar for a farewell beer or two. I had 'palled' up with a soldier from the 'Queens Own Highlanders', Jock; I know, it's an original name. He was a Corporal in their mortar platoon. We got on very well and on the last evening he went to the bar to get our drinks. He returned with a bottle of 'Famous Grouse' and two glasses. Oh dear! I later I bought the same round also. Oh dear, again! The detail of evening remains a vague memory. Jock had a letter 'W' tattooed on each of his buttocks; he showed everybody in the bar. The WRAC ladies were very impressed. 'WOW' they said together!

Helicopter Handler

7 Armoured sent me off to RAF Gutersloh to do a 'Helicopter Handlers' course. Apparently, every Major unit needed to have a helicopter handler and I was going to be ours. My only clue was what I had learned during NI training with the 14/20th a few years before.

I was the only REME soldier on the course, the other twelve or fifteen were infantry and gunners from various regiments and battalions.

The course was taught by RAF Corporals and very knowledgeable they were too. A lot of the course work was technical stuff with which I was well familiar with being REME. There were essentially three elements to the course.

Firstly, there was 'Underslung loads'; The British forces like to carry equipment's around by helicopter, giving them range, speed, and accessibility to difficult and normally inaccessible areas. Equipment's were vehicles, light tanks, artillery, generators, land rovers, a very wide range of stuff. Whatever can't be fitted into a helicopter can be underslung beneath it. If the helicopter can lift the weight the equipment travels. There's a manual that gives precise information about each established piece of military equipment. What strops and chains to use, where and how they are attached. The load needed to be appropriate, secure, and balanced. The fixings had to be sure and firm. The last thing wanted was for equipment's to fall away (they have done so), or for strops to break and wrap around the helicopter causing it to crash (that has happened). Smaller or irregular items could be placed in nets or baskets and underslung in a similar fashion.

When helicopter blades slice through the air the friction generates static electricity which remains in the frame and body of the aircraft. Consequently, the aircraft, helicopter aircraft that is, must be earthed before the slings and strops are attached to up to three hooks on the belly of the aircraft.

Here is a common scenario –

You are tasked with preparing an eight-ton vehicle for air lifting by Chinook; it could lift to twelve tons. You set about rigging the vehicle ensuring you have the right straps and strops and spend a good while securing the vehicle and checking for competence and safety. It's dark, it's cold, and it's raining (it's always raining), and you are operating tactically. You and one other are standing atop the vehicle holding up the straps which are attached to the loops that you are going attach to the load bearing hooks on the belly of the Chinook. Your fingers are freezing, almost numb, they always are, it's the army way!

You are wearing thick rubber gloves and holding a very big copper earthing probe. Trailing from the end of the probe is a copper cable down to a spike driven into the ground. The Chinook can be heard long before is seen, a deep resonating Wop, Wop, Wop. It gets louder and louder. A team member is on the ground alongside you, and he is there to give signals to the pilot to guide him in for the 'earthing and hooking'. In daylight it's hand signals, at night its dim torchlight.

The Chinook, deafeningly, moves slowly in on you, literally 'on you'. You are about twelve foot above the ground, in deafening noise, with a massive twenty-ton double-rotor helicopter hovering inches or less above your head down to the point of contact. The down-wash is smashing into you pushing you down to the ground, any accompanying rain or snow or dust is accelerated to hundreds of miles per hour; and it's all coming your way. The Chinook, moving at stunned-slug speed, takes an age to get close enough, it's got to be close enough to touch-to-earth.

The wind is beating, the noise is unbelievable, the buffeting is knackering, all you can see is the dark mass of the huge machine edging closer and closer. You are willing it on, you must make 'earth' before touching the Chinook or you'll be off in an ultra-bright flash of yellow and orange sparks before lying on the floor in a singed, smoking heap. No fun there; no ambition for that. After an exhausting eternity the giant Chinook arrives on plot, arms reach above your head, you reach out and hammer the probe onto the belly hook. Throwing the probe to the side, you and your equally uncomfortable and stressed colleague loop the strops and straps over the belly hook(s). The wind continues to crush, you catch a fleeting glance of a helmeted and microphoned crewman through the open floor hatch of the Chinook. You think he gives you a thumbs up. You start to climb down, the cyclonic draught from the massive rotors helps you along the way and you crash onto the floor, scrambling and rolling away. All your senses urging you along. Standing a few yards clear you hear the Chinook start to take the strain. The engine pitch becomes deeper and faster, the helicopter noise becomes firmer and industrial like and slowly, very slowly the great beast starts to rise and move forward, slowly but surely gaining height and speed. Within minutes it has gone, noise, wash and cargo receding into the darkness. You are left with a gentle patter of soft rain and a cooling breeze as your breath and adrenalin levels ease. Thank fuck for that!

Character building? Hell yes.

Secondly, there's Troops on and Troops Off – for reasons that need no explaining the British military like to carry troops around in helicopters. There are a couple of principles that must be adhered to. The embarking and debussing must be orderly and disciplined. The ultimate control rests with the aircrew. Always approach with line of sight of the aircrew and at their behest. Be very careful on slopes, the rotors may be twelve feet off the ground on one side and only four or five feet off on the other; flat ground is always best.

Hanging out of helicopters and sliding down long ropes into battle is for Hollywood and elite special forces. Good luck to them.

The third and final element of the course was the making and preparing of helicopter landing sites. Although helicopters go up and down, the preferred method is to fly in and out much like fixed wing aircraft. I guess it saves on fuel and gives better vision to the pilots. Finding suitable ground was interesting and laying 'landing lights' was also thought provoking. Over the years I made several landing sites and the lining up of vehicles with headlights on seemed to be the preferred and simplest option.

Log-Pot

Exercise Log Pot. Short for Logistics Potential. Somewhere a high-ranking person sitting behind a desk thought it would be a good idea to invent an exercise where the ability of the logistics arms could be tested to assess their fighting potential. He called it, with army originality, Exercise Log Pot.

I must have been out of favour with my boss at the time, I never was a in favour, because I was chosen to be a section commander for this novel endeavour. I was given eight soldiers to command, fortunately mostly Recy Mechs, who were probably the most soldier-like of REME soldiers. A big bonus for my section was Gaz Eckett, who had transferred to REME, to be a Recy Mech, from the 2nd Parachute Battalion (2 Para). Infantry soldiering had been his bread and butter for several years.

We had a month's training before the actual exercise, which was to be a competition. There would be teams of REME, RAOC, RCT, Intelligence

Corps, ACC, and anybody else they could think of who didn't want to be there.

The exercise would consist of shooting, tactics, camouflage, map reading, defensive positions, making camp, field cooking, night moves, attacks and defences, NBC environments. Practically the full gambit of fighting skills.

Although I was the section commander, I was wise to give Gaz practically full reign. He knew his stuff and knew it well. We took his advice and ditched a lot of stuff we didn't need to carry as there would be a lot of route marches and physically demanding stuff. One shirt, half a towel and so on. As lightweight as possible carrying only necessary stuff. So, we trained.

We fired thousands of rounds at different ranges on different ranges, we skirmished and zig-zagged the world, we threw ourselves over assault courses, we bivvied (camped) in fields, ditches, barns, sheds, woods, and hedges. Gas, Gas, Gas repeatedly. We set map reading challenges, we camouflaged ourselves and everything else. We section attacked every building, barn, trench, hill, garage, vehicle, and object we could find. We threw thunder-flashes, lobbed smoke grenades, fired schermulies (parachute flares). We forded rivers and streams, swam lakes, climbed trees and buildings, and vehicles. We fought-through, fought-around, consolidated, regrouped, replenished, time and time again. We jogged and ran miles and miles. Eventually the exercise Log Pot was upon us.

On arrival we had to report one by one to a table where our kit was checked. As section commander I was first. At this table we had our kit checked to make sure we had all we needed, there were marks for this; it was a competition. Also, at this table we had to strip and reassemble our SLRs', it was timed. So, this soldier is standing in front of me with a stopwatch, and he says 'GO'. I strip my SLR, I've stripped and reassembled it a thousand times in the last month. I can do it blindfolded. I can do it under a blanket. I can do it taking all the parts from with a sealed box by touch alone. And I can do it very quickly indeed. So, this chap with the stopwatch is watching and his eyes can't keep up with me, I strip the SLR to its component parts in seconds. It's not a great skill, it's just practice. He looks at me surprised and says, 'Fucking Hell, how did you do that'? He forgets to stop the stopwatch, so I must do it again.

This time he measures it, and it's a good time. I'm in the lead which is easy because I'm first! If he thinks I'm fast he's in for a surprise because there are blokes in my section much quicker than me. One after the other my section goes through the first task, at the end of which we are in the lead. It's a good omen, well done boys.

The exercise rolls on and we are in the lead or thereabouts throughout, our training is paying off. We pick up a lot of points on a deep river crossing thanks to Gaz. He has brought black bags with him. The water is deep. We strip off, put our kit inside the black bags, blow them up, place our rifles on top of the floating bags and we dog paddle across, we put our dry clothes back on and we are checked by the staff for all our equipment; dryness is a bonus.

Keeping dry in the wet.

Our shooting and assault course traverse is good. Who can map read better than Recy Mechs? nobody that's who. Radios are spot on as are NBC tests. We ate the assault course. Our team finished in second place from about sixty teams. Well done boys. Thanks Gaz. When we get back to the unit is there a 'Well done' or any other such acknowledgement. Not a chance.

Character building? Hell yes!

REME v The USA v The Welsh Guards

It is decided we will take a selection of our ARV's onto Hohne Ranges and fire our mounted machine guns. 7.62mm General Purpose Machine Gun (GPMG) pronounced 'Jimpy' was fitted to the Chieftains, and Browning .30 Medium Machine Guns, pronounced 'three-oh!' mounted on the centurions. We have the guns; we have the mountings fitted to the ARV's. We have the means of securing the guns to the mounts with, believe it or not, mounting pins. We have thousands of rounds of belted ammunition, including tracer. We have crews who have fired the guns not mounted on the ARV's. We have the crews to fire the guns fitted in the mountings on the ARV's. What we haven't got are crews who have fired the guns while they are fitted in the mountings on the ARV's.

To add a bit of competitive interest, on the apron of the range we are allocated there are 12 parallel stands, we are allocated four on the left, Americans are allocated four in the centre and the Welsh Guards have the four on the right. It's a fully packed apron.

The first thing we find is that the mounts on the Centurions are useless. Apparently, they had been cannibalised off Saladin armoured cars and were supposed to fit. Even the armourers on the range with us were unable to help so we had tripods for the three-Oh's and fired them off those; either free standing on the roof of the Arv's or by just placing the tripod mounts on the floor at the front of the ARV's. The accuracy was ok as they were famously reliable machine guns. When I say ok, I meant the bullets went forward down the range. I don't know if we hit anything.

The Chieftain mountings were less than useless. We could fit the guns to the mounting, but once mounted there was no way the firer could get in any position to use the gun safely and accurately. The sights fitted, again cannibalised from old army vehicles, just didn't marry the mount with the gun. Useless. The best we could do was sit atop the ARV alongside the GPMG point it down the range and hope for the best. We were however, being entertained by the Americans alongside us.

They had every conceivable firearm from little ones to big ones. Where our ammunition was contained in about four boxes in the stowage bins of each of our ARV's, the American vehicles each had a separate trailer stacked high with ammo parked up behind each of their vehicles. The American vehicles were Bradley fighting vehicles and compared to our solitary machine guns each Bradley had a missile system, a chain gun system, a very big machine gun, five-oh, I think, and little guns like ours. They had everything and tons of ammo. Mind you they were, unlike us, fighting vehicles.

The Welsh Guards, on the other hand, appeared to have less than us. They had arrived in a couple of four tonner lorries and set about mounting about six

GPMG's to large tripods, bigger tripods than ours, on the soft ground just at the front of the apron. There were about four Guardsmen to each gun. Behind each gun they stacked many boxes of belted ammunition. They appeared much more professional and soldierlike than the Americans, and certainly more so than us.

Eventually the range was opened, and we were cleared to fire. We fired first. The good thing was that our bullets were going forward from our vehicles. That was about it! We were unpractised with the guns; the mounts were less than useless. We were firing over open sights at 'figure' targets a couple of hundred yards downrange. If we hit anything it was luck; we may have scared some. We adjusted our aim by watching the fall of the tracer rounds, about one glowing red shot in every six. We were more accurate with the ground mounted three-Oh's than with the Jimpy's loosely mounted on the Chieftains. Our plan evolved to getting shot of all our ammunition as quickly as we possible could and get out of there. It didn't take long, minutes in fact, as we packed away the Americans opened with all they had.

FUCKING HELL! It was like a firepower demonstration. There didn't seem to be any order, or target even. They just fired round after round after round. It was quite a cacophony of exploding gunpowder and clattering expended shells. The missiles whooshed off with a roar and the five-Oh's thumped mightily making the small chatter of their smaller guns unimpressive. They seemed to shoot endlessly. It was difficult to see what they were aiming at. Their shot blasted off in all directions forward without appearing to hit anything. The missiles didn't strike any of the targets we could see and seemed to fall just about anywhere. They were still partying when the Welsh Guards joined the fray.

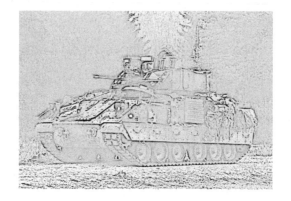

THE BRADLEY FIGHTING VEHICLE IOS AN EXCELLENT COFFEE MACHINE

The Welsh Guards were a whole different ball game. They had appeared to spend some time setting up their guns, sighting them in, measuring ranges and preparing their firing points. Although having six guns at about five-yard intervals they opened-up independently, and in order. The guns fired at the same place which looked to be a road intersection about a mile distant. I was watching the line of tracer and fall of shot, which was unwavering. Each gun took its turn and fired at the same distant crossroads. After all, six Jimpy's had fired independently they all fired simultaneously. Unexcited, no fuss they just got on with it. Anything on the mile distant crossroads would have been obliterated, or at the very least an enemy denied the ground. Had it been us REME trying to do the same the enemy could have had a picnic on the crossroads, and if it had been the yanks; well, who knows!

Later I chatted with the Americans and the Guards. The Americans were new to Germany and had picked up a lot of surplus ammo from the unit they had taken over from and the 'sell-by' date was looming and they were disposing of it for administration purposes. The guards were running a machine gunners' course and this day's element was sustained fire. The Americans had by far the best coffee!

If I was scoring on the day, it would have looked like this (maximum of five)

	Welsh Guards	Recy Mechs	USA
Coffee	2	2	5
Knowledge	5	2	3
Accuracy	5	1	2
Professionalism	5	2	3
Total	17	7	13

Welsh Guards win. It was a fabulous experience, showing the contrast between the different units. The Welsh Guards and the Americans thoroughly enjoyed climbing all over out ARV's. however, it was unanimous that our British Army coffee was shite!

I can say, with certainty, if it was a battlefield recovery competition the REME would have been unbeatable. Horses for courses.

Character building? Hell yes!

Fallingbostel Anecdotes

London University Economics Students

One day at 7 students from the London School of Economics were visiting us. We were briefed to take four or five ARV's out onto the 'Ulu' and show the students over them and let them have a drive. The Recy Mechs were falling over themselves to get in on this as about half the students were very smart young ladies. Ever optimistic those Recy Mechs!

One of the young ladies was very striking. Let's came her Jane, a stunning well-proportioned brunette. Curvy, with tight jeans and massive personalities. She smiled and laughed and the Recy Mechs were falling over themselves to impress her with their recovery prowess and knowledge. The students, Recy Mechs and Jane clambered over the ARV's asking questions, pulling levers, and switching switches.

455

Jane - an exceptional photographer

Jane had a very impressive and obviously expensive camera. It was in an equally expensive, quality camera bag, and she had many, many rolls of film. She photographed everything, the ARV's from every angle, the posing Recy Mechs, her fellow student, the 'Ulu' scenery, everything. There was no end to her photographic enthusiasm.

It was decided that the students would drive the ARV's for about a mile each. They were Chieftain ARV's, easier than driving a dodgem; we couldn't have done it with Centurions because of the driving complexity and time restraints.

Each ARV had one Recy Mech sitting atop the driver's hatch giving instructions to the student driver. The remainder of the students, about five or six on each ARV, sat atop the ARV's in the commanders' seat or on the decks. Off they went for an hour or so leaving about a dozen Recy Mechs behind for fags and tall-story time.

Jane, bless her, was the first of her group to drive. She found that the camera around her neck was very impracticable to wear in the ARV driver's position. There just wasn't the room for Jane and her camera, so she took her camera from around her neck and laid it on the ARV alongside her position. Shuggy McGurk, an erstwhile Scots Recy Mech was clearly concerned for Janes camera, and he told her that where she had placed it was unsafe and it may get damaged when the ARV bounced across the rough ground of the 'Ulu'. Shuggy, gentleman Recy Mech that he was, offered to look after it for her, to keep it safe from damage and he would give it back to her on her return. Jane flashed him a lovely smile, handed the camera over to Shuggy, lowered herself into the driver's seat and under the instruction, of I believe Andy Spiby, moved slowly off across the 'Ulu'.

The students had a fab time. They all had a go at driving, taking turns as the Recy Mech instructors guided them through the nuances and skills required to traverse rough ground, hills, slopes, water, and ruts and so on. After about an hour and a half the students returned to where the surplus Recy Mechs had been waiting. The students, mud splattered, some sore, but all happy enthused how much they had all enjoyed and they were assuring us that 'Recy-Meching' was the best job ever. Jane was ebullient and smiling and said she'd had a fabulous time and the Recy Mechs were great. Andy Spiby was grinning from ear to ear.

Jane collected her camera from Shuggy, and she asked if she could take a group photo of the students and the Recy Mechs together. Of course, she could. We set the ARV's up in the good old REME fashion of inverting two ARV's together and we all clambered on to the tops of them and adopted our best poses, students, and soldiers alike. Jane wanting to be in the photo also, placed her camera on a third facing ARV, set the timer, and clambered aboard to pose with the rest of us. How we laughed and joked while we counted the timer down. It was sure to be a fab photo and jane promised to send us copies when she had it developed in the UK. It was a fun day and we all returned safely back to our unit.

Following the student visit we often mused over Char in the Recy section what the reaction of the film processor at Janes chemist would be when he or she developed Janes films. There would be a selection of about twelve Recy Mech penises to compare, all from varying angles and at different sates of arousal. Pusks massive hanging foreskin would no doubt be commentated on with some amazement as it featured prominently.

Jane would also have this comparison dilemma when the lovely young lady received her photographs.

We further pondered and mused as to what the developers judgement of the Recy Mech anuses would reveal, particularly the ones apparently smoking cigarettes and one even drinking from a bottle of Herforder Pils.

Character building for Jane and the developer? Hell yes!

FAG BUTT!

Perinium – a New Word

We were on a range day and being taken to the range on the back of four tonners, as was the army way. We were dressed in full combats carrying weapons, mostly, if not all SLR's, the soldiers favourite rifle.

On arrival at the range, we dropped the tailboard of the four tonner and jumped down from the bed of the lorry. I was one of the first out. I heard a cluttering behind me, and I turned quickly and saw that one of the soldiers jumping from the lorry had dropped his rifle and it had hit the ground, butt on the floor, and had remained upright. The soldier, I've omitted his name for sensitivity reasons, followed a split-second later and straddled the rifle.

There was ear shattering scream. He had landed square on the upright rifle and driven by the full down-weight of his fall the rifle had entered his body between the back of his ball-bag and his anus, medically known as his 'perinium'.

461

The end of the steel barrelled rifle consists of a flash hider, which appears as a slatted tube forming the last four inches of the barrel. Also, on the end of the barrel is a steel 'bayonet-boss', used for securing a bayonet. Both the flash-hider and the 'bayonet-boss' had disappeared inside the soldier. He lay screaming on the floor, the rifle stuck fast between his legs.

An ambulance was called for, there was one allocated for the range day. I was mindful that the soldier would have to be taken to the medical centre. I could see there was a magazine attached to the rifle; why I don't know. I was also mindful it would be wise to 'clear' the rifle to make sure it was safe and not loaded with ammunition; particularly so, as there was a magazine attached.

Making a rifle safe involved the removing of the magazine, a simple clip to press, and no problem. The second part of making a rifle safe to open the 'working-parts' by pulling them to the rear with the cocking handle. This would automatically eject any round in the chamber and enable me to look in the chamber to see if any ammunition was present.

Mindful that about six inches of the rifle was stuck in the soldier I got one of the other soldiers to hold the rifle firm and still while I removed the magazine and opened the working parts.

I told the injured soldier what I was going to do and told him to 'shut his bleating' as I needed to concentrate. The other soldier holding the rifle still had his eyes shut and his teeth tightly clenched. I don't know why as for him this was a painless process. I unclipped the magazine and removed it, laying it on the floor nearby. So far so good.

I then pulled out the cocking lever, took a firm grip on the rifle and pulled back on the cocking lever. It wouldn't budge, not an inch. I tried again, no success, and a third time. Still no movement. I would have to be a lot firmer.

I grabbed a firmer grip on the lever and using my fist and with all my strength I jerked the lever back. The soldier screamed, louder than before. The working parts shot backwards, and a stream of blood spewed out of the chamber and splashed over my hand, soaking the soldiers combats in the process. The chamber was empty apart from a trickle of blood. I eased the working parts forward once again sealing the chamber. If he was going to continue bleeding it was going to be at most a barrel full. I reassured him the gun was clear and what the bloody hell did he have a magazine on it for anyway? He murmured and whimpered and was soon taken off by the ambulance. I cleaned his blood off me and went on to the ranges. He made a full recovery. I hope he cleaned his rifle properly!

Character building? Hell yes!

<u>Sgts Mess Barman</u>

Corporals at 7 were, on a rota basis, appointed to be the Sergeants Mess barman for a period of three months. On this one occasion the duty fell to me. I hated it. Some of the senior ranks there at the time were the most whinging deceitful, accusing, backstabbing people I have ever encountered. Being the one sober person there, behind the bar, I saw it all.

The Sergeant that did the accounts and stocktaking couldn't, he constantly got it wrong. Lost barrels of beer, and bottles and bottles of spirits. He regularly accused me of diverting stock to the rugby club. I never did, but if I had have done and he would have had to account for it, it would have been worth it. He had a big personal drink problem, and he didn't know it. He wasn't the only one.

A few of them were always asking for credit for booze. Credit that they expected me to underwrite, no fucking chance. I was surprised at how many of them stuck all their wages into the fruit machine, they never won. They would then spend a month trying to borrow. They had petty, pathetic arguments, and woe betide any person who left a group in conversation, he could be assured he would be the very next derogative subject of conversation. One artisan S/Sgt was such a 'bully' to Sergeants, he should have had a right kicking. I was glad to get out of there.

It's that Twat Gonzo - Again

One evening in a Sergeant's mess function while I was barman, 'Gonzo' my old useless ARV commander turned up there as a guest of one of the Sergeant Majors (who happened to be a top man), and somehow, he had been promoted to artisan S/Sgt, fucking unbelievable. The slimy, backstabbing, horrible useless little fucker must have arse-licked and brown-nosed endlessly.

The orderly Sgt on this evening, a truly decent man, came into the mess. He was chatting with me at the bar when Gonzo started accusing him of saying something derogative about his wife. He most definitely hadn't, not a word. She wasn't part of that or any other conversation. Gonzo, a very small, metaphorically as well as figuratively speaking, man, with a bit of rank on his arm was the worst kind. Hiding behind his rank, gobbing off at the Queens expense, belittling his position, the very worst of what the REME had to offer. He was every bit the slimy little fuck of a useless brown-nosing ARV commander he had been years previously. Ineffective, disrespectful, just a gobshite, quick to accuse and abuse others of lower rank.

The orderly Sergeant left the mess a wiser and more discerning man. Gonzo, drunk more and more got louder and louder and more abusive as the night went on.

Vodka & Lemonade
(vodka free)
For twats only!

His wife drunk lots and cackled and giggled also getting louder as the night wore on; she flirted outrageously with any person there who was a higher rank than Gonzo. I began to think, because of her behaviour that I was witnessing, her promiscuous generosity might have been the basis of his promotion. Eventually they left the mess well pissed. Strange really because they were drinking large vodkas and lemonade, and I wasn't putting any vodka in them. Pricks.

<u>Dodger and the Enemy Ducks</u>

Sergeant Majors of the British Army have a famous reputation for being hard but fair, many RSM's have gone down in history as 'the loudest voice' or toughest disciplinarian and so on. Soldiers encounter their own Company Sergeant Majors (CSM's) more so than they do RSM's. At 7 Armoured there was 'Dodger'.

Company Sergeant Major (CSM) Dodger Green had a style and manner that once seen was never forgotten. He was a man with a distinctive disposition of speedy intolerance. Imagine a tall skinny nasty, version of Alf Garnett and you're on the way to seeing Dodger. Bald, with round, metal framed, Japanese sniper style glasses, tall and always upright and marching. I think he hailed from a place of regular unpleasant people but I'm not positive.

His favourite word was 'Cunt'. But he pronounced it as 'Kant', and he pronounced it loudly and often. I'm

469

sure his job description was shouting at people and calling them 'Kant's'.

One or two examples of his style were as follows.

I was the guard commander at 7 Armoured. The telephone rings and I answer it promptly, the military way.

> "Guardroom 7 Armoured Workshop, Cpl Rees speaking Sir'.
> "Kant", was yelled down the phone and the handset slammed down. It was most certainly Dodger.

On another occasion we were doing pre-Northern Ireland training and we had been on a five miler with kit and rifles. Andy Brosnan and I were running as a pair and for the last few hundred yards Andy was struggling. I pushed and pulled him along and eventually we finished both of us collapsing exhausted on a grass bank outside our training office. We were in a heap blowing, sweating, and sucking it in when along comes Dodger. We heave ourselves to our feet and it would be normal for the

NCO or officer passing to stop and compliment us on our efforts or ask how it had gone. But this was Dodger. Without breaking stride or even looking in our direction –

"Kant's"
"Sir".

That was it.

However, I did discover a foil to Dodger in the guise of my good friend Les Payne. Les was an instrument technician, rugby player and all-round good guy. Funny and helpful, Les was sociable, amenable, and great company. He was a bugger for drinking dark rum and he drank it in great quantities. He still does. Dodger hated Les.

So, the foil to Dodger, was to stand near Les because whenever Dodger saw Les all his foul mouth venomous rhetoric went, like an arrow, straight to Les. I thought it was fab. To Dodger, Les was the ultimate 'KAANT". The 'Dodger and Les' double act was always fabulously entertaining and injury and insult free for the rest of us. Well done, Les!

On one occasion Dodger was giving a classroom lesson on target acquisition and range finding. It was an exercise in identifying easily seen obstacles and calling in the target from there. There were countryside panoramas on the wall from which we gained the information to adduce our instructions.

Shouting the fire order loudly It would go something like this –

> *Centre of Arc*
> *Range 300 metres*
> *Stone tower*
> *Looking left, clump of trees*
> *Look to the right of the clump of trees a pond.*
> *Left side of pond enemy*
> *'Rapid Fire'*

My turn to give the fire order, I noticed on the pond on the panorama there were ducks on the pond.

> *Centre of Arc*
> *Range 300 metres*
> *Stone tower*
> *Looking left, clump of trees*

Look to the right of the clump of trees a pond.
Centre of pond enemy ducks
'Rapid Fire'

Dodger went off on one. I can't understand why, there were ducks in enemy territory. I was a 'KAAAAAAAAANT' for the rest of the day. Where was Les Payne when you needed him?

In fairness to Dodger, he was a good soldier. Despite his abrasive, foul mouthed, pointed manner, he looked out for his troops with their best interest at heart. His bark was certainly worse than his bite, however his bollockings skills were right up there with the best of them!

Character building? Hell yes!

ENEMY DUCK – VERY DANGEROUS

<u>Taxi for Mr Boulton</u>

7 Armoured were keen on Combat Fitness Tests (CFT's). this involved us all parading at a given time outside garrison gymnasium. We would be in full combat kit carrying everything possible in the way of battle equipment. Webbing and packs, water bottles full, weapons and ammunition. Helmets were sometimes worn and S6 gas respirators were a must. Our kit was weighed and had to be a minimum weight before setting off.

It was eight miles around the concrete range road, which was hard going for running at the best of times, let alone in DMS boots, and carrying weight. No range road convoy-lob on these occasions. We had one hour and fifty minutes to complete the distance. One hundred yards at double time, one hundred yards at quick time, one hundred yards at double time and so on. Double time is running, or jogging in unison, quick time is a fast walk or march.

It doesn't take long before the body temperature starts to rise, sweat starts to flow, the webbing straps bed-in and the weight begins to take its toll. Rifles get heavier and kit adjustments are made. The first mile or so is uncomfortable but a rhythm develops, and body temperature stabilises, breathing is deep and regular. The witty will quip, the usual suspects will moan, NCOs encourage even if they themselves are struggling. It's a slog. For a few of the one hundred yard stretches respirators were worn. Ever was it so difficult to breath, it just makes everything harder, the last mile is welcome, well into the rhythm, a few may have fallen out with issues or being just plain knackered. Shin-splits are a real fucker!

BODY TEMPERATURE STARTS TO RISE, SWEAT STARTS TO FLOW

Finally, the end point back at the gymnasium hove's into sight and its welcome. At 7 Armoured, I don't know about other units, the CFT didn't finish with the run. Then we had to do so many press-ups, sit-ups, star-jumps, and other treats. Finally, there was the unsavoury dessert of picking up another soldier, including his kit and rifle, in a fireman's lift and carrying him one hundred yards as fast as possible and throwing him up into the back of a four-tonner lorry, at a height of about four and a half feet. It was meant to be casualty evacuation simulation.

The run and exercises finished we'd gather on the grassed area, take a gulp of water, and prepare for the challenging carry. I normally weighed in at about sixteen stone, much heavier than most, and I would normally find myself in a clear space as others avoided having to carry me. My kit and I were heavy. I used to find the carry as no issue, most soldiers were three or four stone lighter and I managed easily. After one range road bash I was standing, alone, looking for someone to carry because as

usual the wise regulars had scattered. However, one man hadn't, standing about twenty yards away looking at me and smiling, he was always smiling, was my good friend and fellow Recy Mech Kev Boulton. 'BOLLOX' I thought.

Kev was a big, big man, about six foot three and a solid twenty stone plus kit. There was only Kev and I unpartnered, it wasn't rocket science or brain surgery to figure out why!

We closed together knowing what was coming. I agreed to go first to get it other with. I gave Kev my rifle. I continued to wear my kit, as did Kev wear his. I bent forward, Kev leant over my back, I took his weight, straightened my legs, and stood upright with Kev on my back.

FUCKING HELL! Ever was there such a load. Me at sixteen stones, Kev at about twenty stones, two sets of equipment (XXXL) and two rifles at seven pound each. I estimate the total payload of more than forty stone, a grand cargo if ever there was one. I was warm from the run and well stretched. The weight on my shoulders and arms was fine, my legs were OK, but the downward pressure on my hips was immense. I'd never felt anything like it.

FUCKING HELL! Ever was there such a load.

I started off on my marathon one hundred yards, slowly at first, sucking huge gulps of air, controlled deep breaths as I would do during particularly demanding scrummages on the rugby field. Air, move, air, move, build a rhythm, push a little harder, suck it in, control it out, push on. The one hundred yards might have been miles. This was a big challenge by any standards.

I was aware that most of the others had completed their runs and were gathering in lines along my route to watch this titanic spectacle of a struggle; and it was truly titanic. The soldiers began to shout encouragement and cheer me on, it's a thing that soldiers do and it's a good thing. I picked up a little speed, mindful not to overbalance and tip my laughing load to the ground. Boulton was enjoying himself – the bastard. I began to curse and swear, what I didn't name him wasn't worth naming. About thirty yards into the hundred I knew I was going to complete the run. I still wasn't sure about the lift into the lorry, but I was confident the hundred carry was in the bag. I settled into a rhythm, accepting the weighty huge pressure on my hips, I managed my long deep breaths, and ensured my posture was as economical as could be. The soldiers cheered and shouting. 'Come on Taff, you can do this', louder and louder. It was fabulous and valuable encouragement and it helped spur me on. I was also enjoying the abuse Kev was getting, 'Get off and walk you lazy fucker', 'Taxi for Boulton' and so on.

For the last thirty yards I was planning how to get my load into the back of the lorry. I decided I would not break my run but as I approached the lorry I would turn at the last moment and try, with all my scrummaging legs, to hoist Kev up and onto the flat bed. I shouted to him that I was going to do this and told him to keep the rifles held tight and to trust me. 'OK Boyo' he shouted back. Kev always called me Boyo; still does!

As I closed in on the last ten yards, I tried to pick up a little speed, I wanted the extra bit of momentum to ensure my lift. Sucking huge gulps of precious air, I closed on the lorry back. About three or four yards from my target I began to spin anti-clockwise to my left, throwing everything I could muster up and towards the lorry. As I turned fully backward, I raised my arms and shoulders and heaved backwards planting all twenty stones plus of Kev, kit, and rifles, squarely on the back of the lorry. Thank fuck for that!

Amongst cheering entertained soldiers, I drop to sit on the floor. I turn my head up to look at Kev, he is smiling his huge west country smile, and I am blown out but delighted. That was some achievement, I was feeling the warm afterglow of a job well done. An eight-mile forced march, in full kit, respirator events, exercises and a hundred yards carrying Kev. Yep, I was 'chuffed' to NAAFI breaks.

Next it was Kev's turn to carry the sixteen stones, kit, and rifle of mine and do the same. He did it effortlessly laughing all the way, 'Come on Boyo, I don't know what you were making all the fuss about, its piece of piss', and it was for him.

Character building? Hell yes!

<u>Exploding Forehead</u>

A significant event for me is where my forehead exploded. We were in bivvies in a marshy area on Ex Log Pot, and I'm sleeping in my green maggot (army sleeping bag). There are mossies' everywhere, buzzing their high-pitched whine all night long. I wake in the morning and my forehead is itching, madly itching. I sit up, open my eyes and I can't see. I put my hand to my face and feel a flap over my eyes. It's my forehead. The only part of me exposed through the night in this marshy ground was my forehead. It must have been a landing pad on a restaurant for every mozzie in Germany. They had feasted on my forehead all night long. My forehead was filled with liquid, swollen, and drooped and fell like a thick flap over my eyebrows and down across my eyes. If I didn't hold the flap up, I couldn't see. There was no pain or discomfort, just the flap. I tucked the flap under my beret and went off to seek medical advice.

RELENTLESS FOREHAED EATING GREEDY LITTLE FUCKER

I came across a Captain at the exercise HQ and told him I needed to see a medical officer. He asked me what was wrong, and I took off my beret. My forehead flopped down over my eyes. Using the back of my hand I lifted my flap up over my head and placed my beret back on to hold my forehead in place. I could now see the Captain trying hard not to laugh, but he failed miserably. Through giggles and mirth, he directed me to the medical tent where in front of the medical officer I removed my beret once again. Yet more laughter. I got the funny side of it; my forehead was pain free but a flappy nuisance. I was given cream and the assurance it was a mild reaction to the mossie bites. I was assured there was no danger, and that the liquid would disperse, and the swelling go down. I was for two or three days a popular attraction on the exercise and every soldier there came along and viewed me for a laugh. The cream worked, the swelling went, and my forehead returned to normal.

Forehead building? Hell yes!

I want my Money Back

I was driving a Scammel Crusader, a very large and long low-loader lorry. It was snowing and as I was driving through a German village a civilian car came toward me. I was wide on the road, so I stopped the Scammel, but the German civilian carried on trying to squeeze through the narrow space. I watched as he scraped his car along the side of the trailer causing a big gouge along the length of his car. I was stationary throughout. After he had passed my trailer and damaged his vehicle he stopped, got out of his car, and waved his fist at me. What? It was all his fault; I knew the space was narrow and I had stopped accordingly.

I alighted from my cab and walked back to the German. He saw me coming and quickly jumped back in his car. He had nothing to fear from me. He had a decent scrape along the full length of his car. He was sitting quietly in his car not looking at me. I was gesticulating for him to get out of his car, and he did so after a short while. He wasn't happy and was remonstrating with me about the damage to his car. I was trying to tell him it was his fault and that he should have stopped. We were having language difficulties my German was poor and if he had good English, he was too agitated to use it. I told him to call the German police and he did so.

The police arrived and spoke good English son we both explained what had happened. The police listened and decided there was no action for me to face. I gave them my details and unit address and continued my journey. There was no damage to my vehicle. On returning I reported the issue to my S/Sgt, who had made it known to me previously, that because I had EPC(A) and he couldn't pass the qualification, that he would make my life uncomfortable (very petty and he did), who in turn informed the company commander. I have no doubt he put a negative spin on his report to the OC as was his way.

Next thing I know I am on OC's orders charged with the traffic incident in which the German police, who were on the scene, had deemed there was no case to answer, and that the German Civvy was at fault for not stopping.

I get the option of accepting the OC's punishment (that meant he thought me guilty before he had even spoken to me) or going before the commanding officer (where a higher level of punishment is possible). I edge my bets and opt for the OC, and I get fined DM120. I'm told I must be seen to be putting something back in. Something back in? What the fuck was that all about? It wasn't my fault and I get a fine. Fucking annoying, even to this day. It was the only disciplinary blemish in over twelve years of service. It was a travesty. It was an injustice; It was an aberration of institutional power. I want my money back, all of it!

This episode was reinforcing my consideration to leave the army.

<u>Trout Anybody 2</u>

The Forward Repair Group (FRG) is on exercise, and we are parked up for a few days. Fortuitously for our bland army diet we are very near a trout farm. This farm is more sophisticated than the previous trout farm from which we had, over enthusiastically, fished using plastic explosives some years previously. A reconnaissance reveals the trout are of many different sizes the largest of which are in huge plastic barrels. It's as if they have been placed there prior to transportation elsewhere. Placed there for us? It's easy for us to get into the ground in the dead of night where the trout are conveniently placed near the perimeter fence. The foraging party is successful and there's enough trout for one each. Fresh trout for breakfast is the order of the day. We cook our own and for the most part they are roasted over an open fire or fried in margarine.

The trout farmer discovers his loss and putting two and two together he suspects that the nearby British soldiers may have been involved in this piscine crime. He comes to our encampment and is escorted into the centre where he speaks with the officer commanding and FRG commander who is eating his breakfast. The farmer tells the officer he suspects the soldiers may have been involved in the trout disappearance because prior to the soldier's arrival there had never been an issue with trout loss. He goes on to say the trout were very valuable and his loss was considerable.

The officer assures the farmer his soldiers would never contemplate such an act. He goes on to say that he feels sorry for the farmers loss. Even more so he goes on to tell the farmer he will instruct his soldiers to keep an eye out for anybody with trout and that his soldiers will keep a watching eye on the trout farm for the remainder of their stay in the area.

The officers' assurances seem to pacify the farmer and they shake hands, and the farmer leaves the area on good terms satisfied the British troops are not involved.

All the troops are very impressed with their officer because throughout the dialogue the Captain had manged to keep his trout overflowing mess-tin concealed behind his back. His trout had become cold, but he said it retained its flavour and was worth the wait.

All Because!

It's the all-ranks Christmas party at 7. The party venue is the garrison gymnasium, and it is expected to be an excellent turnout. The Andy Capps Commandos would do their usual exceptional festive effort. There was to be a band and a singer followed by a disco. Drink would be cheap and plentiful.

The commanding officer and his good lady were attending, and the party organising committee were considering laying on something special to mark their attendance. 'Pusk' was on the committee, and he decided that he would take care of this high-profile issue.

At the time there was a regular advertisement on the television concerning 'Cadbury's Milk Tray' chocolates. The catch phrase was 'All Because The Lady Loves Milk Tray'. The advertisement proper was a 'James Bond' type character dressed in a tuxedo and he would deliver the chocolates to a lady. However, his delivery route was beset with all kinds of obstacles such as having to dive off a very high

490

cliff into shark-infested waters. Swim and battle through the sharks to board a yacht and place the chocolates on to her bed; all accompanied by dramatic music.

MILK TRAY - FFS!

'Pusks' plan was this.

Milk Tray music would start to play loudly, he would then run into the building through a fire door and 'forward-roll' into the middle of the dance floor.

Rolling straight to his feet he would then run and jump onto a strategically placed chair from which he would catapult onto a prepared table.

Jump from that table to another and then somersault onto the floor and run out of an exit door and up onto the gymnasium 'weight's' balcony where there were four or five 'arches' overlooking the main function area from which he had started.

He would run along the balcony and dive through the third 'arch' whilst forward-rolling and land square on his back on top of a couple of gymnasium matts situated where he was intending to land.

After landing he would rise to his feet stroll casually over to the Commanding Officers wife and present her with the box of chocolates. At which point the music would cut and loudly 'All Because The Lady Loves Milk Tray' would play from the speakers. The Commanding Officers wife would be delighted to receive the chocolate, the partygoers would be entertained. The Commanding Officer would be very impressed with 'Pusk' and it would be a fabulous opener to the party. So Pusk practised and practised, timing, music loud enough, route planned, correctly placed furniture. It was going to be perfect!

Well, that was the plan!

Come the night; the Milk Tray music started playing loudly, Pusk charged in through the fire door and executed a superb forward roll, propelling himself straight to his feet in the middle of the dance floor. Without hesitation he ran and launched himself at great speed onto the strategically placed chair, then up onto the first table. With a mighty leap he landed on the next table and flew through the main exit door and up the balcony stairs. Accelerating as fast as possible he ran along the balcony length and dived like an arrow through the arch. The wrong arch that is!

He 'piked' into a forward roll and landed, as intended, squarely on his back, missing the mats by about ten feet.

With an almighty crash he slammed 'REME precision perfect' onto the middle of a round table of twelve party revellers who were anticipating him landing on the mats alongside. Everything went 'tits-up' glasses, bottles, drinks, candelabras, the lot. The table collapsed; the revellers were knocked to the floor; it was momentary, instant mayhem.

Everybody was aghast. The blokes stared agog; the women held their hands to their mouths in concern. The speaker blasted out, on cue, *'All Because The Lady Loves Milk Tray'*.

It was a fantastic start to the Christmas entertainment. A standing ovation for such an unexpected and spectacular display. The applause continued as he was stretchered out! The chocolates were taken from him and delivered much less spectacularly. The Commanding Officers good lady wife was very grateful for her chocolates!

Merry Christmas everybody.

Operation Banner (Again) - NIRW

REME RECOVERY in Northern Ireland

Throughout the troubles there was a continuous REME RECOVERY presence all through the province provided by the Northern Ireland Roulement Workshops (NIRW). The headquarter unit was based in Belfast and there were outlying units at other parts of the province. We had the large Volvo, Foden and AEC recovery vehicles on 24-hour standby for the recovery of broken down, damaged or bombed Pigs, Saladin's, land rovers, coaches, and all other marked military vehicles. We would either tow the vehicles or if they were severely damaged put them on a large trailer. These 'green' recovery vehicles would also recover and deal with covert military or police vehicles that had been 'compromised' i.e., shot at or blown up normally. Sometimes this would take a while and was invariably in a 'hard-area'. Despite the infantry escort and cordon it always took forever and we always presented a huge target for snipers. Some of the cargo we brought 'home' on those trailers was most unpleasant. A sad duty!

Every part of the province was covered, and we generally moved with a two land-rover infantry escort when travelling around. High up in the cab of a 25-ton army recovery truck driving through West Belfast or the Bogside was a character-building experience and outside of the SF bases themselves, they were the biggest targets for bricks and snipers.

We, the REME that is, also provided a covert recovery service throughout the province for the duration of the troubles. We had smaller civilian registered vehicles, normally some sort of pick-up or land rover painted red or blue or whatever. They were purposefully kept dirty and unkempt just like a bog-standard Irish civilian recovery garage. They sometimes had markings of civilian garages on them such as 'Murphy's Garage' but no other details.

There were generally three or four on duty cover throughout the province at any given time.

The crews of the covert recovery vehicles would consist of a Recovery Mechanic and a second volunteer REME tradesman. There was no shortage of volunteers. In addition to doing the NITAT green army training these covert crews underwent specialist covert training in anti-ambush drills, escape, and evasion, firing from moving vehicles and other such skills. It was great fun firing through the windscreen of a car from the inside; however, not so funny when the very young first Lieutenant, who is a passenger in your car, gets carried away and shoots out your rear-view mirror, car radio and heater controls. There were SOP's for encountering army and police patrols and road checks as well as illegal VCP's and so on.

The crews wore civilian overalls and jackets, hair was generally long with an equally lengthy, droopy seventy's style classy porn-star moustache. Apart from the vehicle and recovery equipment we carried a personal radio, which was always out of range or didn't work or, the HQ formation in the area we were working in had never heard of us.

We carried 9mm Browning Automatic Pistols and Sub Machine Guns (SMGs) in the footwells of the recovery vehicles, along with a couple of smoke grenades. These covert vehicles worked alone and throughout the entire province and unofficially in, around and over the border. The covert capability was occasionally used by military commanders for purposes other than recovery such as reconnaissance, conveyance of supplies, equipment, and personnel to and from covert ops or locations.

There were some 'hairy' moments, particularly when encountering army or RUC (I always thought they wanted to shoot me) VCP's or patrols. Difficult enough trying to identify yourself as SF at the best of times. A real danger for us was encountering an illegal VCP set up by the terrorists somewhere near the border in the dead of night, or the Garda over the border, no comms, trying to work out of it was legit or illegal. If it appeared illegal, then backing out or driving through; and even if it was legit still the same issue. Every VCP or patrol incident carried danger and welcome relief. Always prudent to react to even the slightest suspicion about vehicles or people ahead, there were a few times where we erred on the side of caution and reversed quickly back down the road or took a wise and speedy diversion.

One dark night on the Limavady to Londonderry road my oppo Kev 'Cheeseboard' Milward and I were travelling along in our covert role Landrover.

(So called because Millward became Millboard then Jim Burberry and Glyn Mountjoy turned it to Cheeseboard which was endorsed when Jim Burberry and Kev had a cheese and wine session on their FV434; why wouldn't you?)

In the beam of the headlights, we saw an object in the middle of the road. We slowed and approached it cautiously ever wise to the slightest measure of terrorism. As we got closer to the object the hairs on my neck began to rise. Cheeseboard and I looked nervously at each other. Fuck this, we're out of here. I began to three-point turn the Landrover and we ended up, side-on to the object giving us a better view of it. It was very clearly a weapon much in the style of a Thompson Sub-Machine Gun. Why was it there? Was it a come-on? Was it booby-trapped? We got out of there sharpish!

It might have been nothing (who leaves machine guns lying around?) Were we fortunate to have been in covert clothes and vehicle? Would it have been different had we been in uniform? Who knows? Extreme caution was an outstanding philosophy to practice!

Everybody I worked with in Northern Ireland, and there were many of every cap-badge and service,

were professional in the extreme and for the most part I look back on them with fondness.

<u>Worst Officer.</u>

I was the resident Recy Mech Cpl at Fort George, Londonderry, and my partner and fellow crewman was 'Cheeseboard', we had a full green role, but we also had a covert role with a land rover fitted with towing kit for recovering covert cars and 'other things'. We carried 9mm browning pistols, sterling sub machine guns, radios, and smoke grenades. We had undergone special training to deal with 'contact' events. Our main tactic was to stay out of trouble, not get into a firefight and be as inconspicuous as possible in a recovery vehicle. How can you be inconspicuous in a recovery vehicle? We were very busy with work from the local HQ, the resident battalion, the UDR and others anonymous and less well knowns.

Our new REME OC from Belfast came to visit at Fort George in Londonderry, this Captain guy was so ignorant of our situation and role. I can't even remember his name. He took over from Ben Tyler (who was a proper officer) at NIRW. The new Captain was totally clueless as to what our role was or what we were being asked to do by the brigade headquarters and the resident infantry unit. His knowledge appeared to be no more than a BAOR or mainland UK unit commander would have. He seemed to have no perspective about terrorist activity, hard areas, border work, the requirement to be situationally aware regarding intelligence and operations. He told Cheeseboard and I to get a short a back and sides!

The Worse Kind

He needed to get out a bit more and find a civilian Recy Mech or mechanic with neat short back and sides that we could be compared with. He gives me a bollocking (as bollockings go it was minor league and probably not worth a mention) for having hair over my collar but says nothing about my classy porn star moustache. He thinks it's not a good idea for recovery crews (overt and covert) to be armed. So, tells us we are not to carry firearms on recovery jobs, covert or overt. What?

The infantry company commander, who was accompanying him out of courtesy, puts him right. The Captain had a totally insufficient grasp of our situation, location, or role. One 10-minute visit then clears off back to his cushy desk in Belfast. Inspiring leadership? I think not.

At one-point Cheeseboard and I had two 9mm pistols, two 9mm sub machine guns, and one 9mm bullet between us; ONE FUCKING BULLET!! a breakdown in NIRW logistics? This was

Londonderry FFS and we were working covertly in and around the border with the south and regular infantry escorted forays into the Bogside. We ended up borrowing 'loads of ammo' off Felix, the bomb disposal teams, with whom we shared accommodation. It took weeks to get our own issued.

That useless Captain reminded me a little of 'The General' by Siegfried Sassoon, of whom I used to read often.

The General
"Good-morning, good-morning!" the General said
When we met him last week on our way to the line.
Now the soldiers he smiled at are most of 'em dead,
And we're cursing his staff for incompetent swine.

"He's a cheery old card," grunted Harry to Jack
As they slogged up to Arras with rifle and pack.
But he did for them both by his plan of attack.

Not the best of analogies, but it's what I thought of him at the time. Character building? That Captain needed some! Where do they get people like him from?

Often our HQ element at Belfast just didn't get what we were up to and against at the outstations. There was a real shooting war going on and people were regularly getting killed. For example, on one occasion we were issued with gleaming white overalls. Gleaming white? I hear you ask! What Recy Mech or mechanic ever wore white overalls? Painter and decorator? – yes. Milk parlour worker? – yes. We stood out like 'falling plates' (targets on a rifle range). Cheeseboard and I were having none of it and resorted to whatever 'rags' we could find if they weren't army green or white. FFS.

Trying to build our characters? Maybe if they knew what character was!

NIRW Anecdotes

<u>Slight Altercation in Belfast</u>

'Cheeseboard', and I are in a plain car, plain clothes, and we're off to Belfast. We have a duty job to do there. Hollywood Barracks in Belfast, it's a different ball game to Fort George in the Bogside. Hollywood is a 'soft area' Fort George certainly is not. We are spending the night in Belfast. There is to be a disco in the camp with local women allowed in and beer is available; things Cheeseboard and I are not used to. No such luxury west of the Foyle. We have a few beers and chat to soldiers we knew and hadn't seen in a while. I know all the soldiers there but not the women. I tire of the disco and intend to get to bed early but could do with a bite to eat. I know there is a duty driver on call with a plain car and Cheeseboard and I are fancying the luxury of a Chinese meal before bed, something impossible in Fort George. So, I speak to one of the MT Corporals and ask him if he can provide transport for me to go out and get some food. He says no. Ok, no problem I'll go without.

I return to the disco for a last beer before bed. I learn that that same Corporal, whom I knew, was using the unit transport, the one he had declined for me, to shuttle civvies around in. Mmm! I think to myself. That's a bit off. I've come out of a hard area for one night and my own parent unit can't provide me with the curtesy of a short lift. Moreover, the car I could have had a lift in is being used elsewhere. I speak to the duty driver of the car Ralph 'Meddy' Medlock, who I know and had taught to drive an HGV2 lorry, and he has been told by the MT Corporal not to give myself or 'Cheeseboard' any access to the cars. 'Meddy', confirms he is driving civvies about. I'm not happy so I confront the MT Corporal once again and ask him what's his game and how come civvies get the use of the cars but not troops (me and my oppo Cheeseboard). Effectively he tells me to 'fuck off' back to the Bogside and how he managed his transport was fuck all to do with me. So, I punched him.

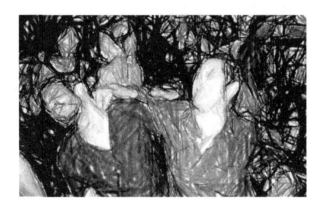

SO, I PUNCHED HIM!

I punched him three times, twice to his face and once to his ribs and he fell to the floor. Two other Corporals, RD staff and mates of his, intervened by grabbing me. I punched one, knocking some teeth out and the third ran away; perhaps he is still running. My disappointment satiated I went to bed in the transit accommodation. I'm sitting on the bed reading a newspaper and in comes WO2 Alf Simpson the Q bloke, and Sgt Nigel Hancock (Nigel was an extrovert character in his own right, no doubt he thought the situation amusing). They have been told that I have gone berserk and was causing a riot. They have come to sort me out. They weren't expecting to see me relaxed on a bed reading a newspaper. They asked me what had happened, and I told them exactly the way it was. Both knew me quite well, they knew I wasn't a lunatic, nor a troublemaker. In fact, Nigel played full back for the rugby team of which I was Captain. They said they would speak to me in the morning.

The next morning, I get sent for by the officer commanding Captain. Ben Tyler, another fellow unit and REME Corps rugby player. I stand in front of his desk, and he says to me-

'Morning Taff, what happened last night?'. I knew he would have already made enquiries and fully appraised himself of the events of the previous evening.

I tell him word for word, exactly how it was. He tells me that the first Corporal I punched is in hospital with two broken eye sockets and broken ribs, the second has lost a few teeth, and the third isn't saying anything and is planning on staying out of the way until I've gone. I didn't know I'd hospitalised the one with broken bones, but I had an inkling about the teeth. I didn't know nor care about the third.

Ben asked me how I felt about it all. I told him I thought the Corporal was in the wrong and that even so, I was sorry I'd hit him so hard; I didn't mean to and was sorry he was in hospital.

Ben said to me-

'No, no Taff, if you're going to punch somebody do a proper job of it. Have a safe drive back to Londonderry'.

and that was it. I left his office, a little perplexed, and Cheeseboard and I went back west to the Bogside. I was expecting something more in the way of discipline and repercussion.

Weeks later I heard, from an impeccable source, that Ben had considered that what I had done was do him a favour. Apparently, there was an awkward problem developing in the unit where three senior Corporals were fucking the lads about on a grand scale and it was affecting morale. The situation was going to be difficult to deal with, but my knocking them about had brought them down a peg or two and off their high horse. I knew nothing about this, nor did I care; all I wanted was a Chinese before bed.

The Fastest Soldier in the Army

My good friend Dave 'Buck or Tojo' Rogers, a man of enduring military enthusiasm, has a tale to tell. He is called Buck because of his surname and Tojo because he has 'Japanese' features. Back in the day he looked like a Japanese sniper, thin and wiry. Today he's more like a Japanese general. Dave initially joined the Royal Welsh but transferred into the REME after a few years. He's a good Cardiff man.

At the start of this speedy adventure, Dave is at Ebrington barracks on the waterside part of

Londonderry, he needs to come to us at Fort George. He is wearing a combat uniform and is carrying a nine-millimetre browning pistol. The smallest weapon in our armoury, it's good for about twenty-five yards of accuracy and after that its pot-luck. Dave is looking for transport and from the command room he learns that a patrol of two land rovers of 'Royal Anglian Infantrymen; are going over to the Bogside and they will give him a lift and drop him in Fort George. Dave gets into the back of one of the land rovers.

As they cross the Craigavon Bridge into the Bogside the word 'Contact' and a location, comes over the radios. Contact means that a unit is in contact with the enemy. In this instance a serious fire-fight with terrorists has broken out in the Bogside and the patrol with which Dave is having his lift responds sharply to get in on the action and support the units involved. The patrol quickly gets into the shooting area. Terrorists have opened fire with machine guns on a foot patrol. The foot-patrol have returned fire, and a serious fire-fight is developing. Other foot patrols and mobile patrols, including Dave's, is converging on the scene. As Dave gets closer, the sound of the firing increases considerably, there's a lot of it, it's a serious business. The IRA would employ the tactics of opening fire on a patrol, then withdrawing as the patrols responded, only to open fire from a second or third or even fourth position as the soldiers advanced to the shooting points. That is what was happening here. The British Army seldom, if ever, initiated the fire-fights unless they were special forces on a planned operation ambush on known terrorist activity.

Dave's lift got to where they needed to be for the firefight, and they dismounted and got involved into the action. Dave also dismounted but being armed with the smallest pistol in the British armoury, there wasn't a great deal he could do. Also, the infantry guys were drilled and capable and having Dave do anything would only complicate things. The heated fire-fight continued with Dave's patrol returning a considerable amount of rifle fire. Rounds were coming back, and the ricochets were buzzing and clanging around and nearby. Dave took hard cover, mindful of the precarious situation, certainly wanting to avoid being hit by anything. The gunmen withdrew from their first line and the infantry moved after them. The section commander of Dave's lift called his soldiers in and very quickly they mounted the Landrovers' and moved forward to a new position to continue the hot pursuit. There was no hanging about, this was a contact situation and swift and decisive action was the order.

In the heat of the action – they forgot Dave! He was in the middle of the toughest part of the Bogside, crouched, taking cover, in a hard area of known and fatal terrorist activity, in which gunfights were common. Alone and friendless, armed with the smalless pistol in the British armoury, this was not good, not good at all!

Dave had heard stories of soldiers being isolated and the gruesome accounts of them being mobbed by women and having their genitals cut off and stuffed in their mouths. Or of soldiers being taken prisoner, tortured, and shot, their bodies thrown in a ditch. He knew he was in a dangerous situation. The Royal Anglian had a fire-fight on their hands, they were unlikely to remember him and return anytime soon. He couldn't follow them into the fire-fight; besides he didn't know where they were. He couldn't stay still, the longer he did so the higher the risk of being identified as alone and lightly armed. He had to move to a safe place which was going to be an Army base or a Police Station. The closest one he knew the location of was Fort George. He didn't know how to get there directly but he knew it was alongside the river which was behind him. If he got to the river and turned left, he would eventually get to Fort George which was on the banks of the river Foyle. So that's what Dave wisely decided to do, it was his best option. He would run, as fast as he possibly could back and down to the river, then along the river to Fort George.

DAVE - RUNNING LIKE FUCK!

It was about two miles along the paved street some crowded with pedestrians. Dave reckoned he did the two miles in less than eight minutes, on a par with the finest of athletes. New name 'Dave 'fast as fuck' Rogers'.

Character building? Hell yes!

<u>Helicopter for Taff and Cheeseboard</u>

'Cheeseboard' and I were at Ebrington Barracks on the waterside. We were in uniform and needed to get over to Fort George in the Bogside. We were strolling along the side of the parade square heading to the control room to try and scrounge a lift. Hopefully not with the 'Royal Anglian' after Dave Rogers's world record sprint. I hear incoming aircraft noise and on looking up we saw a Gazelle helicopter coming into land on the square, Kev and I stopped to watch. I always enjoyed watching the choppers, just as much as I enjoyed watching tanks in action. The Gazelle pilot, the only occupant, switched off, alighted, and walked towards us. I jokingly extended my thumb up as in thumbing for a lift. He asked us where the cookhouse was, and we gave him directions. However, I told him, that this cook house was shit (it wasn't) and that the one at Fort George was more A' la carte, and much better food. Also, that if he gave us a lift over the water, we would join him for lunch. He readily agreed. Cheeseboard and I got in the

Gazelle, strapped ourselves into our first-class lift, 'our now private', five-seater reconnaissance chopper, donned headphones and had an unplanned surprise aerial sightseeing tour of Londonderry and surrounding areas. It was exciting we swooped and turned and twisted over the city, seeing it all from a new perspective. What a small place Londonderry was for creating so much trouble and danger!

THE FOOD HERE IS SHIT. TAXI!

Chatting with the pilot we learned he was an infantryman, a substantive Lance Corporal, Acting

Corporal and Local Sergeant. He had recently qualified as a pilot and was loving every minute of it. I suspect it was the novelty value still with him that underlined his generosity to us. I wasn't complaining. We landed and enjoyed a decent lunch in the cookhouse. The Slop Jockeys (ACC) putting their hands up again; well done Andy Capp. Big thanks to the pilot.

What a fabulous way to travel, a superb lunch at the end and great company to boot, and so unexpected.

Character building? Hell yes!

What Happened to Fido?

Whilst at fort George in Londonderry 'Pusk' came to be my recovery crewman for a while. I knew him well and got on with him, I enjoyed his unusual behaviour and found him to be an interesting, if highly unusual, character. An object of perpetual curiosity and a rugby playing non-drinker, which is a clue to his complex personality. Hence his military christened nickname 'Pusk' 'Pissed Up Sober Kunt'.

He had unusual features in so much as he always looked as if he was dead. A permanently miserable facial expression with ashen complexion sunken eyes and gaunt features. His eyes were dark and solemn as were the shady rings around them. In his covert role he wore dark civvy clothes which were best described as 'rags'. His droopy long moustache gave him a forlorn Mexican bandit face. He was tramp-like and during his time at Fort George he was a solitary, independent character apparently without friends through choice. He was a candidate to be the first miserable 'Goth'.

A small friendly dog appeared in the camp, a small white terrier, probably of the Jack Russell breed or something similar. This little terrier took to following 'Pusk' around as he would feed him tit-bits and chocolates (I don't know if they were good for the dog, but they appeared to do him no harm). 'Pusk', rather originally, named the terrier 'Fido'. They seemed inseparable and wherever 'Pusk' went, Fido was sure to go. They walked the camp internal perimeter regularly and Fido came out in the vehicles with us on recovery jobs. Fido would even eat in the cookhouse from one of the metal food trays we all used. 'Pusk' would sort his food from the same selection as us, Fido particularly liked custard. Everybody made a fuss of Fido, but not of 'Pusk'.

As their relationship grew 'Pusk' went and bought Fido his own dog bowl. It was a grand thing for a dog bowl, far too big for Fido, he could probably have slept and bathed in it. It was a shiny aluminium dog bowl and 'Pusk' had stencilled 'FIDO' on the side of the bowl for good measure. 'Pusk' would queue in the cookhouse with his own food tray and Fido's bowl. Fido would obediently 'heel' along, there was food as a reward. 'Pusk' would then find a distant unoccupied table and eat there with Fido. Fido's bowl on the table as he stood on hid hind legs on the chair choosing from the wide selection 'Pusk' had brought (Andy Capp excelling again). This amused many in the camp but was occasionally frowned upon by an inspecting officer, but it went on for a while.

Then one day Fido was no longer around. Nobody knew where he went, he just disappeared. We looked everywhere for him without success. We could only surmise that he had had a gutful of 'Pusk', or of being pampered, or of army food. Whatever it was he was gone, and it appeared for good.

'Pusk' became morose and crestfallen. His only friend had gone and no matter how much I tried to raise his morale, I had no success. But 'Pusk' found his own restitution, he decided to eat from Fido's bowl!

Every mealtime 'Pusk' would join the cookhouse queue, looking dead and Mexican, dressed like a tramp, he would stand patiently in line holding Fido's bowl before him. He would be barked at, growled at, 'miaowed' at, asked to 'fetch', to 'sit', asked for his 'paw' and any other canine colloquialism you can think of. He ignored it all.

On arriving at the hotplate, he would put all his food into the one bowl. Main meal and dessert at the same time. Sausage, egg, and chips, sidled up alongside spotted dick and custard. His only cutlery was a sharpened spoon which he would use for cutting and portioning his food. He continued to sit alone on distant tables, and he appeared to care not a jot for what anybody said or didn't say.

One day I was walking alongside the helipad when a black Gazelle helicopter came into land. I stopped to watch the landing and saw three people alighted from the chopper, the pilot and two others. I assumed the two were special forces. Probably SAS. They had the look about them. The gazelle was totally black which was unusual the two were hanging in black rags, they carried short rifles, not the standard issue SLR's, they had back packs, radios and were covered in camouflage cream. I assumed they had been on or were going on covert observation work. There was a lot of it going on at that time.

The Gazelle engine wound down and stopped. The three alighted and walked towards me. The pilot, who was in conventional uniform, a Sergeant, asked me where the control room was, and I directed him there. The other two, now that they were close, were clearly knackered. They were almost asleep on their feet. They asked me where the cookhouse was and I pointed them in the right direction, and off they walked. Clearly food was a priority.

A short while later I went to the cookhouse for a meal. Filled my tray and I sat with some of the infantry guys whom I had got to know. The two 'special forces' gents had got themselves some food and were sitting alone at the far end of the cookhouse. They looked all-in.

I saw 'Pusk' enter and join the queue with his Fido bowl. He filled it with food and coming from the hot-plate he looked around for a suitable place to sit. His eyes fell on the two who had arrived by Gazelle. He must have felt an affinity with such dirty, scruffy individuals because, loaded with a full Fido bowl of food, he headed directly towards them.

Without speaking 'Pusk' sat directly opposite the two special forces guys. A trio of tramps. 'Pusk' dived into Fido's bowl and began spooning the food into his mouth one load after another. He didn't say a word. He didn't smile. He made no acknowledgement whatsoever, he just masticated and stared. The two just looked at him. Special forces or not, this must have been an unusual encounter. Special forces are normally revered in the military, not treated to an indifferent display of a dead tramp eating from aluminium labelled Fido bowl with a sharpened spoon.

The two special gents gathered up their gear and weapons and just left, leaving their food on the table. 'Pusk' just carried on eating and showing total indifference. Not a word had been spoken by any of them. The cookhouse was deathly silent.

Character building? Mmmm....

<u>Staring Down a Barrel 2</u>

Cheeseboard and I were at Fort George on the Bogside in Londonderry. We needed to get to Ebrington Barracks across the River Foyle on the Waterside to pick up a covert vehicle for a job. We were dressed in civvy outfits, customary long hair, classy porn-moustaches, black donkey jacket, jeans, brown desert boots. We went to the infantry command room to see if we could get a lift. There was nothing available or suitable in, so the control operator went out on the radio to ask if anybody could assist. There was a positive response from a RUC patrol who said they would pick us up at the side gate of Fort George in about ten minutes. Suited us just fine.

FULL OF POLICE, GUNS, AND BULLETS!

527

The side gate was armoured, with a six-inch square of green armoured one-way glass in the centre at head height. There were heavy springs on the door which slammed it closed tight if it wasn't held open. The door would then lock into a non-return latch and could not be opened from the outside.

Cheeseboard and I stood inside the door looking through the glass for the Grey Hotspur Landrover that was coming toward to pick us up. We saw the grey Landrover approaching along the Strand Road and not wanting to have them waiting around for us, this was after all Londonderry Bogside, we exited the gate to meet them. The gate slammed shut behind us.

The approaching Landrover drove straight past us and on along the road out of sight. It must have been a different Landrover and not ours.

We were standing on the street having just exited a military base with no way of getting back in the camp. We decided to stroll along the road with the hope that our lift would arrive soon. We walked about fifty or sixty yards when another Landrover, ours, hove into sight. The Landrover stopped outside the gate we had exited and was clearly waiting for us to come out of the camp. Only we weren't in the camp.

The grey Hotspur RUC Landrovers at that time were formidable vehicles. Fully armoured they had a powerful V8 engine, and they took a lot of punishment. The carried the scars of riots and disorder, dents, cracks, and black scorch marks. Likewise, the RUC officers within were very formidable. They were more like commando squads than police. Courageous, heavily armed, and always in the thick of it. They faced life threats and danger every working day.

Looking local in long hair, porn-star moustache, donkey jacket and jeans 'Cheeseboard' and I turned and walked back to the RUC ç. I approached the back door, gave the handle a twist and yanked it open. Instantly I was looking down the barrel of a very big revolver, a Magnum .357, that had been shoved in my face. The hand holding the revolver was shaking and the eyes behind the outstretched arm holding it to my face were very wide under the peak of the dark green police forage cap. I was in deep, deep, shit, and I knew it.

'British Army', British Army' I shouted in my very best Welsh accent, 'British Army' I kept repeating with my empty hands held high in the air. The police officer motioned for me to move backwards, I did so, and bumped into Cheeseboard, who was doing the same as me but without the Welsh accent. We're soldiers I told him; we are waiting for a lift to go over the water. Cheeseboard was nodding to my every word.

We just stood there, motionless, the police had the upper hand and a 'fucking big gun' pointed at my head. I was going to do everything they said.

The situation eased but only slightly, our identity and purpose were confirmed. We climbed into the back of the Landrover with the police and they drove us across the Craigavon Bridge to the waterside. It was an uncomfortable journey. They never took their eyes off us nor their hands of their weapons. Both Cheeseboard and I were carrying loaded, shoulder holstered 9mm Browning's and we daren't go near them. Not a chance. It had been tense, and very dangerous and could so easily have gone tits-up. We got out of the Landrover without a word of thanks nor a goodbye, just relief. Tough boys those RUC Commandos.

Character building? Hell yes!

That evening we were having a beer in a bar inside Ebrington Barracks. I was stood at the bar getting some beers and the guy next to me asked me how I was doing. I didn't recognise him. He told me the last time we spoke he was holding a Magnum to my forehead. He told me he had shit himself when I pulled the door open and for a split second, he nearly pulled the trigger.

He now thought Cheeseboard and I were some special operations people reporting in but at the time he had no clue who we were. I told him we were Recy Mechs, he knew of us having been recovered by army Recy Mechs previously. We would meet again briefly alongside the 'Free Derry' house in the Bogside at the scene of overturned burning cars, riot waste, soldiers, and police. He was a good man, as was his mate and we had a few beers together. I hope he got through the troubles safely.

<u>Top Cover in Derry</u>

I used to get on well with the infantry company from the Queens who were the resident battalion at Fort George. I'd often join them for a brew or a banjo in the cookhouse and they would come to our workshop and climb over our vehicles. They seemed to like big trucks.

Sadly, one day a soldier named Neil Clarke was shot and killed by a sniper while on mobile vehicle patrol in the Bogside. Neil was top-cover in the Landrover, meaning he was standing, with his upper body and rifle through the top hatch. He died on the street having been hit in the back of his head. I learned the details by chatting with his brick commander. The Queens, good infantrymen that they were, were not in any way shape or form not going to be patrolling the area and even though they had lost one of their own, they were going back to show it was their turf. Neil's Corporal was a man down and they were going back out on patrol and needed somebody to take on top-cover. I had all the requisite skills having been a brick commander on a previous tour. I donned my combats and borrowed a rifle (I only had a sub-machine gun and a 9mm pistol) and ammunition and mounted the Landrover. We were the front Landrover of two.

We left Fort George and after a short while we arrived at the Bishops Street scene of the shooting. Both Landrovers debussed and the Queensmen took cover and held the ground. They were making a point. The Corporal walked me around the area and talked me through the murderous shooting. He tells me his patrol were moving slowly along the road when they were attacked by rioters who threw petrol bombs made from sweet jars from a high building. When his uniform caught fire, Neil Clarke jumped from the back of the Land Landrover he was travelling in and as he did so, an IRA sniper opened fire. Neil was struck in the head by a single round and died instantly. Two other members of the patrol were also slightly wounded in the attack. Neil was twenty years old. A man from Londonderry was arrested for his murder and imprisoned. It was an emotive and solemn visit. I could sense the Corporal reliving the event as he spoke to me. We milled around quietly for a few moments before we mounted our vehicles and resumed patrol. I never met or knew Neil Clarke, but I think of him often, RIP Neil.

Character building? Hell yes!

7 Armoured Rugby

Cardiff rugby club has for years lain claim to being the finest rugby club in the world. Well in the 80's it wasn't. I can assure anybody that mantle lay squarely on the shoulder of 7 Armoured Workshop RUFC.

7 had always had a significant and worthy rugby reputation. Always a hard side to beat, it epitomised the very best of REME rugby. Its provenance had been built by sturdy characters such as Terry Pashley, Keith Bartlett, Tony Hibbert, Phil Hope, and many other stalwarts. Notably, at 7 we initially had a rare Recy Mech only front row Phil hope, Sam Oakley, and yours truly; the only time I was aware of such an illustrious trio, and fab it was to.

The famous Rugby Club was in a basement underneath the main cookhouse. Down stone steps and then along shady basement walls covered in purloined trophies of every shape and form, every trophy harbouring a tale of an away foray to an opposition venue the return from which was never empty handed, either in terms of sporting victories or away-day souvenirs. The two main trophies were a 'Stuffed Fox', 'borrowed' from the Hamburg Police, it was homed in a glass case the alert looking animal became the club badge. Sitting, staring, looking for its next kill. (Where is the Fox today?).

The second main trophy was a 'Ships Bell', bolted firmly to the wall alongside the bar. Any ringing of the bell necessitated the immediate purchase of a crate of twenty beers by the ringer whether he or she be 'pressed' or otherwise. The crate being then consumed by whatever thirsty brave souls were present. On many occasions the numbers of crates exceeded the number of people in the club.

Army Regiments, British or otherwise, like to signpost their unit lines and camps with proud signs, always in regimental colours, always very large, always proclaiming their position or standing, and always held to a wall or post by a few screws. 7 was after all an engineering unit and screwdrivers were aplenty. From all over Germany and beyond were in 7, probably the finest unofficial selection of acquired militaria in existence.

In my second season at 7 and following the departure of Graham Downes, an excellent REME CORPS centre, I was voted in as Skipper (It's that

English thing again). How do you improve an already very good side. I thought fitness was a good place to start so we set about pre-season training with a will. Twice a week, gym, and field. I pushed and pushed and cajoled and bullied, got heavily on the case of any player who didn't show for training. Introduced a few new, for 7, moves which I knew from other clubs to be tried and tested. My plan was to play a physically hard fast game. Forward domination with quick skilful backs was the order of the day, wasn't it for every successful club? We held a trial for position, I wanted everybody to know they were in a with a chance for a first team place. Jim Burberry and Mark Smith were 'found' at this trial. Fabulous wing forwards and they would play a huge part in our success. No cliques here. We had enough players for three teams; we were formidable. We had about thirty players worthy of a first team place and they were all highly competitive.

When I arrived the team colours were a very disgusting thin hooped orange and purple. It didn't look 'hard', we were going to be 'hard'. So, I ordered a new black strip. White collars, white sock tops, white numbers, and a big square white club badge for the breast. The Fox was to be in GOLD. Just like the 'All Blacks and 'Neath'. Besides, black was slimming! (Les Payne).

Very quickly we set our mark. Within a week we had beaten the Welsh Guards, big strong Welshmen with rugby nous, who had hammered us the season previously. Jim and Mark tackled everything. Three tries to one. Steve Morgan our Abertillery Fly Half scoring two tries and giving an easy walk-in to Ian Crummack, formerly of London Scottish. The same week we took 21 Engineer Regiment to the cleaners, a handsome win in which I scored a scrapping try. The engineers were the current BAOR and Army Champions. Steve Williams of Cwmavon had a ten yard sidestep; he was there then he wasn't. Phil Pontin of Bridgend was a class act (The RRW were to poach him from us with great promises to him). Don Scambler a ginger Scotsman a prolific try scorer on the wing as he was for North Berwick. Tony Williams his usual bludgeoning, never taking a step backwards, self. Pete Mattinson was a consummate back. We had an abundance of handsome props; Glyn Mountjoy who had played for a Crawshays XV, Dave Mason young and keen, Les Payne, Taff 'Tits' Thomas and of course yours truly. It was just all clicking into place. Open your eyes and taste the win boys! We carried on like that for a few seasons, hard fast rugby. Win after win. Our third half was a tough and demanding as the rugby itself.

Sadly, and as happened so frequently in the army, the powers that be let us down. I was approached by the commanding officer and asked how good we were. I replied we could confidently beat the best in Germany and if we continued as we were the army cup was ours. I don't know when a REME unit won the Major units army cup, if ever. I was confident. In the semi-final we were due to play the reigning army champions, 21 Engineer Regiment which was effectively the Royal Engineers Corps side, the strongest they had, and we had beaten them twice in the season already.

So, what did we do, prepare our side diligently, make sure everybody was fit and ready, put maximum effort into a sporting venture the REME has never achieved, bring reputation and kudos to the unit? Err no! not a bit of it. We sent half the rugby team to Canada. So, when we took the field against the best sapper-side they could put out we had only half our first team on the pitch. We lost by one lousy point! Fuck it!

Today, years later nobody remembers the Canada thing. Nobody remembers coming second in the semi-final. If we had treated the army cup as seriously as did the other army units, we would be in the record books and people would still be talking about it today. Fuck it!

<u>Generally, Rugby</u>

The British Army is a tough place. The boundaries of social acceptance are pushed and stretched and sometimes broken. The nature of the work will harden and insulate young men who have faced and dealt with extreme adversity. These traits will inevitably spill into military social behaviour. Coral those young men in the competitive atmosphere of a post-match rugby club with beer and sometimes things can get a bit out of hand.

Post-match entertainment at 7 consisted of excellent food, ensured by one of our second-row players, Jim Green, who coincidentally was the 'master-chef'. Frequent 'ringing of the ships bell' determined copious quantities of free, for some, beer. Nobody wanted for anything. After food and a few drinks, the inevitable sing-song would start.

The singing was always loud and raucous. Hymns, filthy bar-room ballads, anthems and made-up on the spot chants and bawls. It was fab. The opposing sides would take turns in some delinquent order, and it was always competitive. Who could be the loudest, sing longest and so on.

At 7 we played a lot of touring sides as we had a reputation for being good hosts. Welsh club sides would tour frequently, they were always good for a tough game. Royal Navy ships would frequent Hamburg or Bremen and they would always put up a good effort. Socially the matlows were world class. They were generally very strong upper body players but troubled at mobility; forfeit of being on a ship I suppose. We played Germany under floodlights at Hannover Stadium a very close game, but Germany had two centres who played at Toulouse in France. That was the difference between us, the third half was no contest. It never was.

About a third of our first team played for 1st Armoured Divisional side (the rest of the divisional were mostly from 21 Engineer Regiment) and about six or seven of us for the BAOR REME Corps side.

We had two army players in Steve Morgan and Paul Arnott who for some anonymous reason didn't get selected by REME Corps. They should have most definitely. A few of us played for BAOR. I played for them about six or seven times while at 7, but I was not a regular BAOR player by any means. Third or fourth choice probably.

One noteworthy game was when three of us from 7 were selected to pay for a BAOR XV against Cornwall County who were touring Germany. Ian Crummack, Ian Simpson, and I travelled down to Herford for the game. It was noteworthy because Graham Dawe the English hooker was hooking for Cornish County side. It was a very tough game and we lost. Even so, between us Ian Simpson our hooker and I managed to take two against the head from the English international; a small claim to fame. Tough boys those Cornishmen.

I also recall playing for a BAOR XV against Durham County. They were a composite of Hartlepool and

West Hartlepool rugby clubs. They were treating this tour as a training tour because on their return most of their players would make up the North of England side against the UK touring New Zealand All Blacks. Phew! That was a tough one. We lost.

Glyn Mountjoy and I were selected to play for a BAOR Welsh XV against the Welsh Guards on St David's Day. Our composite XV lost but what fabulous hosts the Welsh Guards were. Rugby mad they just did everything right. A fabulous experience. Tough boys those Welsh Guards.

I played for the BAOR REME Corps side continuously for five years barring Northern Ireland, Canada, and courses. They were a great bunch of players.

We went on tour to Yorkshire and played several games one of which was against Ripon. The No 10 for Ripon was a chap called Peter Squires. He was a county cricketer but more relevantly he was an England and British Lions winger. I remember admiring his fantastic skills as I and the rest of the Corps team trailed in his wake. A class act is a class act! Having a beer with him afterward he was an absolute gentleman and a fine ambassador for Ripon and rugby.

Another memorable tour was going down to Frankfurt to play the Americans. There were two games played, the first against the regular 'Frankfurt Americans' RFC, which was their regular side. The second game was against the 'USA All Wonderful Hollywood Stars Dancing Super Elite Perfect Select Combined International Europe Way-Over-the Top RFC,'. The Frankfurt Americans were the tougher game which we won by about seven points.

Their all singing and dancing select XV were a much easier side to beat; they didn't have the cohesion of a regular team. Their selection had a substantial 'American Football' influence; they were all like Captain America. Huge and hard, no necks, broad shouldered and loud, very loud. Happily, for us they lacked 'rugby savvy' so we took them apart. Their No. 8 was massive; he had a short hair style a huge square neck, the widest shoulders and smallest waist I have ever seen; obviously gymnasium manufactured. He tackled with a clear American football influence, very fast and diving straight. He made a noise like an accelerating jet engine – Vroooomphh. It was a little disconcerting. Near our try line there was a scrabble for the ball, and I found it in my hands. I tried to clear the ball, but I was under huge pressure. I could hear a Vroooomphh getting louder and louder behind me. I knew I was in his sights. just as I kicked the ball out, he side-wined me. I was felled like a tree, just cut in half. The tackle rattled my teeth, shook my bones, numbed my nerves, knocked the wind from my lungs and laid me flat on the floor. I was winded and stung. I had to get up and heaved myself slowly from the floor. I was in great pain and hurting all over. The tackler got up alongside me and I turned to him and said in as gently and concerning a voice as I could muster 'Are you OK?". If looks could kill! He'd given me his best shot and I was querying his condition. Yanks just don't get understatement. As I walked away, I was

rattling inside. His hit was one of the three hardest I ever experienced the other two coming from an RAOC No.8 and one from a certain Mr Terry Pashley of REME fame.

However, the All-Stars after-match hosting was probably the best I ever experienced. The proceedings were in a large magnificently decorated ball room and there were hundreds of bottles of beer just lined up in ice buckets. It was all free. The wide selection of food was expertly laid out and the centrepiece was the most gigantic lump of beef I had seen since seeing a whole Ox roasted on a spit in Hamburg. The lump of beef was the size of a very big TV set and the chef carving it, resplendent in his whites and very tall hat, was generous in his distribution. Steve Milner, George Raw and I absolutely gluttoned ourselves. Beer and Beef – it's the way forward!

After the meal I was having a beer with my opposite number to whom I had given a torrid time in the tight.

He was from New York, and he kept pressing beers into my hand. He was loud and opinionated as I have always found New Yorkers to be. 'You British sure are tough motherfuckers!' he kept repeating. Oh well!

Character building? Hell yes!

Cadavers Burp?

We toured in Wales where we always had a remarkable welcome. On one tour to the valleys, we played eight games in fourteen days. It was tough rugby, we socialised hard, we played hard, and we ran it off every morning. Great days.

It's been a slog of a week with about four matches and the socialising along with it. On the Sunday morning we need to go to the local accident and emergency unit to get patched up. We need stitches putting in, stitches to be taken out, joints to be bandaged and supported. Most of us have some issue that need looking at.

We go to Prince Charles hospital at Merthyr Tydfil, we all go, about fifty-five of us on our coach. As we all enter the A&E department, I see there are about thirty civilians waiting there and we sit amongst them. Those soldiers that need treatment book in at the reception, the rest of us sit quietly visiting the vending machines and so on. It's a slow process and we are hanging around for quite a while. Not a good thing as the boys begin to get restless, and I know something will happen. Nigel Hancock and 'PUSK' go for a walk.

I'm sitting with Toy Williams chatting away. My attention is drawn to a doctor in a white coat with a stethoscope around his neck pushing a hospital trolley into the waiting room area. The trolley has on a white sheet pulled over what is obviously a body, a dead body? The doctor and trolley pass along the front of the waiting people and as he draws centre with the waiting room the doctor stops pushing the trolley, and raises his hand to his chin, then rubs his chin as if musing something. The doctor then turns

551

around and walks out of the waiting room to where he came from, leaving the trolley with the body and white sheet stationary at the front of the room. The room has gone quiet. Everybody is looking at the trolley and people can't believe a body has been left in front of them. The doctor has disappeared. It is very disturbing. The waiting room has gone very quiet, and people are clearly perplexed and uncomfortable. There is a very low murmur of conversation. I, for my part, had clear knowledge that the white coated, stethoscope wearing doctor looked remarkably like Sergeant Nigel Hancock, REME military technical storeman and 7 Armoured RFC full back!

I sit quietly watching what will happen. Tony Williams, very unusually for a Sergeant Major, is also quiet. So are the rest of the 7 guys. Their silence adds to the foreboding atmosphere. The soldiers are quiet in anticipation; the civvies are quiet in unsurety. The moment lingers on. Nobody moves, people strain to look where the doctor went, hoping he would come back and remove the body.

Suddenly, an arm falls from below the sheet and dangles motionless downwards. There is an intake of breath, still nobody moves. All is quiet.

There is a burp. A burp! It seemed to come from the trolley. It couldn't have, dead people don't burp. Do they?

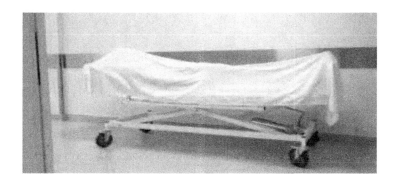

Dead people don't burp. Do they?

There is a brief moaning sound coming from the trolley then slowly but surely the body sits upright. The white sheet slips down and there on the trolley the dead body has risen. Then risen body has

553

unusual features, though he looks quite dead. A miserable facial expression with ashen complexion, sunken eyes, and gaunt features. His eyes were dark and solemn as were the shady rings around them. His droopy long moustache gave him a forlorn Mexican bandit face.

The risen dead body slowly turned toward the waiting people. There was a momentary pause and all the civilians rose as one and hurried to the back of the waiting room, away from the miracle, and out the doors.

The rugby players rolled about laughing hilariously. 'Pusk' and Hancock were, true to form, being their mischievous selves'.

Character building? Hell yes, even for some civvies!

Tastes Like Shite

For that same tour Jan Christofferson, in charge of beer, bought thousands of cans of the cheapest beer he could find. It was called 'Edel Pils', it came in small white cans and tasted shite. The talented JJ Bateman was so disgusted with the beer he penned a song. I'm sure every tourist remembers the song to this day.

Edel Pils (To the tune of Edelweiss)

Edel pils, Edel pils,
every morning you greet me,
small and white,
taste like shite,
I'm on tour so I'll drink thee;
it's the pits
it gives me the shits,
me the shits
all morningggg...
Edel pils, Edel pils,
It's the best thing
for ring sting!

<u>Korean Bell or Our Biggest Fuck-Up Ever!</u>

It's a very hot day and we send a club team, by white army coach, down to Hildesheim to play against 1 Royal Tank regiment. Our club team isn't a very strong side it's a mix of first and second team players. I and other first team regulars are on the bench and it's a hard game. The weather is clear sunshine, the ground is like iron, and the Tank regiment are putting up a decent fist of it. Half time and its ten-nil to the tankies. We put everybody on, and we finish eleven points to ten winners. Its close run, but the game is ours' always a pleasure to win. The boys are sweating big style, they have really built up a huge thirst, and they are very keen to have it quenched. A quick shower and it's off to the RTR rugby club bar for cold beers, lots of them, but there's an issue!

The 'cooler-pumps' in the bar are broken. Apparently, according to the barman, they have overheated with the abnormally high temperature

and there's no cold beers or cider. The barman goes on to say the only cooler that is working is the one sourcing white wine. That'll be very cold white wine. Ok so very cold white wine by the pint.

The boys get stuck into pints of cold white wine. They deserve it. A good win with a club side, why not enjoy the post-game festivities, especially as the wine is so cooling. Just be mindful the wine is three or four times stronger than beer, so be moderate in your imbibition. FAT CHANCE!

There was no change in drinking behaviour other than the entire club was rat-arsed in short order. We cleaned the bar out of wine and then drank warm beer, which tasted shite. Eventually it was time to go and the usual foragers in the club went looking for a memento of sorts to add to our clubhouse collection at Fallingbostel.

During the Korean War the Centurion Tank Equipped 1st Royal Tank Regiment was deployed, their main role was to dominate "No

Man's Land" and this they did with tremendous success, bringing down fire on enemy positions more effectively and quickly than the artillery could. In the six months that the 1 RTR spent in the line, the Regiment fired nearly 24,000 rounds of main armament in support of the Commonwealth Division. The Regiment and its echelon support never wavered in its duty. The Korea Bell, which stands outside of the 1 RTR guard room was made from some of the empty 20 pounder cases and hangs from a miniature "Torii". It was presented to the Regiment by Brigadier G C Hopkinson, who commanded the 1st RTR from January 1952 until September 1953.

Some of the lads while foraging, saw a very attractive Brass Bell hanging from an ornate wooden structure outside the unit guardroom. They thought it would make an excellent addition to our purloined trophy range back at the clubhouse. With the wine-fuelled motivation of an elite special forces raiding outfit the foragers succeeded in removing the bell from the structure and made to secrete it in the boot of our coach for the return trip to Fallingbostel. However, they didn't go unchallenged. The second in command of the guard that day happened to be a REME Lance Corporal, let's call him Jock. He approached the bell removers and for his trouble and interference he was also bundled into the boot of the coach and held there under duress. As a 'coup de grace' the same foraging team removed the 1 Royal Tank Regiment regimental sign, measuring about five feet by five feet, and that was also found a place in the boot of the coach; and so, the coach left on the return journey.

As the effects of the wine began to wear off the enormity of the probable consequences of having away such artifacts began to dawn on the rugby playing minds. It wasn't the sign that would be a big issue, a sign could easily be replaced. It wasn't the second in command of the guard, Jock, that was a big issue; he was by now happily drinking away in the back of the bus, and a replacement lance Corporal could be found. But the bell!

A "serious pucker battle memorial", forged from brass cases fired in battle, presented by a Brigadier, hung proudly at the front of the unit for over thirty years. Oh Bollox!

RESPECT

A plan was hatched. We would not go directly to the clubhouse but would hide the bell in a volunteer married soldiers house before journeys end. The second in command of the guard 'Jock', who was now well pissed, would be got out of his uniform, dressed in civvies, and was told to keep his mouth shut. The regimental sign would go with the bell. The

coach would then carry on to the clubhouse as if nothing had happened. That was the plan; it was, of course, doomed to failure from the start!

As the coach pulled up outside our clubhouse there were more military police on parade than there were players on the bus. Military Police are not known for their good humour and 'bonhomie' and this occasion was no exception. They lined us up, rather harshly I thought, and conducted a thorough search of us all and the bus, including the boot and found nothing. They had no reason to believe that Jock wasn't one of our own.

Why were they searching people's pockets for a hundredweight heavy bell, a five-foot square sign, and a Lance Corporal?

Nothing found we were sent on our way. I knew that was not the end of matters and I was correct.

Early the next morning the entire rugby club, including those who hadn't even been on the trip, were ordered (ordered mind you) to assemble in the clubhouse. Also present were Captain Crummack, our second row and rugby officer. Also, Company Sergeant Major Tony Williams, another second row and the highest-ranking soldier in the club. They were both delighted they hadn't been at the match. Probably 'career-safe' delighted!

Crum and Tony laid it out as it was. The Royal Tanks weren't happy, far from it; they were FUCKING FURIOUS! The tankies wanted their commemorative battle bell and sign back. It appeared they cared not a jot for their REME Lance Corporal. The bell was everything. Crum and Tony continued to lay it on thick and fast. A Landrover was brought to the clubhouse, the bell and sign placed therein, and they were post-haste returned to Hildesheim. The bell and sign were accompanied by a massive apology.

The issue numbed our activity for a short while; threats were hanging over our heads about club behaviours and so on, and in all fairness we mellowed. That is until we played Germany at Hannover stadium and some of the lads found a pitch-side bar could be dismantled and would fit, with a squeeze, into our coach. That's another story.

As for Jock the kidnapped second in command of the guard. He was after all REME, just like us, and he knew a few of our lads. He found a bed that night at the married quarter of one of our players, a fellow Scotsman. They arrived at the quarter four sheets to the wind. Our man went to bed and Jock was to sleep on the settee in the living room. Our man's wife was up first in the morning and on entering the living room it wasn't particularly the naked drunken snoring second in command of the Tank Regiment guard that disgusted her; it was the fat brown turd he had laid on the telephone table.

The Hooker!

The first female soldier at 7 Armoured!

I was Skipper (that English thing again) of the rugby team and one lunchtime I was sitting in the Hackett Club eating my NAAFI sandwich and drinking a coke. This new female soldier comes up to me, up to that point I had only seen her at a distance, and she says to me.

> *"Are you Taff Rees?"*
> *"Yes" I replied.*
> *"Do you organise the rugby?" she said.*
> *"Yes, I do" I replied, wondering where this is going.*
> *"Good" she said, "I would like to play".*
> *I thought this had to be a wind-up. I looked around to see if any of the rugby boys were present but could see none. I thought I'd call her bluff.*
> *"Ok" I said. "What position do you play?".*
> *She kept a serious and straight face. "Hooker" she said.*
> *This was a wind-up; OK I would play along. "No problem" I said. "Be at the gym one o' clock on Saturday; we have two games at home I'll see what we can do".*

"OK, great, thanks" she said. She then turned and walked away.

I mused on the matter for a while but quickly dismissed it. A clear wind-up by some devilish rugby soul.

The following Saturday I was sitting on a bench in the foyer of the Gym sorting the teams for that afternoon. A few of the players had arrived early and were milling around. I then heard an unfamiliar click-clack, it was the sound of high heels. I looked up and there she was made up in civvies, a yellow blouse, black pencil skirt, high heels and under her arm was a towel wrapped around a pair of rugby boots. I was taken aback.

I quickly considered the situation; this was an extended wind-up, at any minute the boys present, who were standing there looking gobsmacked, would roll about laughing at my expense. I decided I couldn't be outdone and made a quick decision.

"Ok I said, what's your name?"

"Sheree Haddlesey" she said, "but everybody calls me Fred".
"OK Fred" I said, "You're hooking in the seconds this afternoon".
"OK thanks" she said and trotted off in her heels to join the lads.

The upshot of this tale is that it wasn't a wind-up, she was genuine, and she did play that afternoon against 21 Engr Regt 2nds. Taff 'Tits' Thomas propped alongside her. She had a good game. She joined in fully in the clubhouse after the game, where she showed me her 'Tits's hand sized bruise' on her left breast, and she was, I recall, a good member of the club. How the world was changing.

Character building? Hell yes!

The Edinburg Constable

Company Sergeant Major Tony Williams, optimistic and persuasive soul that he was, thought it would be a fine idea to hold an Inter-Company Boxing Competition at 7. It wasn't by any means a 'boxing' unit and the combatants would have to be found, training undertaken, and the main event organised. It was going to be a full-on Regimental Boxing evening. Mess dress for officers and senior ranks with mess functions following the boxing. Compulsory attendance in No. 2 dress for all other ranks. Who was going to box?

Tony went about the unit identifying participants; I'm not sure 'volunteer' is the right word but eventually enough 'gladiators' were found to fill all the weight divisions for each company. I was volunteered. My volunteering went something like this –

'How do you fancy boxing Taff'?
'No thanks.
Yes, I'm sure you'll be good at it'!

'No thanks.'
'It'll be a good night'.
'No thanks'.
'Yes, I'm sure you'll be fine'.
'No thanks.

That was it, I was B Company's reluctant heavyweight contender in the inter-company boxing. My opponent from A Company was Neil Gordon, our rugby team No.8. an Edinburgh Police Constable before joining the army. He stood about six foot four inches and had a reach about a yard longer than me. I knew from playing alongside him on the rugby pitch he was a very strong man with a punch like a mule. Bollox!

Training was organised with all the accoutrements such as boxing gloves, punch bags, weight-benches. A full-size boxing ring was setup in the garrison gymnasium. Each boxer was allocated a 'corner-man'. Mine was 'Oggy Horton', driver by trade, paratrooper by badge and a man of permanent informative conversation. I enjoyed 'Oggy's' company and listening to his tales of adventures. Particularly the one where he left his wife for the two strippers that performed at the 'Hackett' (7 NAAFI) club one evening.

We set about training for over a month. I was reasonably fit through the rugby; I was strong and prepared to have a go despite being 'pressed' by Williams. What I didn't have was any boxing skill. I'd never really taken an interest in boxing, but I was quickly learning it was an art. The rules of amateur novice boxing were explained. It was going to be bouts of three rounds, the first two rounds of one and a half minutes, the third of two minutes. I was also learning what a long time two minutes was, it could be stretched into a never ending eternity. Boxing was physically exhausting, and the exhaustion came on very quickly. We spent about a month sparring, punching bags, learning to roll with punches, keep our arms up, look for gaps, move forward, keep aware, focus on your opponent. Even so, I knew I wasn't very good at it. So, I developed a plan. I didn't mind a close-up wrestle, or a head clashing intimately personal confrontation; I was well used to such things in rugby.

My fight plan was to keep both hands high to protect my face and head from Neil Gordons 'sure to come bombs', keep moving forward constantly, and because of my opponent Neil's height, try to uppercut from in close. Well, that was my plan; the six-foot four former Edinburgh Police Officer had a different one.

It's the night of the match. The gymnasium is rammed. There are about eight bouts and mine is last but one, they found some capable welterweight boxers who were to be the last and probably best match. I didn't watch the preceding bouts I stay in the changing room. I was nervous and concerned I was going to get my fucking head knocked off, I had seen Neil punching. Fuck it!

Eventually it's time for our bout. There is a 'kettle drummer', borrowed form an infantry battalion, in red tunic and pith helmet who precedes each of us into the ring. He plays his drum, increasing the tempo as we draw near the ring. The soldier audience are loving it. Each company yelling enthusiastically for their representative boxer. Great cheers as the boxers are drummed in. Great cheers as the boxers are announced. I sit in the corner; I've got to appear hard and intimidating I stare at Neil across the ring. He's not looking at me. Oggy is giving me all the advice from his years of experience; he's never boxed in his life! The bell rings.

CONSTABLE GORDON – PUNCH LIKE A MULE!

I rush straight to the middle of the ring. I intend to press forward from the word go. I must bully him. We close in the middle of the ring. Fucking hell, he's huge. I try a few punches which land on his arms. I push forward. He lashes out, I see it coming I raise my arms in defence, it's a solid punch and he rocks me backwards. He can punch. I press again and try to hit him, succeeding in only hitting his arms. I keep pushing forward. He thumps me again. I feel the punch, it's a corker, but I feel no pain. The bell rings.

I sit on my corner stool, Oggy, professional that he is feeds me water, fans me with a towel, and advises more of the same. Back into the fray. The second round goes much the same as the first. I can't get close to him. He is punching me and I'm absorbing the punches on my arms. I try a few upper-cuts from in close, but he easily steps aside. Second round over and I'm back in my corner on my stool. More of the same from Oggy.

It's the last round. I'm blowing and so is Neil. There are about four hundred soldiers cheering their heads off and I can't hear them. I'm getting punched hard, and I can't feel a thing. As Neil lands a bruiser on the side of my head the ref pauses the fight and moves in towards me. He holds my chin and looks close into my eyes. It's not love he has, its concern. He holds up four fingers. I tell him four and that he's to get out of my way. We continue, time is not with me. I see an opportunity and I let go my biggest punch of the nigh; if it connects, he's fucked. Neil sees it coming, steps back a tad, and it skins his face, he looks relieved I missed, but oh so, so close. I push him, and bully him, and harry him all around the ring; but I can't land any telling blows and eventually the final bell rings. Both Neil and I are heaving for breath. I don't think I've mastered him. The referee congratulates both boxers on a worthy match and Neil is pronounced the winner. Deservedly so.

There is a riotous evening to follow. All the messes have functions, and the boxers are feted in all of them. Drinks and toasts and so on. It was a fabulous and memorable night.

Character building? Hell yes!

The next day my jaw didn't work. I couldn't eat for a week. It was soup and beer only. Sergeant Major Williams, you bastard Sir, I said NO!

<u>Double Tragedy</u>

One of our players is getting married in the Channel Islands. It's going to be a fabulous wedding and I'm sure a lot of beer will be put away. Two of the team, Phil 'Ginge' Heaton and Tony French, are travelling to the wedding, driving down all the way through Germany. Tragically they are involved in an accident, and both are killed. It's an immense shock. Fit young men in the prime of life. The shocking event hits the rugby fraternity very hard. Both were excellent club members participating and playing in everything the club did.

Tony Williams, a Company Sergeant Major, and fellow rugby player, discussed with me the possibility of the rugby club forming the burial party. Tony has the commanding officers permission, so we put it to the club for volunteers, as it was always going to be, they volunteer to a man. It's going to be two full military funerals. Ginge to be buried at Hannover military cemetery and Tony at Reading. We are going to be in full No. 2 dress, rifle volleys over the grave and a last post bugler.

We set about rehearsing for the sad event, it's a matter of personal pride and respect to our lost colleagues that we put on a perfect performance. We start rehearsing under the expert eye of Company Sergeant Major Williams. As Captain of the rugby team I am designated right hand marker.

The burial party ceremony is quite complicated and involves drills we haven't done before. There is a bearer party element and a firing and escort party. Much of the drill is at slow march and much of the rifle drill is unfamiliar to us as they are carried upside down. We practice for hours and hours. Our uniform is immaculate, our boots are highly bulled, our drill is perfect. As for firing the volleys we do it as one. Its personal.

Ginge is first at Hannover. His parents, sister and brother-in-law have travelled to Germany for the funeral, they stay at my quarter. Ginge's father is a

Chief Petty Officer in the Royal Navy, and he is resplendent in his best uniform. The funeral is very moving and goes along perfectly. That bugle doesn't half drill your soul.

I am shocked to see that I know or know of, about ten of the people who are buried in the same row; soldiers all and good men.

We repeat the process at Reading Cemetery in the UK for Tony. His family are present and some civilians who I don't know. They are very shocked and startled when our volley is fired.

I don't have the words to fully explain how moving a military funeral is. If you know those being buried, it's tough. If your part of the burial party and you know those being buried its tougher still. Rest in Peace gents' fine men that you are!

Character building? Hell yes!

Respect RIP Lads

6th Unit – Royal Scots Dragoon Guards

Final Posting

My last and shortest posting. I'd returned to the UK with the intention of leaving the army and seeking pastures new. I'd gotten a little demotivated at 7, due almost entirely to the very poor quality of the Recy mech SNCO's. I was very disappointed that people who could be so good a first line units sank to the sort of behaviour I had encountered the last few years. I didn't want to be like any of them.

I enjoyed my short time at the RSDG LAD, including wearing my new grey coloured beret. The Royal Scots Dragoon Guards cap badge was a 'French Eagle' inspired from when Sergeant Ewart of the Scots Greys Captured a French Eagle at Waterloo.

He said, when describing the Capture.

> *One made a thrust at my groin; I parried him off and cut him down*

through the head. A lancer came at me - I threw the lance off by my right side and cut him through the chin and upwards through the teeth. Next, a foot soldier fired at me and then charged me with his bayonet, which I also had the good luck to parry, and then I cut him down through the head.

Today the Standard and Eagle are kept on display in the Royal Scots Dragoon Guards Museum in Edinburgh Castle. Ewart himself is buried on Edinburgh Castle esplanade, a Scottish hero, and the only person to have this honour.

I was the RSDG HQ Squadron Recy Mech. The Recy Sergeant was Don Martin. He was fabulous, just like the senior Recy Mechs prior to 7. There wasn't a lot of recovery at Tidworth. I had a twenty-seven-ton Foden to play with and occasionally I would help the squadron Recy Mechs moving tanks about. I was not in any way challenged.

The Regiment had a famous bagpipe section having made national fame with 'Mull of Kintyre'; I could hear them all the time.

Writing in Scots

One thing about the Jocks that I could never understand, and still don't to this day is why so many of them try to write in a Scots accent; I just don't get it.

> For example -
> *Ma tank is deid cuid ye c'mere an mibbe noo fix afore am roond ma hoose.*

> Translation-
> *My tank is dead, could you come here now and maybe fix it before I go home.*

Last Exercise – Escape and Evasion

My last military exercise was with the RSDG LAD. It was an escape and evasion style exercise which, what I had been through the preceding twelve years was small fry.

The LAD deployed into the 'Ulu' with full personal kit. As we set up camp, we camouflaged our faces and hands with cam-cream and started building bashers. Almost immediately we were bounced by the enemy, and we were all Captured. Even though it was an ordered exercise scenario I didn't like being Captured, neither did anybody else. It went against the grain. I didn't want to comply and made myself as awkward as possible for our captors, making them work hard to get us to do what they wanted. We were stripped of our equipment and forced to put on only green army coveralls. We kept our boots, but no laces. We were given a right-angle army torch, of which I immediately checked the batteries. That was it. We sat in a circle in a field, guarded, for what seemed forever. Eventually we were split into groups and each group was appointed a group leader. I was one.

The group leaders were taken to one side and given a briefing. We are told that at the arrival of darkness, it was January, we would be taken to a yet undisclosed place where we would be given a map and told to make our way, as quickly as possible to another location. It was 'escape and evasion' and we were to avoid all contact with anybody whomsoever. We would have to identify our start point ourselves when we were delivered there, no clue would be given. I went and briefed my allocation of four or five soldiers. I didn't have much to tell them. I asked for their input, one of them had some cash, in notes, he had secreted in his boot. That was it.

It had been raining for weeks beforehand and the ground was very wet. It began to rain yet again. We hadn't yet started and we were already cold and wet. Just after darkness fell a Chinook Helicopter landed in our field. It was surprising because the weather was so bad, the cloud base was so low, it wasn't the best flying weather. I was a RAF qualified helicopter handler and knew the aircraft well. We were ushered into the back of the aircraft, still only in coveralls and unlaced boots. The Chinook took off. It flew for quite a while, not flying high but making many turns and weaves. At one point I thought they might have been lost or been unsure of the way because we hovered very low above a well-lit motorway signpost; the sort that was huge, blue, and said things like 'M1 The North'.

I surmised we weren't travelling a very long distance because of the amount of turning we were doing. I thought we were flying around for an hour in much the same area. Eventually the Chinook landed in a dark area. I could see no lights or indeed anything outside. A section was told to get off and they did so. The Chinook took off again and soon dropped off another section. Eventually it was our turn and we egressed into a field, the Chinook took off and

disappeared into the dark night sky. It was pissing down. It was dark wet, and the only noise came from the heavy falling rain. The army certainly knows how to professionally fuck people about!

I gathered the lads together, here's the situation; we're in an unknown field, we are wet and cold, we have a map and a torch. One of you has some cash.

Here's our plan; we keep moving to keep warm, we find something to lace and tighten our boots, we locate where we are, we make best speed to our end point, which is a grid reference on the map.

We start moving out of the field. Luckily the gate out was tied shut with baling string. We quickly unravelled the rope into string and made improvised laces. Boots were now tightly on, a good start. We left the gate unsecured.

We were clearly in a very rural area, I could see no street light glow, hear no traffic noise, see no landmarks. We had come out of the field onto a single-track tarmac road, it didn't appear to be well used as there were loose chippings across it. We are going to stay tightly together; I didn't want to lose anybody. We started to walk briskly off along the road in the direction we did for no reason other than it was there to walk along.

Eventually we came to a small crossroads which, joy of joys, had a signpost on it; even so it took ages to locate us on the map, in the rain with a shitty army torch. I estimated we had about thirty miles to get to our target location. Thirty fucking miles? In this shit weather!

We had choices to make, stick to roads or cross country. Roads were better for walking on, but cross country offered some decent shorter options. I'd decide as the options arose on the map. For the first move we were going directly across a field which would save us a mile or two. Two hundred yards into the field and we are up to our waists in swirling cold water. Fuck this, about turn, back to the crossroads and stick to tarmac.

We were walking along the road, soaking but warm and morale was good, cracking jokes, slagging the army off and so on. Eventually we came to a small hamlet of a few houses with a tight crossroads in the middle. Not a sound, other than falling rain, nor any light. I heard a vehicle approaching.

It was a short wheelbase Landrover, a farmer's type of vehicle. The Landrover stopped at the hamlet crossroads. I stepped up to the driver's window and rapped on it sharply. The driver shit himself, crashed it into gear and floored the throttle to get away from the soaking, camouflaged face apparition, trying to get to him. The engine roared, the Landrover jerked forward and stopped. In his fear and haste to get away he had stalled it. He appeared to be quite young, and he was clearly panicking. I shouted to him 'it's OK, It's OK, we're soldiers. Army'. He just sat there staring at me through the rain-soaked widow. I told him to open the window as I wanted to speak with him. He opened it about a half inch, still very much unsure.

I explained I was army on a night exercise, the weather was shit, and I could do with a lift. We chatted a little more and he agreed. I then called the lads forward; it was the first time he had seen them. He was OK with it, and I got in the front seat and the lads piled into the back. Many sighs of relief.

I showed him on the map where we needed to go, he knew the place and was happy to take us there. We chatted all along the way with him asking all the questions. He visibly relaxed as we travelled for about an hour, and he began to revel in his unexpected adventure. I asked him to drop us off a few miles from our destination, I didn't want to be seen having a lift into our target location. As far as anybody else was concerned we had done the whole shamonka on foot as we were supposed to.

Nearing our destination, we found some shelter on a closed garage forecourt and relaxed there for the extra hours we would have been tabbing. At an appropriate time, we moved off and strolled the last few miles to our final grid point. We were met by camp staff who gave us hot food and drink, dry clothes (ours were there) and a hot meal and a big army tent to sleep in. We had after all tabbed thirty miles, through the night in the shittiest of weather, and had finished in an excellent time. No other team completed the course, no willing clandestine Landrover I suppose. They were all eventually rounded up by directing staff in vehicles.

To the young gentleman driving the Landrover, many thanks. I bet you've told the tale of that night over and over.

Character building? Hell yes!

<u>Rugby at Tidworth</u>

I was in the process of arranging to leave the REME and had no intention of playing rugby for fear of injury before starting my new career, but unavoidably rugby is in my Welsh blood.

The RSDG had a decent regimental rugby team. It was OK but nowhere near 7, or the REME Corps side, for whom I started playing again in the UK.

The RSDG had a very noteworthy winger by the name of Andy McLellan, tall, powerful, and fast, he was a prolific try score and had a kick like a mule. He played for Salisbury RFC on the weekends, and they were the premier side in Wiltshire and further afield. Andy encouraged me to go along to Salisbury RFC with him.

Salisbury RFC were a very typical English rugby club. I was told before I arrived at Salisbury that they actively encouraged military players and this initiative had no doubt strengthened their player

base. The club had fabulous facilities, and superb clubhouse and an abundance of pitches. They also had about seven or eight playing sides. So, I started training with them two evenings a week. As I recall they had names for their sides, colloquial names such as 'Druids', 'Stones' and other peculiarities. Initially I was selected to play in what was their seventh team. For the few months I was at the club I rarely played in the same team twice. I was surely moving up the selection ladder, and I was, as always, enjoying the game.

At the time Salisbury played in the Courage Rugby Club Championship and were classed as one of the top 50 - 60 clubs in the country and were deservedly allocated a place in Area League South, level 4 of the national club hierarchy The standard of the first and second teams was very good.

My debut game for the first fifteen was at Salisbury against top London side Rosslyn Park, a very strong side. Salisbury narrowly lost the game. It was quick and tough. A bonus for me was that the referee was none other than Royal Artillery Master Gunner Roland 'Taff' Hill. He was the most able of army rugby referees I had ever encountered, and he had been a regular official for our games at 7. It was good to catch up with him. Salisbury was a good club.

As a bonus, whilst playing at Salisbury, they put on the best 'Beer Festival' I have ever been to, either before or since. Well done Salisbury Rugby.

SALISBURY RFC - BEST BEER FESTIVAL EVER

Last Day with the Colours

My last day in the army was Friday 5th February 1988 I had handed all my kit in, obtained the relevant signatures through the week, had a few drinks at a leaving do, and I was intending to head away about midday. I was in civvy clothes walking around the unit, shaking hands, saying goodbye. The unit clerk, who was also leaving the army soon to become a civilian airline pilot, caught up with me and said the Captain would like to see me in his office straight away. I made my way to his office.

I knocked and entered the Captain. was there, and so was a REME Lt Col; I didn't know him. We had a brief conversation about my plans. The Lt Col was particularly inquisitive. Eventually he asked me if I would reconsider my leaving the army. He offered me promotion to Sergeant immediately and any posting I wanted within reason. I know he wasn't there specifically about me, I was incidental to his visit, and I guess my Captain, with whom I had a similar conversation previously (but without the higher authority) had brought up the subject of my leaving. I asked the Lt Col for a moment to consider.

I thought about my time in the REME, I was at the absolute top of my game and had been for years. I was qualified to Warrant Officer Class One. I had eight consecutive recommendations for promotion to Sergeant, I had extensive experience of armour, infantry, and workshops. I had toured Northern Ireland in an infantry and REME role, both covertly and overtly. I had helicopter qualification and experience, I had managed recovery and transport sections, I had managed G1098 stores. I had written, organised, and taught courses. I had written and published technical papers on recovery, I was a qualified all-subject instructor. I thought of all the good times, and of all the outstanding 'Magnificent-Bastards' I had worked with; there were many. The outstanding Recy Mech bosses I had in Dennis Jones, Roy Allen, Kev Boulton, and Don Martin. The superb officers I had worked under like Mike Pearce,

Peter Garbutt, Ian Crummack and Ben Tyler. I thought of the rugby and the tours and the great times. My official conduct was endorsed 'EXEMPLARY'.

Then I thought about the not so good things. The REME could have promoted me to Sergeant in any of those previous eight years, but they chose not to.

I thought of the poor quality of senior ranks who were for a time, in the Majority at 7 Recy section; I could end up in a shower like that lot. No thanks!

I thanked the Lt Col for his consideration but declined; I didn't expand on the 'why of it'. I felt a little personal satisfaction in declining.

For the most part it had been a very good twelve years. I had crammed a lot of life in. I had grown from a very young seventeen-year-old to a mature confident man taking big strides along the way.

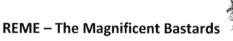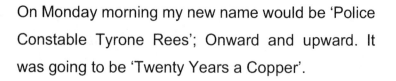

On Monday morning my new name would be 'Police Constable Tyrone Rees'; Onward and upward. It was going to be 'Twenty Years a Copper'.

Time to leave for pastures new. **AetM.**

Reports on Discharge

Officer Commanding's Discharge Report

Period covered by report:

From: JUL 87   To: JAN 88 (ON DISCHARGE)

Rank held and how employed during period

CPL AT TRADE HQ LAD UK ARMD REGT

Assessment of soldier

I have been extremely impressed with all aspects of Cpl Rees' performance. He is an exceptionally strong character who commands great respect. He is intelligent and hardworking and is an active leader of men. He has, alas, decided to make a career in the police force, and purchased his release from the army. A very able man who could have made a good recovery mech ONES/00

Signature of C.O. or officer under whom employed

Name BETTERIDGE Rank   Appt   Captain
Commanding LAD REME
The Royal Scots Dragoon Guards

Date 14 JUL 88

Initials of soldier and date   19

RECOMMENDED FOR 10 RE-ENLISTMENT

597

REME – The Magnificent Bastards

<u>Commanding Officers' Discharge Report</u>

Army Form B108Y

Description of Soldier on leaving Army Service

Hair	BLONDE	Height	1.82	cm
Complexion	FRESH	Eyes	BLUE	
Marks and Scars visible	SCAR LEFT EYEBROW			
		Blood Group	A POS	

Assessments of Military Conduct and Character

Military Conduct   EXEMPLARY

Note   The range of Military Conduct Gradings possible are:
1) Exemplary   2) Very Good   3) Satisfactory
4) Fair   5) Unsatisfactory

Testimonial   *(To be completed with a view to civil employment and with relation to the Certificate of Qualifications and the Job Description)*

Corporal Rees has had a very successful 12 years in the Army. He was quickly promoted to Corporal and each year of his service has received a very good report. He has served as a recovery mechanic with armoured regiments, an infantry battalion and engineering workshops, and has spent four months commanding soldiers on internal security duties in Northern Ireland.

He is an intelligent and articulate man who put his maximum effort into all he does. He has commanded the respect of both his seniors and juniors through his down to earth manner, his honesty and his hard work. He has a mature personality and has a sensible perspective on life.

During his service he has represented the Army and his Corps at rugby, and he has given much of his time to the game.

He has been a loyal and valued member of the Army and I expect him to do well in his life outside of the Service.

The above assessments have been read to me

Signature of Soldier

Signature of C.O.   Lt Col
                                            Commanding
LAD REME   The Royal Scots Dragoon Guards
27 JUN 1988   Date   27 JUN 88
THE ROYAL SCOTS   Address   BHURTPORE   BKS
DRAGOON GUARDS   TIDWORTH   HANTS   SP9 7AC

Epilogue and Remembrance

I served twelve years and three hundred and nine days and twelve hours in the army; I wasn't counting. It was from the age of seventeen through till thirty, my most Informative years. Though I was REME I was also in the British Army. My experiences of the REME and the Army ran alongside each other. They are the same but also separate, similar and yet not. An oxymoron of experience and course. Consider somebody being in the Royal Artillery for twelve years. Our Army experience would be similar, but our Corps experience would be different. I am fashioned thus.

My military memories seem to fall into two categories 'heavy' and 'light'. The light memories surface often and are enjoyed, talked about, and shared with friends and family alike. Sometimes to the point of boredom for them. Many are written about in this memoir.

The 'heavier' memories surface less often. Normally when I am alone or in the company of someone who was 'there' and who understands, and to whom I don't have to explain or defend.

I suspect this applies to many ex-service people, men, and women, to different degrees.

Post army my remembrance days go much like this, and I have much to remember.

The service this year was at St Edith's Church in the village as it is every year. A poignant day for me as with many service men because I can personalise the day remembering good people whom I knew in my service days and who are no longer with us. Somehow as I get older the more important the day becomes.

I wear a black suit, REME corps tie and my two medals along with my veteran's badge and a paper poppy. I personally think all poppies should be the paper ones made by the RBL, that way they get the money. I always arrive early accompanied by my daughter; on arrival she goes off and joins the Girl Guides contingent of which she is a member. It's a big day for them full uniform and a flag to follow.

On the way into the church, I pause a moment and look at the names of the fallen on the memorial stone from both the big wars. A few years ago, I researched all the names on the monument there are thirty-eight and each has a story to tell. They cover all areas of the globe and all arms of the services. One particularly poignant story is that of Lt. David Cuthbert Thomas.

> *" David Cuthbert Thomas", Second Lieutenant, Royal Welsh Fusiliers. David was the Son of Evan and Ethelinda Thomas, of our village Rectory. He was commissioned into the 3rd Battalion,*

Royal Welsh Fusiliers, and after training was posted to the 1st RWF, on the Somme. On 18 March 1916, David oversaw a working party, which was repairing wire emplacements in No Man's Land when he was shot in the throat. He walked to the First Aid Post for treatment but began choking and died shortly afterwards.

David had been wounded in the neck, his wound had been treated and he was expected to survive. Whilst lying on the stretcher he was told to lie still but he reached to his breast pocket for a letter he had received from a lady friend in Glamorgan. It was this movement that re-opened his wound and he tragically choked on his own blood. David had lived in the rectory which is the closest house to the church and is now lived in by friends of mine.

I read all the names on the memorial, mused over a few I knew the history of, and walk into the church. I know most of the people present and I choose a pew near the back where sit the other old fogeys like me, sporting medals and ribbons and exuding a confident air of 'I was there'.

We wait for the church to fill, which it does with regular church goers, occasional visitors and the once or twice a year special event attendees like me. The last to enter are the community council who take the credit for organising the service. They all look the same in black overcoats, dark hats, gloves, and glittering chain of office where appropriate. They try to appear solemn and important; the local MP is amongst them and some assembly members. Tellingly not a medal ribbon in sight!

The vicar, Dennis, is a top bloke. He's been the vicar here for about ten years. He's a cockney with a broad bow bells accent. He is enthusiastic about the Welsh language, but his pronunciation is appalling to the point of being very, very funny. Whenever something happens in the bible, which is the least bit suspect, as far as Dennis is concerned, they are "Bang out of order"; terrific. But he tries with gusto and gets ten out of ten from me. Moreover, his sermon is spot on target. He hasn't got a good word to say for the politicians, ridicules political correctness and goes on to tell us about wars and his family.

He tells us how his grandfather used to show him his medals and then the hole in his back where the round exited. He tells us about seeing a photo of Uncle Jim on his parents' mantelpiece at home as a child, and that when he asked where Uncle Jim was the answer was 'still in Burma'. He finishes with the story of a German landmine attached to a parachute landing on his father's house in London during the blitz. The landmine scraped along the roof eventually detonating on the house next door killing all the family therein. Very poignant, very relevant. He goes on further about more recent events and current conflicts he doesn't like them, neither do we all, but he understands duty and conveys the personal sacrifice in a moving and respectful manner.

We sing a few hymns; some school children read wisely chosen passages. The Mayor of the council reads some verses from the bible; he's a youngster as politicians go, he doesn't get my vote. How could you vote for a dignitary at a remembrance service who reads a message but hasn't cleaned his shoes and hasn't done his top shirt button up. He's missing a trick here.

Mrs Thomas plays the organ as well as she always does. We sing a few hymns in Welsh and English; the singing isn't great but it's ok. We then sing God Save the Queen and Hen Wlad Fy Nhadau, the Welsh National anthem.

The church wardens Gareth, Tom, and Ray go around with the collection plates. I think everybody donates and each plate has a substantial pile of notes on it. The collection is for the RBL poppy appeal. Proper order too.

We file outside, the councillors following the guides and brownies with flags and congregate around the memorial. A trumpeter, a local lad, plays the last post. Very moving, the church predominates over the valley with the river below and the notes are clear and crystal and long. Immediately takes my mind back to some military funerals from years before where I was 'Right Marker' in the firing party; I feel a tear forming in my eye, but

I wipe it away before it emerges, and somebody sees it. Not having any of that nonsense.

It's a bit disorganised outside the Church, a Queue has formed to get out and most of the people are still stuck inside because the council who are the first out have stopped as soon as they get to the memorial. In a quiet unsure non-military voice, a man who I don't know, calls forward wreath layers. The MP, the assembly member, the council chairman with dirty shoes and an undone top button; the local branch of the legion, the local rugby club, local aid charity and the RAFA. The last wreath is laid by a young girl in RAF uniform she is the smartest there, smartness being a military thing, she is very proud, salutes and has done a good job.

We then have two minutes silence the trumpeter keeps looking at his watch and I am thinking of good friends and my squash playing partner Micky Dowling MM, who needs no introduction to this forum and of Frank Evans killed in the same action in Iraq. Neil Clarke a private in the Queens who was shot and killed in Londonderry and whose place I took as 'top cover' on a subsequent patrol, and Keith 'Frenchy' Lepine of the Royal Hussars killed in Canada, and of his young daughter asking me for fags for her non-smoking mother when she learned of his loss. Happy and chatty recently married Carl Sharples killed in Germany, Phil Heaton and Tony French, fellow rugby men, who also lost their lives in Germany. Three young Grenadier Guardsmen who I never knew, but helped carry their bodies off a helicopter, killed in Northern Ireland.

All young men, all met violent death, all so very sad.

The trumpeter checks his watch for the last time and plays reveille, the brownies and guides raise their flags. The service is done. My daughter and two of her friends run to me. I send them deep into the graveyard to look at a plain white Commonwealth War Graves Commission headstone of an RAF lad who died from wounds in 1945. He's the only deceased serviceman buried in the small cemetery the others are memorised only on the granite stone. They come back and tell me about the details on the stone. He is not forgotten.

I am one of the first to enter the small church hall where the Mother's Union have laid on tea and cakes. It looks very nice, and I am tempted but in come the councillors all congratulating themselves on how well they arranged the service, and they quickly lapse into their normal sycophantic behaviour. I can't be doing with that, and I head home, I am sure my daughter and her friends will finish off my share of the fancy cakes.

As I leave the Church Hall, I see Dennis the vicar walking toward me. I tell him he's done well, the best service I had witnessed at St Edith's and tell him it was very poignant, which it was. He tells me that someone else had told him that and he was pleased. He is a good man. We shake hands; he has, like me, a firm proper handshake. I like that in a man. Politicians don't do that, soldiers do.

I am very pleased at the Vicars performance, message, and attitude, it warms me. In the past the council have invited 'guest speakers' from afar. For a few years they called upon the services of a Chapel Clergyman from further down west. He politicised the entire service, didn't understand or consider personal sacrifice or duty and said some very controversial things to the point where cross

words were spoken in the church grounds (not by me I might add).

I get home, change into casual clothes, and put away my two medals and veteran badge. They are not for bravery but merely state that 'I was there when it counted'. They may come out of the draw again next year. I walk into the kitchen; my wife Nicola has been cooking cake. The kitchen smells mouth wateringly wonderful, it's Christmas cake in the oven. Christmas is coming!

AetM

Printed in Great Britain
by Amazon

37906606R00337